Praise for
How to Travel the World on $75 a Day

"*How to Travel the World on $75 a Day* is a great resource for when you're sitting and home and dreaming of travel, for when those dreams turn into travel preparation, and for when those travel preparations take you out the door on your dream trip."
—Rolf Potts, internationally bestselling author of *Vagabonding*

"Matt is a budget travel expert and his advice has helped millions of people travel cheaper. This book puts all his knowledge into one place and is sure to help you save money and get off the beaten path."
—Samantha Brown, host of *Samantha Brown's Places to Love* on PBS

"Nomadic Matt is one of the world's top budget travel experts. His writings and teachings will help anyone get off the beaten path and save money no matter where they are going in the world."
—Onieka Raymond, Emmy Award–winning travel journalist

"Matt's helped millions of people travel cheaper and he's one of the savviest travelers I know. This book is definitely going to help you save money no matter how long you want to go away for!"

—Brent Underwood, *New York Times* bestselling author of
Ghost Town Living

"Matt is the travel expert I always tell my friends to reference when planning their trips. He has a ton of firsthand experience traveling on a budget and seamlessly shares all that knowledge in this book. It's easy to digest and jam-packed with helpful tips."

—Renee Hahnel, author of *Roaming America*

How to
TRAVEL the WORLD
on
$75 A DAY

Also by Matt Kepnes

Ten Years a Nomad: A Traveler's Journey Home

How to
TRAVEL the WORLD
on
$75 A DAY

Travel Cheaper, Longer, Smarter

MATT KEPNES

BenBella Books, Inc.
Dallas, TX

BenBella Books, Inc.
8080 N. Central Expressway
Suite 1700
Dallas, TX 75206
benbellabooks.com
Send feedback to feedback@benbellabooks.com

BenBella is a federally registered trademark.

Printed in the United States of America
10 9 8 7 6 5 4 3 2 1

Library of Congress Control Number: 2024050107
ISBN 9781637746646 (trade paperback)
ISBN 9781637746653 (electronic)

Editing by Keith Gordon
Copyediting by Michael Fedison
Proofreading by Jenny Bridges and Ashley Casteel
Text design and composition by Jordan Koluch
Cover design by Erin Tyler
Cover image © Adobe Stock / Eigens
Printed by Lake Book Manufacturing

To all the people I've met on the road—
you changed my life in ways you'll never know.

Author's Note: All prices, resources, and information were correct at the time of writing. All prices are in USD for easy comparison and based on exchange rates at the time of research. Since things in travel can change quickly, some resources and companies may no longer be available and prices may be different due to varying exchange rates or general price increases that happen with time.

Contents

PART THREE: BREAKING IT DOWN BY REGION

Introduction

When I was growing up in the '80s and '90s, any dreams of long-term travel would have been considered far too expensive and impractical. Fancy group tours, big hotels, flashy resorts, five-star meals, and budget-blowing flights were supposedly what travel was all about. The travel industry kept that perception alive with glossy advertisements for luxurious holidays in far-off destinations where we could escape the stress of our day-to-day lives ... if only we ponied up the money.

Travel was a vacation. A respite from the monotony of modern nine-to-five life. You'd go off, spend a lot of money, and come back from your two-week trip reinvigorated (and with a tan to make your coworkers jealous). Then you'd spend the rest of the year in your cubicle saving up for another trip, dreaming of the excitement that would come with it.

But those ads—and that entire concept of travel—were lies.

After all, you can't run a media company by selling hostel dorms, budget hotels, discount transportation, museum passes, or cheap tours—the kind of stuff that makes travel affordable for the masses. You need ad revenue, and the luxury travel companies were more than happy to spend money to promote the dream of big, splashy, expensive (and lucrative) vacations.

So mass media promoted a style of travel that was more up-scale (and thus more expensive) than it needed to be.

It wasn't until I *actually* traveled the world that I understood how misleading and wrong those big travel companies were—and just how affordable travel could be.

Back in 2003, I was planning my first trip overseas. I had just graduated from college and was working in hospital administration. I was putting in forty-plus-hour weeks and looking forward to my precious two weeks of vacation. I booked a trip to Costa Rica (how I chose it as my first international destination, I don't know—time has faded that memory) and spent two weeks falling in love with travel. I loved the sense of adventure. I loved how every day held something new. I loved the feeling of endless possibility that each day brought, a stark contrast to my well-structured days in the office.

The following year, I used my entire annual allotment of vacation days in January because I couldn't wait to get overseas again. I had picked up the travel bug in Costa Rica—and there was no going back.

My friend Scott and I ventured to Thailand—and that's where my life changed.

While we were in the northern city of Chiang Mai, I left Scott to visit a temple outside the city. I shared a tuk-tuk (the name for inexpensive shared taxis in Asia) with five non-American back-packers. On the ride we began discussing vacation time, and they were amazed that, as an American, I got only two weeks of vacation per year. They all received at least a month off in their home countries, and they were doing all this travel on a budget—staying in hostels, using local transportation, eating at street stalls, and finding deals that allowed them to stretch their savings.

To say I was jealous would be an understatement. I wanted *their* freedom more than anything, and our conversation made me rethink my life. I was heading down a road I realized I wasn't ready for—marriage, house, kids, 401(k)s, playdates, college funds. While those things aren't bad, at twenty-three, those weren't the things I was really sure I wanted. I loved the freedom travel brought and wanted more of it. Before I met these backpackers, I didn't think traveling long-term on a budget was possible, but now I knew it was.

A few days later, while lying on the beach on the famous island of Koh Samui, I turned to Scott and said, "I'm going to quit my job, finish my master's degree, and travel the world for a year. Just like those backpackers." I knew the second I told him that I was making the right decision. Everything in my being told me so. That evening, I went to the only English language bookstore on the island and bought *Lonely Planet's Guide to Southeast Asia* to seal the deal. In my mind, it was my unbreakable commitment.

Once I got back home, I promptly quit my job, finished my MBA, and, in July 2006, I hugged my parents goodbye and set out for the open road. I used the money I had saved and invested from working my hospital job to fund that initial trip.

That adventure was supposed to last a year. It turned into eighteen months, and then eighteen months suddenly became forever.

There was a lot I didn't know when I first started. But the more I traveled, the more I found ways to save money without sacrificing comfort.

Since this book's first edition in 2012, travel—and the world—has substantially changed. The internet, the sharing economy, social media, smartphone apps, and countless blogs have changed people's perceptions of travel. Long-term travel, digital nomading, and career breaks are far more common and popular than they were even just a few years ago.

The rise of the "social media influencer" has made young people realize that travel doesn't have to be expensive and that they don't have to put off their dream trip until retirement. They see people online traveling to far-off destinations and say, "I want to do that too." They want to YOLO now, not when they are seventy.

The FIRE movement (financial independence, retire early) turned thirty- and forty-year-olds into penny pinchers so they could retire early and roam the world. COVID changed how we work, and digital nomading and remote working are no longer the sole domain of bloggers, techies, and influencers. People from all industries have been unchained from their office jobs and can be found in cities and communities around the world. They, too, want a better work-life balance and more time for experiences and adventure.

Whether it's two-week trips, staycations, or folks quitting their jobs to travel the world, more and more people are saying yes to travel and heading out the door.

But time and time again the number-one concern would-be travelers still express to me is: "But how can I afford it?" The reality is most people *still* believe travel costs large sums of money—and that it's something they'll do at some nebulous future point in their life.

Yes, it is true that travel simply isn't as cheap as it was in the years leading up to the pandemic (even a seasoned travel expert like me has to look harder and harder for deals).

But that doesn't mean it's impossible to travel on a budget. In this book, I'll show you how to travel the world for $75 a day (or less). I'm here to tell you that you don't need to tap a trust fund to travel. You don't need to win the lottery, and you don't need your parents to foot the bill. Anyone can travel cheaply and comfortably if they know the secrets to saving money on the road.

Nothing I tell you in this book is a "secret" to those who have traveled. I didn't need to join a special club to learn these things. I didn't take a course. Experience on the road showed me what most travel companies don't want you to see. Working in the industry and traveling for a long time—along with years of experience on the road—allowed me to peer behind the veil, and I saw that travel is *genuinely* affordable because a host of budget options exist for tours, accommodations, food, and flights. They just aren't well-advertised.

The goal of this book is to put travel within your reach, even if you don't have a lot of money. (I didn't either when I started.) My approach is not about avoiding certain highlights or activities— it's about *traveling smart*. I don't go to Italy to avoid nice meals. I don't go to Bordeaux to avoid a wine tour. I don't dream of visiting Australia and camping in the Outback only to say, "No, that's a bit out of my budget. Maybe another time."

And neither do you.

I want to help you experience destinations fully while also ensuring you don't break the bank.

As you read through this book, you'll find a lot of advice geared toward people taking long-term travel. After all, this book is about traveling the world, right? But not everyone is going to jump overseas for months on end. Some people just want to save money on their two-week holiday.

Don't worry if you go away for only a week or two—this book is still for you. My tips can be used for a trip of any length. Whether you are going to Paris for two weeks or two months, you'll still need to know how to get a cheap flight, affordable travel insurance, affordable accommodation, and authentic meals.

The more deals and tricks you know, the more you can stretch your budget. And "cheap" doesn't mean traveling like a pauper. It's about traveling (as the cliché goes) like a local. After all, when you are home, you don't spend a lot of money per day—and neither do the locals where you are visiting. If you know just a few general tips and some location-specific advice, you can always have a first-class experience without paying a first-class price.

This book is your first step out the door.

So, grab a drink and a map while you read, relax, and learn to save.

Sincerely,

"Nomadic" Matt Kepnes

PART ONE

PLANNING YOUR TRIP

1

GETTING OVER
YOUR FEARS

The most difficult part about traveling the world isn't actually the logistics of a trip—it's finding the courage to go in the first place. It takes a lot of courage to leave your life behind and journey into the unknown. It's this initial step that most people never get past. For me, it took a trip to Thailand to get me to make the leap. For others, it's a lot more difficult. Instead of the nudge I required, some people require a full-on shove.

While most of this book will talk about the practical, financial side of travel, I want to begin with the psychology of travel because it's usually where people need the most initial help. Let me start by saying that any fear, second-guessing, or anxiety you have is *normal*.

It's natural to second-guess yourself when making a big life change, and leaving everything behind to travel the world is certainly a big change. But let me tell you: it's going to work out just fine.

As a travel writer, I get emails all the time from people asking me whether or not they should travel the world. Do they quit their job and go for it? Are they in the right stage of life? Will they find work when they return? Will everything be OK?

These emails are peppered with nervous excitement over travel's endless possibilities, but there is also always one underlying message in the emails:

"Matt, I want to go but I'm afraid. I need someone to tell me it will be all right."

Well, I'm telling you right now that it's going to be all right.

In my meetings with strangers, they always tell me how they dream of traveling the world. "It must be such the adventure," they tell me. "I wish I could do it." And when I ask them what stops them, they come up with a book full of excuses as to why they can't:

"I can't afford my trip."

"I have too many responsibilities at home."

"I won't be able to make friends on the road."

"I don't want to be alone."

"I have too many bills."

"I'm not sure I could do it."

"I need [insert new product] so I'm saving my money for that."

"I'm simply too scared."

"I don't have the time right now. X, Y, Z social event is coming up and I can't miss it!"

It's not that these aren't valid excuses—but that they are *surmountable* excuses. They just don't get tackled because of fear. It's easier for someone to stay home in his or her comfort zone than to break out and travel the world. As the saying goes, "People go with the devil they know over the devil they don't." Home is our safe zone. We know it. We understand it. We may not always like it, but we get it, and that is a powerful force. In the end, held back by their own fears, most people stay home and dream of that "one perfect day" when all those obstacles disappear and they are finally ready to go.

But you know what? That day never comes. There will never be a perfect day.

Tomorrow, you will still have bills.

Tomorrow, you still won't have just the right amount of money.

Tomorrow, you will still have someone's wedding or birthday to attend.

Tomorrow, you will still second-guess yourself.

Tomorrow, you'll find another excuse as to why you can't go.

Tomorrow, people you know will still feed the doubt in your head.

Tomorrow will come and you'll say, "Today isn't the right day. Let's go tomorrow."

Dropping everything to travel takes a lot of courage, and while many people claim "real-world responsibilities" prevent them from traveling, I think it is the fear of the unknown that really holds most people back.

When I first set out on my nomadic lifestyle, I was terrified! I had no idea what I was doing. There was no easy way to come home. No quick FaceTime with my friends or family if something went wrong because FaceTime (and widespread use of smartphones) didn't exist yet. Wi-Fi wasn't ubiquitous, social media didn't exist, and there wasn't a lot of information online about how to get around, where to stay, or how to stay safe.

But I knew if I didn't do it, I'd regret it.

Since you bought this book, you are probably already on the

right track. Maybe you are already committed to a long-term trip, or maybe you are still on the fence about it. No matter what side of the coin you fall on, know that even the most experienced travelers had doubts when they began. I had tons—and I've never met anyone who didn't.

But I want to reassure you that you are doing the right thing. Because once you start traveling, you will realize a few things that will help you get rid of your fears.

You aren't the first person to travel abroad. One of the things that comforted me when I was first starting out was realizing that lots of other people traveled the world before me and ended up just fine. While long-term travel might not be popular in the United States, it is a rite of passage for a lot of people around the world. People as young as eighteen head overseas in droves for long-term trips, and there is a well-worn travel trail around the world where you'll find support from other travelers. As you read this paragraph right now, millions of people are trekking around the world and discovering foreign lands. And if millions of eighteen-year-olds on a round-the-world trip came home in one piece, I realized there was no reason I wouldn't either. The same goes for you.

That realization helped take away some of my fear because I knew there would be other travelers on the road to comfort me. Let that comfort you too.

You are just as capable as everyone else. I'm smart, capable, and have common sense (or so I think). If other people can travel the world, why can't I? I realized there was no reason I wouldn't be able to make my way around the world. I'm just as capable as everyone else, and so are you.

Early in my travels, I turned up in Bangkok without knowing a single person, and I wound up living and thriving there. I made friends, I found a girlfriend, I rented an apartment, I got a job, and I even learned Thai. It was sink or swim, and I swam. Back in the early 2010s, I navigated my way through Ukraine, a country where few people speak English and even fewer signs are in the Roman alphabet (as they use the Cyrillic script there). I had to say, "Choo choo" to a taxi driver to tell him I needed to go to the train station. I once had a friend cluck in Laos so the server knew he wanted chicken. Nobody steps out into the world knowing it all. They learn along the way. Don't doubt yourself. You get by in your regular life just fine, and the same will be true when you travel.

The world isn't as dangerous as the media says. CNN, Fox News, MSNBC, and other major media outlets often make the world outside our borders look like a pretty scary place. They paint a skewed picture of a world filled with violence, terrorism, anti-Americanism, rampant natural disasters, and lots of crime. We always hear about the latest calamity or the current war, but not about the locals taking care of tourists or fighting for gender equality. Like the saying goes: if it bleeds, it leads.

I think one of the main reasons why the world seems so dangerous is because we have instant global communication for the first time in human history. Whenever anything happens, we can know about it right away through twenty-four-hour news networks and social media. Earthquakes and typhoons have always happened, but now we hear about them in our social media feeds in real time.

Moreover, the media—traditional and online—always paints a skewed version of events. My mother constantly tells me when I go anywhere in the world to "be careful," as if the world is a big, scary place. She'll tell me how nervous she is if I end up in a country that she once heard about in the news . . . in 1975. I try to tell her that the world is not that scary and I could get mugged just as easily in New York, Miami, or Houston as I could in London, Beijing, or São Paulo. Sometimes she'll agree with a hesitant, "I guess you have a point."

But it's not just worried mothers who might bring the fear. Years back, when my friend joined me in Thailand, one of her coworkers said to her, "Why would you want to go there? Hawaii has beaches. Do they even have electricity in Thailand?"

Everyone around the world wants the same things that you want. They too have jobs, families, and a long list of chores. They too want their kids to be safe, earn money, and live prosperous lives. Mostly, they want to be left alone. They aren't looking for trouble. Travelers from all corners cross the globe every day without any problems because, like anywhere, people are too busy to care about you.

As a whole, the world is no more or less safe than any part of the United States. Your common sense will serve you whether you are in Phoenix or Phnom Penh. Use your street smarts to avoid dodgy situations, and you will be fine.

You will make friends. People always ask me how to make friends on the road. They tell me they're not very social and that it's hard for them to connect with strangers. After all, not everyone can walk up to a stranger and say hello. You might spend the first few days traveling by yourself, afraid of making that first contact. I was really shy when I first hit the road. I could talk my friends' ears off, but whenever I'd get around new people, I'd go quiet. Now I have no problems talking to anyone I meet, and I can thank travel for that skill.

The good news is that when you travel, you are never alone. There are many solo travelers making their way across the world, and they are in the exact same boat as you. They want companionship. They want friends. You'll find people who will come up and talk to you out of the blue. I was recently having a beer alone in Bangkok, and another traveler at my hostel came up to see if I wanted company, and we struck up a fantastic conversation. I met two of my best friends because I said hello to them in a guesthouse in Vietnam. I've attended the weddings of friends I met while asking to join their Frisbee game on the beach. After a while, it becomes normal to strike up a conversation with a complete stranger.

Travelers are friendly people who want to make friends. And one of those friends is you.

You are never too old. Budget travel, backpacking, round-the-world trips—these trips aren't just for the young. While I was in Poland, I met a sixty-five-year-old American in my hostel. He was traveling around Europe before heading to India, and he was sharing stories from his youth while drinking a few beers with the younger backpackers. My friend once met a man in his seventies making a big trip around the world because, as he said, he didn't have much time left and wanted to see the world. He had lots of ailments and carried many prescriptions, but he knew it was now or never so he went for it.

I've seen families with their children on buses in Southeast Asia and retirees camping in Australia. Some of my favorite encounters on the road have been with older travelers, as they always have the best stories. As they say, you are only as old as you feel.

You can travel with kids. People think that once they have children, they can't travel. But every year, families set off to travel the world. Having a family doesn't need to be a barrier to long-term travel. In fact, more and more families travel the world, thanks in part to a rise of homeschooling options and parents untethered to desk jobs. Some of the biggest social media influencers are traveling families (one of the most famous, The Bucket List Family, has over five million social media followers and a deal with National Geographic).

Don't believe having a family means ending your travels.

You can always come back. If you make it three months into your trip and decide that long-term travel isn't for you, it's perfectly OK to return home. I've met a few travelers who, months into their trip, realized that they really liked being at home. They missed their friends, their family, and their significant others, so they cut their trip short.

There's no such thing as failure in the world of travel. Your trip is your own. You went away for yourself, not for other people—and, in the end, you only to need worry about yourself. Getting up and going is more than most people do, and if traveling isn't for you, there is no shame in embracing that. Whether you are gone for one day, one month, or one year, you still will have learned and grown from your adventure. That in itself is a major accomplishment.

If I've learned anything over the years, it's that these fears, like all fears, are unfounded. In the end, life works out.

Walking away was easy for me, but I understand that not everyone can just cut loose as quickly as I did. Some of us have mortgages, parents to take care of, children to look after. But that doesn't mean it's impossible to travel.

When you dive deeper, you find people don't follow through with their plans because they are too afraid to commit. They looked up some flights, scrolled through some hotels on their phone, and maybe even went to a bookstore to buy a guidebook. But when it came down to committing, they hemmed and hawed and said, "Let me think about it a little. Maybe tomorrow."

Tomorrow is always the day *something* happens. It's the day to hit the gym, start your new diet, read more, or finally book that trip to Paris.

I get it. Change is hard. Getting out of your comfort zone is hard. It takes dedicated mental energy. Turning a dream into a reality can elicit a sort of "Oh crap, this is happening!" moment. There's always a mix of excitement and fear. "Yes!" to doing it but also "Uh, what did I get myself into?"

Soon, you'll be arriving in a city you know nothing about, a place where you know no one and where you (probably) don't speak the language. This is enough to make anyone say, "Wait, I'm not ready!"

But I'm here to take the leap with you and say you *are* ready.

Your future holds mouthwatering meals in foreign countries, tropical beaches you only thought existed in a postcard, winding alleyways in European cities that throw you back into the Middle Ages, or jungles so dense and teeming with wildlife you'll feel like you are living in an issue of *National Geographic* magazine.

In the following chapters, we're going to make that happen.

2

IS TRAVEL REALLY
TOO EXPENSIVE?

et's put the "travel is too expensive" myth to bed with a short exercise. Get out a sheet of paper and write down all your fixed monthly expenses. Write down your rent (or mortgage), car payments, cable bill, utilities, groceries, insurance, cell phone bill, etc. and tally everything up.

Next, write down all your discretionary spending. This would include any dinners and drinks out, movie nights, shopping, that daily coffee from Starbucks, the bottle of water you buy on your way home from work, gym membership, haircuts, change you give away, and everything in between.

If you don't know what you spend money on, you can never save properly. Track your expenses for a month and see what you spend. Don't cheat. No matter how small the expense, write it down.

Once you have totaled up all your expenses, take a moment to reflect on the title of this book—how to travel the world on $75 a day. That's about $2,278 per month, or $27,355 per year.

When you add up all your monthly spending and costs, it's likely more than $2,300. Even if you live in a small town rather than a big coastal city, you're likely spending close to or more than that number.

Assuming your rent is $1,400 per month (which is the US national average in May 2024 according to Apartments.com), that's $43 per day, which is 57 percent of the daily budget set out in this book. Add in food costs, gas, car insurance, health insurance, and cable, and your set expenses are almost certainly higher than the number you need for a year abroad. And that's before you've spent a dime on anything fun like a new outfit or dinner and a movie.

You might have looked at the cover of this book and thought, "I spend way less than $75 per day." I know because many people have told me, "$75 per day sounds like a lot of money." They are positive that they spend way less than that on a daily basis.

But that's because people often don't consider their fixed costs like housing, insurance, utilities, or debt payments when they think about how much money they spend each day. Numerous studies have shown that people spend more when they don't "see" the money leave their account. We think about what we spend when we go out to eat or go shopping, not those recurring bills. We may not go to the ATM every day, but we are constantly spending.

Now, imagine if all your living expenses were less than $75 per day. Everything. Your house, food, transportation, travel, nights out at the movies, or drinks at a bar. How wonderful would that be? How wonderful would it be to live on less than $28,000 per year? Pretty wonderful, huh?

For that much money, you could be out traveling the world instead of sitting at home—and yet many people say to me, "I can't travel. Your advice is great if you are middle-class." "Your parents are giving you money!" "Your website can never work for me. I'm too poor to travel." "This advice is only for privileged people."

Every travel naysayer believes their situation is unique, that they can't manage what someone else did. And it's not just travel. We all make excuses as to why we can't do something we desire. "The gym is too far away." "Just one more cookie won't hurt." "I'm not tall enough to play basketball." We believe we'll never accomplish that great thing we aspire to because we lack the one "secret" ingredient we think is needed to make it happen.

When it comes to travel, people think what's holding them back is money. They imagine they can't travel because they can't tap the Bank of Mom and Dad, or because they are burdened by debt, or because they simply assume folks like me are just lucky.

By believing that everyone else is special, unique, or rich, they put up a psychological barrier that lets them ignore all the reasons why travel is possible. If you wake up today and tell yourself, "I can't travel because of reason X," you'll never look for ways to start traveling. You see only the reasons why you *can't* travel. You'll never peer beyond those roadblocks and ask yourself, "How do I overcome these obstacles like those other people?" The only difference between those on the road and those at home is saying "I can" instead of "I can't."

Wake up today and say, "Yes, I *can* travel too." Start looking for what you can do right now to make it happen. Start small. Each yes builds on the one before it. Look at your day-to-day spending. How much would you save if you bought a water filter instead of a daily bottle of water? What if you gave up Starbucks? What if you gave up a streaming service? Downgraded your phone plan? Walked to work? Sold your unneeded stuff on eBay?

Starting small gives you small victories that help you slowly realize you can do it. The more wins you have, the more you keep going. When I was saving money for my first trip, I started cooking at home more and stopped going out for drinks. Then I gave up going to movies. Then I sold my stuff and found a roommate. Then I found ways to carshare to save on gas.

Each step built on top of the last, and I got more confident in my ability to save. I woke up each morning and said to myself, "I can do this."

Changing your mindset can have tremendous results. Years ago, I met an American girl in Bangkok named Sarah who lived in New York City working a job that barely paid her enough to live. She had to cut a lot of corners, but after two years of saving, she'd scraped together enough to travel the world. She didn't have a lot of money, so she went to Southeast Asia, one of the cheapest areas of the world.

As she put it at the time, "It's true that I don't have much in savings, but if I waited for the perfect time to travel, I'd be waiting a long time. Of course, I was nervous about leaving a steady job and the life I had created in New York. I worried about going broke in the first two months and having to turn around and live in my mother's basement until I found another job. I'm doing this on a tight budget while still paying student loans, but I'm happy to be doing it now rather than waiting an eternity until retirement. You definitely don't have to be wealthy to pick up and travel."

And if the money does run out, there are plenty of ways to work overseas. Travelers around the world work in hostels, work on farms, pick fruit, become tour guides, or get service jobs. When I decided to extend my travels, I stayed in Thailand and taught English. If that doesn't appeal to you, save what you can! It's better to have six months traveling the world than no months at all.

As the saying goes, "Don't put off until tomorrow what you can do today."

3

HOW TO SAVE
FOR YOUR TRIP

I remember when I began saving for my first trip around the world. I had a rough estimate of how much money I would need ($18,000) and thought, "Whoa. How will I ever save that much?" It seemed like an impossible number to reach as a twenty-three-year-old working a low-paying office job.

But, after writing out all my expenses and seeing where I spent money, I realized that if I made a few changes to my lifestyle, I *could* save that much. It would just take a while. I had a job and I could work overtime, so all I needed to do was cut my expenses, take on some extra hours at work, and watch my savings grow. After eighteen months (and on schedule), I got there.

Instead of thinking, "I need to save $18,000," I broke that number down into something much smaller. Our minds have an easier time grasping smaller numbers. If you need to save $18,000 in a year, what does that look like? That's $50 a day. Could you save $50 a day? Maybe. Maybe not. But instead of saying, "Eighteen thousand dollars? I could never save that! That's so much!"

we now say, "Fifty dollars a day? I could probably save that—or at least come close. That seems easier." By breaking it down into more measurable and easily digestible sums, the process of saving for your trip becomes far less daunting.

Every time you take one step toward your goal, the next step becomes easier. Suddenly, this vague goal you don't think you can achieve starts to take shape and becomes realistic. Every time I saved more, I got closer to my goal and I got more excited. It made the trip real. "This is really going to happen!" I started thinking to myself.

Once you get into the savings mindset, it becomes a game. As we just discussed in the previous chapter, wins compound and small changes can lead to big results. You become more motivated. You become more focused. You create a habit. And once it's a habit, it's easier to do.

Here are some proven methods for reducing your expenses and increasing your travel fund:

Eat in. Dinner out is usually someone's biggest discretionary expense—and it's also one of the easiest to eliminate. Instead of buying $20 lunches and $30 dinners, brown-bag it to work and cook dinner at night. When I saved for my first trip, I was spending $70 per week on groceries. I cooked once for dinner and ate the leftovers the next day for lunch. Sure, cooking can be intimidating since not all of us are Julia Child in the kitchen. However, I found cooking to be an invaluable skill, not only because it saved me money before my trip but because it's also one of the easiest ways to cut down expenses when you travel.

The more I cooked, the more I loved cooking. And the more

I saved. (I also got a lot healthier because I knew what was in my meals, which was an added bonus.)

Of course, grocery prices have gone up since the mid-2000s and you're likely spending a lot more than $70 on groceries (I currently spend around $125 per week). But cooking is still cheaper than eating out or getting your food delivered via an app.

You can find a lot of resources for quick and inexpensive meals. There are as many food bloggers as there are travel bloggers these days. I'm a big fan of Rachael Ray's 30 Minute Meals (rachaelray.com/blogs/recipes/tagged/30-minute-meals). I've always found them to be healthy, tasty, and easy to make.

Cut the coffee. Love your Starbucks? Well, Starbucks loves your money. Coffee is the little thing that quietly drains your bank account without you ever noticing. That daily coffee can cost you $90 per month ($3 for a regular coffee, more if you want some fancy Frappuccino). At $1,080 per year, that's a lot of money. What's more important—your daily cup of joe or getting to spend an extra few weeks on the beaches of Thailand or exploring the jungles of Borneo? Give up the coffee, or switch from the cappuccino to a standard brew. Move to tea, or brew your own cup. Folgers might not taste as delicious as a venti triple mocha latte with whipped cream, but it's a lot cheaper (and, let's be honest, healthier).

Drink less alcohol. It may not be appealing to spend your nights at home instead of out with your friends, but alcohol gets really pricey (and excessive drinking is bad for your health anyway). Before I went traveling, I'd go out on the weekends with friends to places where drinks cost around $5 apiece. Now, those same drinks are double or triple the price so it's even more expensive to go out to bars and clubs!

I enjoyed going out, but those drinks really added up. It wasn't fun staying in while my friends were out on the weekends, but that year of semi-solitude paid off greatly, as I had more money to enjoy the food in Europe. If you have stronger willpower than I do, you can still go out with friends but cut out the pricey drinks—you could even make yourself the regular designated driver. Alcohol is where budgets go to die so cut it as much as you can.

Lose the car. Between insurance, repairs, and filling your tank with gas, cars can cost a lot of money. If you can, get rid of yours. Learn to love public transportation, or start walking everywhere you need to go. It took me longer to get to work using public transportation, but you'll find that you don't really need a car as much as you think. I understand this may not be feasible for everyone, especially those in smaller towns that don't have a good public transportation system. A good alternative is to sell your car and buy a cheap used car. You will only need a car until you leave for your trip, anyway. Buying a "throwaway car" will allow you to pocket the money from your nicer car and put it toward your trip. Additionally, consider getting a bike as an alternative to the car altogether. No gas, no insurance, no repairs—it will not only save you money but will keep you in shape!

Get a roommate. Lowering your housing costs will allow you to see huge gains in your savings. Get rid of that apartment or bring in some roommates. Or try to move in with mom and dad. Six months before I went abroad, I moved in with my parents. It wasn't that fun being twenty-five and living at home, but I saved more than $3,000 in rent.

In New York City, where I live, people transform studio apartments by adding a folding screen through the middle of the room. It's not the most ideal living situation, but it does save money. If you're spending hundreds of dollars per month on rent, cutting that figure in half (or reducing it to zero) will give you the biggest number jump in your bank account.

Open a savings account. You can grow your hard-earned travel savings by putting it in a high-yield online savings account so that it can earn interest. This is what I did while preparing for my first extended trip, and it netted me hundreds of extra dollars. I'll talk more about this in chapter four.

Get a new credit card. While I will go into more depth about credit cards in chapter five, a good travel credit card can give you free travel by accruing miles and reward points on your card. And that trip doesn't need to be long—you can use those points on a trip that is two weeks or two months. A free flight is a free flight. After all, the best way to save money is to avoid spending it. You'll see the most benefit from this by starting early. As soon as you decide to travel the world, get a travel-related credit card and begin earning free points on your daily purchases.

Earn extra on the side. The rise of the gig economy has made it easier to earn extra money on the side. Taskrabbit (taskrabbit.com) lets you do tasks that people don't have time for—from cleaning to moving, doing research, or helping with errands. Websites like Fiverr (fiverr.com) and Upwork (upwork.com) allow you to be people's assistants, editors, designers, or a host of other professional roles, while Yoodlize (yoodlize.com) allows you to rent out your unused stuff for money. These sites can provide an easy way to earn money on the side. Be sure to check them out as a way to earn extra money for your upcoming trip.

Additionally, you can become an Uber or Lyft driver, teach a skill on the side, or rent out a room on Airbnb. In the age of the "side hustle," there are lots of ways to utilize your proven skills for extra cash. Get creative!

Buy secondhand. Why pay full price when you can pay less? Use Amazon.com, Overstock.com, and Facebook Marketplace (facebook.com/marketplace) to buy secondhand and used items at a discount. I buy most of my furniture from Facebook Marketplace and have found some incredible deals, and the money I save goes straight into my travel account.

Cut coupons. The Entertainment Book, websites like RetailMeNot (retailmenot.com) and the Krazy Coupon Lady (thekrazycouponlady.com), Groupon (groupon.com), grocery coupons, and company loyalty cards (like a CVS ExtraCare card) can all reduce the price you pay at the register. Clipping coupons might make you feel like an eighty-year-old grandmother, but the goal here is to be frugal and coupons definitely help with that. Don't pay full price if you don't have to. The Google Chrome extension Honey (honey.com) can also identify coupon codes on the Web and automatically apply them to your cart when you check out.

Use Rakuten. Rakuten (Rakuten.com) is an app and Web browser extension that gives you cash back on purchases that range from 1 percent to 20 percent. You can also get American Express Membership Rewards points instead of cash back if you want. I use this service for all my shopping, including all my hotel bookings, since many travel companies are on the service. You can also tie a specific credit card to your Rakuten account and get cash back in physical stores too. They offer many deals and I always check this website before making any purchase. When you combine Rakuten with coupon codes you find on the Web, you have a very powerful combo to save money.

Cut back on streaming services. Cutting the cord was supposed to save us money, but with so many subscription services out there, it feels to me that we are paying more than we did with regular cable. I mean how many streaming services do we need!? Rather than subscribe to all of them at once, try rotating which ones you are using. I watch everything I want to watch over the course of a few months on one service, cancel it, sign up for a new service, and repeat. By doing this, you are never paying for more than one service at a time while still being able to binge-watch what you want.

Sell your extra stuff. As you downsize your life, sell your clothes and extra stuff for cash. Sites like The RealReal (therealreal.com), Poshmark (poshmark.com), and Facebook Marketplace all provide an opportunity to get rid of your unwanted stuff and make some decent money.

Stop snacking. A snack here and there not only adds calories to your waistline but also empties your wallet. It is another example of a phantom expense. We don't think much of them because they cost so little, but they add up over time and eat into our savings. Eat fuller meals during lunch and dinner and avoid the snacks. Every penny counts.

Buy a metal water bottle. Plastic single-serve water bottles are not only harmful to the environment, they are also harmful to your wallet. One or two water bottles a day at $1 per bottle will add up to at least $30 a month, or $360 a year. You can spend a week in Thailand with that much money! Instead of plastic, buy a metal water bottle and fill it with tap water.

Change your light bulbs. Electricity costs money and, since every penny counts, using energy-efficient light bulbs will cut down on your utility bills. Moreover, due to energy efficiency initiatives in certain states, many electric companies will give you a rebate if you buy LED bulbs. Be sure to check out which rebates your local energy company offers no matter where you live in the world. Going green can save you green! Check your local government or utility company's website for information.

Save on gas. Gasoline adds up! Luckily, there are plenty of ways to save. First, use the app GasBuddy (gasbuddy.com) to find cheap gas near you. Second, sign up for all the major gas station loyalty programs. By default, they save you around five cents per gallon. Shell's Fuel Rewards is my favorite because you can attach it to a dining program that can get savings up to fifty cents a gallon. Moreover, use GasBuddy's credit card, which can be tied to any gas station loyalty program for an additional savings of twenty-five cents per gallon. Most supermarkets also have loyalty programs that offer gas savings. If you sign up for Costco, they have huge savings on gas too.

Frugality is the watchword of all great travelers. When I was preparing for my first big trip, I clipped coupons, saw cheap matinees, and did my shopping only when there was a sale. If it was nice out, I walked. None of it was "convenient," but when I went abroad with more money than I needed, it was all worth it. I may not have enjoyed living a monastic life for so long at home, but having that extra money allowed me to stay away longer, have more adventures, and not worry about running out of funds.

At the end of the day, the simple truth is that the more you save, the longer you can be on the road, the more comfortable you can be, and the more activities you can do.

Because when you are on safari in Africa or sailing the Galápagos Islands, you won't care about those missed nights out or fancy dinners.

4

BANKING OVERSEAS

Your trip will go a lot smoother if you budget properly and organize your money before you leave, and this starts with setting up the right bank accounts. Since you'll be accessing your money multiple times a week from locations around the world, it's important to have a good bank that is easy to work with and has few fees.

SET UP A NO-FEE CHECKING ACCOUNT

The first thing you want to do is set up a checking account at a major global bank. While we may hate the major banks for, well, a ton of very good reasons, unfortunately smaller banks don't always have the leverage to get better currency exchange rates or keep operations and ATMs around the world. Moreover, most of the world's major banks have partnership agreements with each other where they waive their ATM fees.

Following is a list of the banks linked through the Global ATM Alliance, the principal international banking network. The banks on the list have agreements with one another wherein if you belong to one bank, you can use the ATMs of all the other banks without being charged an ATM fee:

- Bank of America
- Barclays
- BNP Paribas
- Deutsche Bank
- Scotiabank
- Westpac

Note: Bank of America charges a 3 percent transaction fee on all non-USD currency withdrawals, even for banks within the alliance. Tip: Often, if you call Bank of America, they will refund most or all of this transaction fee.

Beyond these banks, individual alliance members have additional partnerships. For example, Bank of America also waives ATM fees with TEB in Turkey, Ukrsibbank in Ukraine, and China Construction Bank in China. And Westpac has an agreement with CIMB, a bank in Indonesia and Malaysia.

It's important to note that some country subsidiaries of the above banks might not be included in the ATM Alliance. For example, if you have Bank of America, the BNP Paribas waiver only works for its France operation (not anything else), while Westpac only works in Australia and New Zealand but not Fiji.

You can search the bank's website for more information about fees, exemptions, and ATM partners. That said, I've found the "Global ATM Alliance" Wikipedia page has a lot of regularly updated bank-specific information all in one place: en.wikipedia.org/wiki/Global_ATM_Alliance.

However, there are many alternatives to these banks that allow you to avoid ATM and transaction fees all the time. In my opinion, the best US bank is Charles Schwab (schwab.com). While Charles Schwab doesn't have deals with any banks overseas like those mentioned previously, they don't charge any ATM fees and will reimburse any ATM fees from other institutions at the end of each month. You will need to open an individual checking account (schwab.com/open-an-account) to qualify, but there is no minimum deposit required and no monthly service fee.

You'll never pay a fee with Charles Schwab, and their ATM card can be used in any bank machine around the world. If there isn't a branch near you, you can open an account online by going to their website. Additionally, they will two-day FedEx you a replacement card anywhere in the world for $15 (although you might be able to talk them out of this fee if it's your first time). This was a lifesaver for me when I realized I lost my card and was about to go to Sri Lanka, a place where cash—not credit cards—is king. They shipped my card to my accommodation in Dubai right away. To me, this is one of the card's best features because most banks will only send your ATM card to your home address, which does you no good when you're traveling.

To me, this is the current BEST ATM card to have. I never, ever think about fees with it.

If you don't want to get the Schwab card (and I don't know why you wouldn't), I also recommend Capital One's 360 Savings Account, which also comes with an ATM card (capitalone.com/bank/savings-accounts/online-performance-savings-account/). Capital One doesn't have a fee when you use non–Capital One ATMs with this account, but you still might be charged a fee by the owner of the ATM machine.

For Canadian travelers, Scotiabank (scotiabank.com) or Tangerine (tangerine.ca/en/personal/spend/chequing-account) are a part of the Global ATM Alliance and waive ATM fees when using their partners.

Note: If you bank with a small community bank, ask them if they will waive any overseas usage fees. There are thousands of banks and policies are always different. Before you switch banks, be sure to double-check what's available with your current bank.

ATM fees can really add up. If you're traveling for a year, you will probably take out money at least twice a week (and some travelers may withdraw even more regularly). Fees vary around the world, but on average you will pay $5 per withdrawal. That is $10 per week, $40 per month, or $520 per year. Even if you only use the ATM half that time, that's still $260 per year!

That's a few days of travel right there! I'd rather have more time on the road than give a bank my hard-earned money.

Additionally, **you will *need* to have an account at two separate banks.**

If your ATM card gets lost or stolen, it is important to have a backup so you can still access your money. While visiting Bangkok many years ago, my HSBC ATM card stopped working, and at the time it was my primary bank card (this was before Schwab's account existed). When I called them up, they told me they found fraudulent charges on the card from Moscow (I've never been to Russia). Someone had duplicated my ATM card and my account had to be closed. A new ATM card was sent to me in the United States, which didn't help because I was in Thailand. However, since I had a backup bank account, I still had a way to access some cash while HSBC got my money back and a family member shipped my card.

My friend Christine from Gothenburg, Sweden, also had a problem because she didn't have a backup card. As she says, "During my monthlong hike across Spain doing the Camino de Compostela, an ATM ate my only bank card. This happened on the weekend, so the bank wouldn't be open for a couple of days. That meant I would have to delay my trip to get it back (assuming I could even get it back). Fortunately, my partner was able to pay for the rest of the trip. If I was traveling solo, it would have been a huge issue, forcing me to delay (or possibly cancel) the rest of my hike. I now make sure to always travel with at least two bank cards, just to be safe."

You always want to have a backup ATM debit card in case a situation like the above happens. Additionally, put limits on your accounts. You can do this online or by calling your bank and asking them to limit your withdrawal amount. This reduces the damage thieves can do if your card gets stolen. You should also put a second user on all your accounts (such as a parent or a trusted friend) so that if there is a problem with one of your accounts, there is someone who can call and help troubleshoot any issues in case you aren't able to.

OPENING AN ONLINE SAVINGS ACCOUNT

The second thing you want to do before you go away is open an online money market savings account in order to earn interest. Before leaving for your trip, you saved a pile of cash, which you will slowly drain as you go around the world.

Even though you might not be working, you can still earn money by having your savings earn interest. According to the finance website Bankrate, most traditional "brick and mortar" banks (think Bank of America or your local credit union) pay less than 0.58 percent interest on your savings account. At that rate, you'll be home long before you even notice any uptick in your balance. Online money market and savings accounts, however, offer much higher interest rates because they lack many of the overhead costs of traditional banks. According to Bankrate, as of May 2024, the average rate for these accounts is 4.92 percent.

Let's say you saved $27,355 for your trip ($75 per day, if anyone is still counting). If you put your extra money into an online money market account at 4.92 percent, you will be gaining $1,345.87 per year. Now, since you will be taking money out on a regular basis as you travel, I'd say a more realistic number is probably $800 to $1,000 in interest per year (especially if you save the expensive countries for last).

In order to maximize the interest I earn, I keep only two weeks' worth of living expenses in my checking account (which also limits the damage that can be done if someone steals my ATM card as noted above). When I need more money, I simply transfer the necessary amount from my money market account into my checking account. That way my money has more time to earn interest instead of sitting in a checking account earning nothing.

It might not seem like $800 would make a big difference in traveling, but in some areas of the world, you only need about $25–$30 per day to survive so that $800 will go a long way!

Be certain to make sure the banks are insured by the FDIC (Federal Deposit Insurance Corporation) so that if a bank collapses (which is highly, *highly* unlikely) your money will be insured. And, since interest rates change frequently, be sure to check the bank's website for the most up-to-date rates. I use Bankrate (bankrate.com), which monitors interest rates from around the country.

The third and final thing you need to do is link all your accounts. You'll have two checking accounts at different banks (with an ATM card) and one online money market savings account. Link both checking accounts to your money market savings account so you can shift money to whatever ATM account you want to use.

MINIMIZING FEES AND PENALTIES

Every time you use your card in a foreign country, your bank converts the foreign currency you were charged into your local currency for billing purposes. And they charge you a small percentage for doing so (on average about 3 percent).

Since banks take a little off the top of each transaction, you'll never be able to get the listed official exchange rate you find online. You can check currency rate sites like XE (xe.com). If you have a smartphone, the free Currency app (currencyapp.com) is also a good way to monitor rates. Both will show you the interbank rate and, unless you become a bank, you'll never get that.

But there are six things you can do to get a rate as *close* to the official rate as possible:

Use a credit card. Credit card companies offer the best exchange rates and convert your money closest to the official exchange rate. Whenever possible, I always use my credit card for purchases overseas so I know that I am getting the best exchange rate possible.

I hardly ever use cash. I'll discuss more in the next chapter about which cards are the best to travel with as well as which ones waive the fee for using them overseas.

Use a debit card. ATMs offer the best exchange rate after credit cards. They aren't as good as credit cards, since commercial banks take a little more off the top, but it's much better than exchanging cash.

Don't change unneeded cash. Changing cash, especially at the airport, is the worst thing you can do. Unless I am stuck with cash I need to get rid of, or the exchange rate suddenly changes a lot, I never change money. Most exchange bureaus are so far down the financial food chain they don't have the clout to offer good exchange rates. Moreover, nonbanks charge especially high commissions and fees for exchanging money, and if they don't, they make their money by giving you an even lower exchange rate.

Don't use ATMs in weird locations. Using those ATMs you find in hotels, hostels, local 7-Elevens, or some other random place is a bad idea. They may be convenient, but you'll pay for that convenience. They often charge high ATM fees and offer horrible exchange rates. Even if you get the ATM fee waived, the exchange rate will be worse than if you use a major international bank.

Always pick the local currency. When you use your credit card abroad, you are often given the option of being charged in your home currency (for example, being charged in USD instead of euros). Never say yes to this option. The preset conversion rate is always worse, so pick the local currency and let your credit card company make the conversion. You'll get a better rate.

Don't get currency at home (and skip foreign currency cards).
While buying currency at home might seem like a good idea, you'll end up getting a worse exchange rate. Unless you are 100 percent sure you'll need cash right on arrival, avoid exchanging money in your home country.

On a recent trip to Japan, a friend exchanged dollars for yen before she left the US when the official exchange rate was 147 yen to $1 USD. The rate they got? 117 yen to $1 USD. That's a 20 percent difference! Don't be like my friend (who didn't listen to me). Your credit card will get you a lot closer to the official rate.

Additionally, avoid any "foreign currency cards" where you can preload money and lock in the exchange rate. Seems like a good idea, right? Wrong! You are basically trying to predict the exchange rate and betting you can beat the market. You're saying this rate is not going to get worse, but what if it gets better? You don't know! (And, if you do know, you should be placing bets in the market.) Moreover, these cards come with a lot of fees. Just avoid them.

Rather than try to hedge one way or the other, just use the ATM at whatever the current rate is when you travel. And, honestly, exchange rates don't move that much in a short period of time.

It's important to be proactive when it comes to banking and currency exchange. I see too many travelers hit the ATM without paying attention to the latest exchange rates or considering the fees they are paying. They then wonder why their money seems to be draining faster than they budgeted—because no one really accounts for bank fees in their daily budgets! Be smart so you give the banks less and keep more for your trip.

5

CREDIT CARDS

Travel credit cards are crucial to reducing your costs and making your travels easier. They can get you cheap flights, free accommodations, lounge access, and elite airline status. As we discussed in the previous chapters, they can also help you save on exchange rates, avoid bank fees, and so much more. There are many travel credit cards out there that offer different kinds of rewards, from general points programs to branded hotel and airline cards.

If you love travel, having at least one travel-related, points-earning credit card is a no-brainer. Credit cards offer too many benefits to pass up, and in this chapter, we will explore how to use them to their maximum potential.

First, let's talk about credit cards in general. There is a persistent negative image about credit cards, and a lot of that has to do with the fact that we've heard since childhood that they are risky (they lead to debt, they make us overspend, there are always hidden fees, and so on). There is also the common advice that we should avoid having a lot of credit cards to protect our credit score. (But what good is a credit score if you don't use it?) In short, credit cards have become a symbol of everything that is wrong with modern finance.

There's some truth to that: credit cards, especially travel-related ones, do come with high interest rates as well as regular annual fees. And once you are stuck on the debt wheel, it can be hard to get off.

I'm not here to cheer on big banks, but when used properly, credit cards are a better option than using a debit card, especially when you travel. Debit cards don't come with the consumer protections and benefits that credit cards do, and they don't come with as many travel perks, insurance benefits, or reduced fees, especially when used internationally. If someone uses your credit card illegally or you have a problem with a merchant, you can call up the card issuer and dispute the charge before the money ever gets deducted from your bank account. If you pay with a debit card, you have to fight to get the money back, which can be time-consuming and difficult.

When I had my credit card duplicated on a trip to South Africa, I called up Capital One (my card issuer at the time), and they put a hold on my account and wiped the charges. Easy-peasy. However, like I mentioned in the last chapter, when my debit card was duplicated, the money was taken directly from my bank account and it took close to a month to get it back.

If you pay your credit card bill on time and in full, you'll face no penalty, interest, or late fees. Your card is basically printing you free money (in the form of cash back or points). It's a huge win for you, the consumer.

THE LOWDOWN ON CREDIT SCORES

Let's talk about credit scores for a moment. All forms of credit (credit cards, mortgages, loans, or other kinds of debt) are issued based on your FICO credit score. The higher your score, the easier it is to get a loan with a better interest rate or a credit card with a higher credit limit.

In the United States, your credit score is based on the FICO scale from 300 to 850. Outside of your payment history, your credit utilization is the most important factor in your credit score. If you have $100,000 in available credit but are only using $5,000, that's better than only having $5,000 in credit and using all of it every month. A lot of people ask me if having a lot of credit cards hurts your credit score—and the answer is no. Having more cards can actually *help* your credit score by allowing you to have a high debt-to-credit ratio.

As Brian Kelly from thepointsguy.com, a website that teaches people how to use credit cards to gain loyalty points, told me, "While in its own words, FICO says 'opening several credit accounts in a short period of time represents greater credit risk,' that's because you're applying for multiple lines of new credit rather than submitting several inquiries for a single new line, such as a mortgage. In general, however, the impact on your score from multiple inquiries is small—and remember that new credit counts only 10 percent toward determining your overall FICO score. So as long as you are strong in the other areas that determine your score, like payment history and amounts owed, you should be fine to apply for new cards."

Brian is constantly opening credit accounts and has had the

same experience as I have. He recommends that "ideally you should space your applications several months apart." That's the key. Your credit score will slightly dip every time there is a new inquiry, but so long as you space out your applications and maintain good credit along the way, you won't do any long-term damage to your credit. Your credit rating rises over time as long as you maintain it; you aren't going to have a bank officer tell you years from now, "Sorry, your loan is denied because you canceled three credit cards in 2018." I once canceled four credit cards in one day, and the impact on my score? Nothing.

WHAT MAKES A GOOD CREDIT CARD

Travel-related credit cards often offer huge sign-up bonuses of forty thousand to one hundred thousand points. Most of the time, these points are worth *at least* two free flights, which will save you hundreds (maybe even thousands) of dollars. Additionally, those points can also be used for accommodations so you can save on both of your biggest travel expenses.

Before I go into detail on what you should look for when choosing a travel credit card, I want to give you some good credit card habits so you don't bite off more than you can chew.

- **DO** pay your balance in full and on time to avoid interest and fees. You can set up auto-payments to ensure that you never miss a due date (or at least make yourself a calendar reminder)!
- **DON'T** spend more than you earn. Seriously.
- **DON'T** cancel no-fee cards. Since the length of your

credit history is a factor in your credit score, if a card doesn't have a yearly fee, don't cancel it. Throw it in a drawer and forget about it. It only helps you.

- **DON'T** apply for a lot of cards at once. To avoid being declined, don't apply for more than two cards in one day.
- **DO** wait a few months between applying for cards. Applying for new credit cards gives you a temporary "ding" on your credit score, but it will go away after two or three months.
- **DO** remember to switch to a low- or no-fee card before you cancel an existing card. If you are going to cancel a card because of an annual fee, try to get the card moved to a no-fee version instead of canceling to preserve your credit line—and your credit score.

So what specifically should you look for in a card? A good credit card should have the following:

Huge sign-up bonus. A sign-up bonus can jump-start your mileage account and get you close to a free flight. Typical card bonuses range from between 40,000 and 100,000 points, though sometimes they can be as high as 150,000. That's why cards are so great—you get an instant influx of tens of thousands of points for very little work.

As a rule, you must make either a single purchase or meet a minimum spending threshold to receive the large introductory offer, so make sure you can hit the spending threshold in the allotted time frame.

Since offers and bonuses vary, it's important to keep track of the latest deals. The best websites are the following:

- **BoardingArea** (boardingarea.com): A website that contains a series of blogs that discuss how to fly for free and gain airline miles and elite status quickly.
- **FlyerTalk** (flyertalk.com): A forum site where people post the latest flight bonuses and miles specials.
- **The Points Guy** (thepointsguy.com): A website that helps people navigate credit card bonus and airline and hotel reward programs.
- **Prince of Travel** (princeoftravel.com): The best deal website in Canada.
- **View from the Wing** (viewfromthewing.com): An incredible resource for learning the ins and outs of airline frequent-flier programs, travel-related credit cards, and industry news.

Added-category spending bonuses. Most credit cards offer one point for every dollar spent. However, I don't want one dollar to equal just one point. I want the ability to get two or more points every time I spend a dollar so I can get free travel quicker. The best credit cards will give you extra points on certain categories of spending. For example, with the Chase Sapphire Preferred card, you get two points for every dollar spent on travel and restaurant dining; the Chase Ink Business card gives you three points per dollar for office spending; and the Premier Rewards Gold Card from American Express gives three points per dollar on airfare and four points per dollar at restaurants and grocery stores.

I use cards in my day-to-day spending that give me more than just one mile per dollar spent. For example, I pay for dinner with the Chase Sapphire Preferred card, book my flights with the

Premier Rewards Gold Card from American Express, and pay my phone bill with my Chase Ink Business card.

Be sure to get a card that accelerates your points earning or it will take a long, long time to earn enough points that you can redeem for free travel.

Low minimum spending requirement. Unfortunately, to get the great welcome bonuses these cards offer, there is often a required spending minimum. I typically sign up for cards with a minimum spending requirement of $3,000 in a three- to six-month period, which is usually achievable with your regular day-to-day spending.

While you shouldn't necessarily avoid cards with a high minimum spending requirement (as they often have substantial rewards), it's a good idea to start small. If you go crazy and sign up for ten cards in a short window of time, you might find yourself stuck with having to spend $10,000 to $30,000 in three months to get all your bonus points.

Before you decide to sign up for several credit cards, properly research the required spending limits and how much money you normally spend each month to ensure you will be getting the best value possible.

I try to time my sign-up bonuses with major purchases, such as airline tickets, holiday shopping, a new laptop, or seasonal clothing shopping to help me reach the minimum spending requirement. You'll be making a lot of purchases as you prepare for your trip—from flights to insurance to gear—which makes it an excellent time to get a new card because it's easier to hit any minimum spending requirement.

Additional travel perks. All travel credit cards offer great perks, so it's important to focus on the ones that matter most to you. Many will give you a special elite loyalty status, free lounge access, priority boarding, check-in, covered fees for TSA PreCheck, and so much more. Here are the perks I personally prioritize:

- No foreign transaction fees
- Free checked baggage
- Priority boarding
- International lounge access

Using travel credit cards is not just about getting points or reducing fees; it's about the added perks that make your life easier when you travel!

A NOTE ON FOREIGN TRANSACTION FEES

Credit card companies used to frequently charge a 3 percent foreign transaction fee when you used your card overseas. Thankfully, it's become much more common for credit cards to waive foreign transaction fees altogether. In fact, it's very rare to find a card that still charges you 3 percent when using the card abroad, so if you do encounter one, don't get it and move on to the next.

A NOTE ON ANNUAL FEES

Many fees for company-branded credit cards range from $50 to $95 per year (though some are as high as $650). Fee-based cards tend to offer superior rewards schemes that have faster points accumulation, better access to services and special offers, and better travel protection. With these cards, I've saved more money on travel than I've spent on fees.

That being said, most fee-based cards waive the first year's fee for new customers, so you get a year free. After that, you can either cancel the card or move to a no-fee version. Whenever I call up to cancel a card, the company (wanting to keep my business) either waives the fee for another year or switches me to a no-fee card. If they move me to a no-fee card, they usually feature a less-generous rewards program, but by that point I've gotten my sign-up bonus and moved on to a better card anyway.

If the above isn't possible, try to move your credit line to a different card with the same issuer. It's the loss of credit that dings your score the most, so try to keep your credit limit intact with the issuer for as long as you can.

WHAT IF YOU HAVE POOR CREDIT?

Many travel rewards cards are only available to consumers with a high credit score, so if you have a low score (650 or less), you may find yourself declined for a new card.

Sadly, there's no magic bullet to suddenly fixing your credit score. It just takes time.

But one thing you can do to start the process is to get a secured credit card. These cards require you to put down a cash deposit, which then becomes your credit limit. If you decide to put $500 in your secured credit card, you can use up to $500 each month. Over time, you can raise the limit, which will in turn raise your credit score, allowing you to move to a regular credit card.

HOW TO LEVERAGE YOUR CARDS FOR MAXIMUM VALUE

After you have picked your goal and found the right card for you, you'll want to maximize how you use the card so you can accrue the most points possible before you travel. Here's how to do it:

Everyday Spending

The first thing you should do is put all of your day-to-day spending on a credit card. Every dollar spent not using your card is a point lost. I never pay cash or use a debit card unless I absolutely have to. For example, if you spend $3,000 each month on your regular expenses, that adds up to 36,000 redeemable points (at one point per dollar) each year without any extra effort.

However, as I mentioned before, certain cards have category bonuses that give you two to five points per dollar spent. It varies by card, but generally, you can get two to four points on restaurants, two to five points on airfare, and five points on office supplies.

Why just get one point when you can get even more? Make sure you are optimizing your cards for bonus categories. Don't ever waste a chance to get multiple points per dollar spent. With a little forethought, you can easily turn those 36,000 points per year into 100,000 points per year.

A word of caution: Don't spread yourself too thin. If you're using five credit cards for five different rewards programs, it's going to take a lot longer to earn enough points for free travel. If you're using multiple cards that tie into the same program, like I do with my American Express cards (i.e., two Amex cards that tie into their Membership Rewards program), that's OK because you don't dilute the points as they go into the same combined pool.

You want to avoid earning only a few points here, a few points there, and a few points over there. Focus your spending on two or three cards.

Online Shopping

All airlines, hotels, and travel brands partner with merchants—from clothing retailers to sporting goods stores to office supply businesses and everything in between—to be featured on that brand's special shopping portals. By ordering online through these shopping portals, you can earn extra points for the brand in addition to your credit card points.

For example, buying new clothes at your local Gap store gets you one point per $1 spent. But if you check the websites Evreward (evreward.com) or Cash Back Monitor (cashbackmonitor.com), you may find that by buying your Gap clothes through the United Airlines shopping portal, you can earn three points per dollar spent. Suddenly, you get four hundred points instead of one hundred for your $100 shopping spree (e.g., one hundred credit card points plus three hundred United miles)!

It's always important to incorporate using these portals into your online shopping routine as much as possible.

Swagbucks

Swagbucks (swagbucks.com) is a website that pays you "Swag-bucks" (in the form of gift cards) to answer surveys, watch videos online, and try new products. Each Swagbuck is equivalent to about one cent, so if you're dedicated, you can realistically earn about $90 a month doing this. If you have the time, you can mindlessly earn an extra $1,000 per year.

Swagbucks also partners with many travel companies. If you click through the Swagbucks website to buy the flights, hotels, and rental car purchases (which you were going to make anyway), you earn one to ten points per dollar spent.

InboxDollars

InboxDollars is another website where you can earn money by watching short online videos, going through their site to purchase Groupon deals, taking surveys, and so on. You can earn up to six cents per short video, and surveys pay between $0.35 and $5 each.

Dining Rewards Programs

Similar to shopping portals, many airlines also have dining rewards programs. You sign up with your frequent-flier number, register your credit card, and get extra points when you dine at participating restaurants in the airline's network (which rotate throughout the year).

Join one of the programs in the Rewards Network (rewards-network.com/earn/)—they run all the dining programs—and you can get up to five miles per dollar spent.

Note: While you can sign up for every program, you cannot register a credit card with more than one. That means that if your Chase Sapphire Preferred card is tied to your American Airlines account, you can't earn miles on your United Airlines account with that same card.

Double-Dipping with Crossover Rewards

Thanks to a number of partnerships, you can often "double-dip," where each dollar spent gets you points in two or more reward programs. Even though the amount you earn is often small, extra points are always great, especially when you don't have to do anything more than connect accounts and let the system do everything else.

Here are some examples of crossover rewards at the time of writing:

- When you use Lyft, you can also get 1x Delta SkyMiles (2x SkyMiles on US airport rides) or 3x Hilton Honors points per dollar spent.
- When you use Airbnb, you can also get 1x Delta SkyMiles or 3x British Airways Avios per dollar spent.
- When you use Starbucks, you can also get 1x Delta SkyMiles per dollar spent.
- When you use Uber, you can also get 3x Marriott Bonvoy points per dollar spent (on Uber premium rides).
- When you use Uber Eats, you can get 6x Marriott Bonvoy points when ordering to a Marriott property or 2x points on all other Uber Eats orders ($40 minimum).

I always keep an eye out for these partnerships, even if I'll never use them much. It's better to be enrolled and get occasional bonus points than get no points at all! It's a nice cherry on top.

Paying Your Rent

If you're a United States resident, you can use a company called Bilt (biltrewards.com) to pay your rent without any fees. This credit card uses transferable points, has no yearly fee, and lets you pay your rent via ACH or check. It is an incredible way to earn lots of points on rent payments, which has been historically impossible to earn points for. If you are a renter, there's absolutely no reason not to have one of these cards.

———

In the movie *Up in the Air*, George Clooney's character says, "I don't do anything if it doesn't benefit my miles account." Think like that. Everything you do can earn points, whether big or small. But they all add up! And the quicker they add up, the easier it is to get free travel. Get a card, collect points, redeem them for free travel, and spend more time on the road!

6

AIRLINE TICKETS

One of the most common reasons why people don't travel relates to the cost of airfare. And whether you are going to be traveling around the world or just want to go to Brazil for a few weeks, you're going to need to reduce your flight costs.

Since I want you to afford that plane ticket and head somewhere amazing, I'm going to lay out the best ways to score cheap flights. But, before we get into the particulars, let's talk about why airfare is expensive. If you've been flying for the past few years, you might have noticed ticket prices seem to be going as high as the planes you'll be flying.

For starters, the industry has consolidated *a lot* over the last few decades. Thanks to bankruptcies and mergers, there are now only three major alliance airlines (American, Delta, and United) in the United States (though there are a number of smaller airlines). In Canada, there are only two major airlines. In Europe, Air France–KLM, British Airways IAG, and Lufthansa control the bulk of the market. As airlines have partnered up, merged, or gone bankrupt, there is little incentive to provide low fares to win your business.

Second, the price of jet fuel has increased significantly. In May 2017, when the last edition of this book was published, jet fuel cost $1.37 per gallon. In 2024, it is $6.49 per gallon! Airlines have simply passed that fivefold increase on to the consumer.

Third, airline taxes and security fees have also increased over the years, adding potentially hundreds of dollars onto your base fare.

Finally, demand fell following the 2008 recession, and to compensate, airlines reduced both the number of routes they offered and the frequency of their flights. Fuller planes mean more passenger revenue and fewer costs for the airline.

That trend greatly accelerated during COVID. When COVID shut down global travel, airlines mothballed a lot of their older planes and fired a lot of their staff. When travel restrictions were lifted and more people starting flying again, they didn't have enough planes or staff to return to a pre-COVID schedule. This decrease in the supply of flights coupled with the surge in demand for travel meant that airlines had little incentive to lower prices.

Airlines use something called dynamic pricing to determine fares. While no one can really predict when or if a ticket price is going to go up or down (only the airline knows that), there are four major things that drive prices: competition, supply, demand, and fuel prices. On a US domestic ticket, a flight might have ten to fifteen different price points. Airlines want to fill a plane with the people paying the highest price (to get maximum revenue), so they use dynamic pricing models and artificial intelligence (AI) to figure out the maximum value they can get for each seat.

Airlines have developed sophisticated computer systems that constantly compare booking trends to past sales history and constantly look at major events like concerts, sports, award shows, weather, and competitor behavior.

All of this is why one day a flight may cost $100, then $400 the next, and then back to $100 the day after that. As people buy seats on a flight, airlines raise prices, and when demand falls (at a certain price point), they lower prices until fewer and fewer seats are available, then they will raise prices again. It's a delicate balance designed to ensure maximum revenue. It's why prices are cheapest for 5 AM flights, more expensive over the holidays, and through the roof during peak season or if there's a major sports event in town. After all, you can't add more seats to a plane, so all they can do to raise revenue is charge higher fares!

I used to spend hours upon hours searching for airline tickets. I'd search multiple websites, second-guess myself, and worry about when the prices might drop. I would hold off on buying, waiting for that perfect moment. But it was like trying to time the market—it simply doesn't work.

You can't predict prices. The best day to book a flight is generally the day you are looking. And, post-COVID, airlines have waived change fees so if you do find the cost of your ticket goes down, you can cancel it and rebook at a lower price. (The canceled fare can be used as a flight credit on a future flight. That isn't as good as getting your money back, but it's better than nothing, especially if you know you're going to be taking future flights with that airline.)

Rather than try to "time the market," you can often find cheap airfare by using a few basic strategies.

As a world traveler, you have two options for flying: you can either buy a round-the-world ticket or pay for your flights as you fly from point to point.

ROUND-THE-WORLD TICKETS

Round-the-world (RTW) tickets can be a convenient way to fly around the world. They get you where you want to go without having to worry about booking flights along the way. By pre-purchasing all your tickets in one giant bulk package, you can often save money compared to buying lots of individual tickets as you go.

Previous editions of this book provided detailed sections on round-the-world tickets—how to buy them, how to calculate the math, how to navigate the rules, and so on.

However, as of 2024, in an age of points and miles and budget airlines, I don't think these tickets are a good value anymore. Most alliances have gotten rid of their round-the-world tickets, and those that still offer them no longer let you use miles to buy them and have added a lot of other restrictions.

Other travel writers may disagree but, in my professional opinion, round-the-world tickets should be avoided.

POINT-TO-POINT FLIGHTS

Point-to-point flights simply refer to any flight that takes you from point A to point B (even with a stopover). Over the years, I've accumulated a system for finding cheap point-to-point flights, and, in this section, I am going to share all those tips.

But, before we get to that, I want to first dispel some myths about buying flights that get perpetuated and recycled by lazy journalists and bloggers.

First, it is NOT cheaper to buy airfare on a Tuesday (or any other specific day for that matter). Yes, there are times of the day when flights are cheaper but there is no single day of the week when fares are cheaper. It used to be that airlines literally uploaded their flight schedules and fares on Tuesday and competitors would offer sales to follow suit, which is where this trick comes from. But now, with dynamic pricing, prices change (and sales happen) regardless of the day of the week.

Second, there is NO evidence that searching incognito leads to cheaper deals. Now, you're probably saying, "But, Matt, I did this and it worked for me." To which I reply, "Remember what I said about dynamic pricing and a set number of seats on a plane? That's why the price changed so quickly." It's not that you found a hack; it's just that other people might have put the cheaper fare in their shopping cart in the time it took you to change browsers and search again. And, in that time, the price changed.

Third, there is NO exact date or specific time frame to find the best airfare. While there are generally agreed-upon guidelines (a few months for domestic US flights and up to six months for international flights), there's no hard-and-fast rule. Again, it's due to dynamic pricing.

Remember, airlines use artificial intelligence and advanced algorithms to determine prices and run sales based on the time of year, passenger demand, weather, major events, time of day, competitor prices, fuel prices, and much more. If you could predict flight prices, you'd have a billion-dollar business.

If any of the "secret loopholes and tricks" you hear about worked so effectively, the airlines would close these loopholes right away because it would cause them to lose money. And airlines aren't going to do that, so don't listen to anyone who promises secret hacks. Anyone who is telling you otherwise doesn't know what they are talking about. **There is no magic bullet or one secret ninja trick to finding a cheap flight.**

However, there are a few rules and guidelines that, when followed, will ensure you are not the person who paid the most for their ticket.

Be Flexible with Your Dates

Ticket prices vary greatly depending on the day, time of day, time of year, and upcoming holidays. Being flexible with your dates and times is one of the most important ways to save money. The difference of a single day can mean the difference of hundreds of dollars. For example, it's often cheaper to fly midweek than on a weekend because most people travel on the weekends and airlines raise prices for those flights.

Anytime more people want to fly, fares go up. Want to go to Europe in the summer, or Hawaii during Christmas, or Disneyland when the kids are on spring break? So does everybody else! Think about Thanksgiving, which is on a Thursday. Everyone flies to their destination on Tuesday and Wednesday, so fares are higher on those days. Most people return on Sunday or Monday, so fares are high those days too. But, because most people want to stay with their families and shop on that Friday, return fares are generally lower on that day, making it the best day to travel.

The same logic applies to early-morning and late-night flights, because few people want to be up at 5 AM for a flight or fly overnight.

If you're looking to go to Paris in the summer, airfare is likely going to be very high since lots of other people will be doing the same. But maybe fewer people are going to Mexico or Australia, which means fares will be cheaper during that time frame. Be a contrarian traveler and go to places in the shoulder or off-season.

If you aren't flexible in the dates and times you want to fly, you will never be able to find a cheap flight.

Be Flexible with Your Destinations

Instead of going to a place with an expensive flight, go where the flights are the cheapest. Skyscanner (skyscanner.com) and Google Flights (google.com/flights) offer an "Explore" tool that allows you to put in your departure airport and see routes and prices all around the world. Just look to see what destination is the cheapest! If you are flexible with where you want to go (as in "anywhere but home"), this is a great way to start researching your next trip. I always enter in my departing airport and search for "anywhere." Whatever flights are cheapest to a region I want to explore is often where I fly into.

Fly Budget Airlines

In the United States, there are only a handful of budget airlines. In Europe and Asia, there are *dozens*—and this competition has kept flight prices very low in those regions. You will get fewer perks on these budget airlines than you would with "the majors," but you can save a bundle in ticket costs, with fares as low as $20. (Note: Be sure to check out how far the airports are from the city center; sometimes transportation from the airport to the city can actually make a budget airline more expensive.)

Moreover, years ago, if you wanted to fly between continents, you were mostly stuck with traditional expensive airlines, but that's no longer the case. More and more budget carriers are doing long-haul, cross-continent flights (such as Norse to the United States from Europe, Zipair to Japan, or AirAsia from Asia to Australia). Don't snooze on these airlines.

Check Multiple Search Sites

When looking for a flight, search as many flight search websites as you can to ensure you are leaving no stone unturned. All websites have their weaknesses, and none of them will include every airline. You aren't going to find AirAsia, Ryanair, or most other budget airlines on large US-based sites—other websites are better for certain regions of the world. No website is perfect so be sure to check multiple websites before booking a flight.

I search the following three websites whenever I'm looking for a plane ticket:

- Skyscanner: skyscanner.com
- Momondo: momondo.com
- Google Flights: google.com/flights

Find Alternative Routes

Try being flexible with the route you take to your final destination. There are so many budget carriers around the world that taking advantage of a good deal to another city and then hopping on a budget flight to your destination is sometimes the best way to go. You can often find several budget flights that will lower the cost compared to a single direct route. For example, I once found a $900 direct flight to Paris, but with a little digging, I discovered I could fly to Dublin for $600 and get a $60 flight to Paris. It meant more flying time, but the $240 I saved was worth it. By working various airlines and special offers, you can save a lot. This method is more work as you have to figure out lots of different routes and check different airlines, but it will often shave money off your flight, giving you more to spend at your destination.

Use Frequent-Flier Miles

Airline rewards programs are a great way to get free flights, up-grades, and companion tickets. No matter how often you fly, you should sign up for an airline's reward program. I stick to US-based airlines because they are aligned with all the major alliances and you can earn miles on their partner flights. For example, if I fly Singapore Airlines, I can earn United Airlines miles because they are partners. I get Delta miles on Air France flights, or American Airlines points when I fly Cathay Pacific. You should always be earning miles when you fly. (If you aren't from the United States, simply use the airline you fly most and bank miles to them.)

Refer to the previous chapter on credit cards for more information on collecting points and miles.

Don't Miss Out on Sales

No one likes to clutter up their inbox, but by signing up for mailing lists, you'll be able to get updates about last-minute deals or mistake fares (fares priced below normal). Many times, ticket sales are available for a short amount of time, and if you aren't always checking the Web, you could miss out. I would have missed a round-trip ticket to Japan for $700 (normally $1,500) if I hadn't been on the American Airlines mailing list.

The following websites are my favorites for finding deals:

- Going: going.com
- HolidayPirates: holidaypirates.com (Europe-based)
- The Flight Deal: theflightdeal.com
- Thrifty Traveler: thriftytraveler.com

Search Ticket Prices as One Person

Don't search for or buy multiple tickets in a single purchase. Airlines always show the highest ticket price in a group of tickets, so if you are a family searching for four seats, the airline will look for four seats together and show results based on the highest ticket price. For example, if seat A is $200, seats B and C are $300, and seat D is $400, it will return a price as if each ticket costs $400 instead of adding up the individual ticket prices. Therefore, always search for tickets as a single person. Afterward, in the checkout process, you can pick your seats so you and your family/partner can sit together.

Look for Tickets in Other Currencies

If your country's currency is currently strong compared to others around the world, search for airfare in a country where the currency is weaker. For example, I found a one-way flight from

Australia to New York City for $1,000, but when I searched on the New Zealand version of the airline's website, I found the same ticket for $600. It was the same airline, same flight, and same booking class. It was just booked in a different currency.

This only works when you are buying tickets for flights within a country or from that country. If you go to the Australian version of a US-based airline looking for tickets for travel within the US, you aren't going to find a deal. But if you are looking for flights *within* Australia, then the Australian version *may* be cheaper.

Buy at the Right Time

While there is no general best day to pick your flights, there are some general windows that are better than others. The best time to book a ticket is six to eight weeks before your flight, or twelve to sixteen weeks ahead if you are booking during peak season. During this time period, airlines generally know if a flight is going to sell or not and will begin to either lower or increase fares based on demand. Usually this is when prices are at their lowest.

Don't wait until the last second because airlines realize if you are booking close to departure, you probably need the flight and are willing to pay whatever the price is. Conversely, don't book too far in advance because airlines are going to wait as long as possible to release the cheaper fares.

7

BACKPACKS AND SUITCASES

The most important gear you are going to have on your trip is the bag that holds all your belongings. For most round-the-world travelers, this is the backpack. Most seasoned travelers use a backpack instead of a rolling suitcase because it is much easier to travel with. It just slings on your back and you don't need to lug it over streets, across cobblestones, or up the stairs.

SHOULD YOU GET A SUITCASE OR BACKPACK?

Suitcases are a pain in the butt for long-term travel. Your luggage is going to get thrown about and piled high on buses in random countries. It will get used and abused, and it's simply hard to walk up hills and stairs with your suitcase bump, bump, bumping everywhere. Whenever I travel long-term with a suitcase, it always comes back in bad shape. Backpacks, on the other hand, are easy to carry up stairs and pack into tight places. Overall, they just make life simpler. I don't need to pick one up when I get on an escalator. I can just walk with the backpack...on my back! Simple. Easy.

If you have back problems and can't use a backpack, a smaller suitcase with wheels and a long handle can be a good substitute. It will still be difficult to carry it up and down stairs, and it will be annoying as you roll it across uneven sidewalks, but there are many companies (like those listed at the end of this section) that make decent lightweight travel cases. Additionally, there are many hybrid backpack/suitcase products that might be worth looking into.

In my opinion, suitcases are great for short trips or if you're staying in one place for a long time. But if you are moving around a lot, it is far better to have a backpack. Backpacks just make more sense, which is why this chapter is devoted to them and not suitcases.

CHOOSING THE RIGHT BACKPACK

Picking the right travel backpack is one of the most important things you'll do before you leave. If you pick one that is too big, you'll be carrying around too much extra weight. If your backpack is too small, you won't be able to fit everything you want inside. If you pick the wrong material, your stuff will get soaked when it rains.

There are many backpack brands and many, many places where you can purchase one. No matter where or what you purchase, the best backpacks all share the following characteristics that make them durable, protective, and long-lasting.

Material

While it does not need to be 100 percent waterproof, make sure your backpack is made of a water-resistant material so everything doesn't get wet in a drizzle. (Many packs come with rain covers you can put over them in case of a severe downpour.) Moreover, make sure the material is quick drying so your bag doesn't get musty. Generally, I look for material that is a little thick but also lightweight. I should be able to pour a cup of water over it without the contents getting wet. I don't often travel in torrential downpours or monsoons, but I have been caught in small rainstorms, and because my backpack is made from a good water-resistant material, I've never opened my bag to find wet clothes.

Lockable Zippers

Make sure each compartment has two zippers so you can lock them together. While I am not particularly worried about people breaking into my bag and stealing my dirty clothes in a hostel or hotel, I still like locking up my zippers when I am traveling. I'm always paranoid that someone is going to put something in my bag or a grabby baggage handler is going to take my stuff. When purchasing locks, make sure the package says they are TSA-friendly locks. These locks have a special release that allows the TSA to open and check your bag. That way when the TSA checks your bag for security, they don't have to break your locks. You can purchase TSA locks at any large retail store, such as Target or Walmart.

Multiple Compartments

I like a bag to have multiple compartments. This way, I can break up my belongings into smaller sections so it's easier to access the stuff I need. My clothes are in the main compartment, my umbrella and flip-flops are in the top, and my shoes are in a separate side compartment (that way they don't get anything dirty). This saves time since I don't have to dig around my bag. You want convenience, and multiple compartments help give you that.

Internal Frame

Most backpacks today are internal-frame packs, meaning the support rods and frame are built into the backpack and hidden from view. However, there are still some external-frame backpacks out there, where the rods are separate from the actual pack. Think of the backpacks you see in old hiking movies or movies about people backpacking Europe in the 1970s—we're talking a big clunky metal frame. Don't get one of those. An internal-frame backpack not only looks better, but the rods won't get caught on anything and your bag will be slimmer, making it easier to move around. Additionally, internal frame packs tend to be lighter as the frame is composed of a lighter alloy.

Padded Hip Belt

Most of the weight you carry around will be pushing down on your hips, so you'll want a padded belt to make supporting the weight more comfortable. The belt will help provide support and distribute the weight load more evenly, causing less strain and fewer problems. The hip belt should also be adjustable so you can tighten it for extra support. (Plus, they usually have pockets for small items and coins.)

Padded Shoulder Straps

These make carrying your load more comfortable, as the weight of your pack will also be distributed across your shoulders. Good padded straps will put less pressure on your shoulders and also help take pressure off your lower back. Make sure the padding is very thick and made up of a single piece, as it will be less likely to split and thin with time. After close to ten years, the padding on my backpack is only slightly worn.

Chest Strap

A backpack with an adjustable chest strap helps shift the weight evenly across your upper body, making that walk up the hill to the hostel much, much easier. It also takes a lot of the pressure off your shoulders and helps avoid shoulder and back problems.

Contoured/Padded Back

As with contoured chairs, a lumbar-shaped pack allows for a more natural arch in your spine, eliminating one of the most common causes of back pain. Moreover, this type of pack creates a small space between your back and the bag, allowing air to move through and help keep you slightly cool. Lugging your bag around can build up a sweat!

WHY SIZE DOESN'T MATTER

One of the most frequently asked questions I get about backpacks is about size. Everyone wants to know what the perfect size is. Well, there is no perfect size. The smallest backpacks are usually 43 liters, and they can go up to as large as 110 liters. They also come in a number of torso and hip sizes to ensure that everyone— no matter how big or small—can find a pack that fits them.

No one backpack size is better than another. What matters is that your backpack should be both comfortable and proportional to your body. If your backpack is too big or too small, the weight won't be balanced properly and will cause back pain—or maybe even make you topple over. You don't want a skyscraper rising up from your back, but you also don't want a pack that is clearly too small and overflowing with stuff.

You want a backpack that is big enough to hold just a bit more than the stuff you are bringing. Keep in mind that you don't need to bring everything but the kitchen sink when packing for your trip. Besides the essentials like your passport, wallet, and phone, it's not hard to find the things you need on the road. I like to carry enough clothes for seven to ten days, do laundry, then repeat. (See Appendix B for a suggested packing list.)

If a backpack fits everything you want, has a bit of extra room, and feels comfortable, then you have found the perfect size. Manufacturers also have suggested torso and waist sizes for each model they produce, but I've found that the best way to know if a backpack feels right is to simply try it on. Any good camping/outdoors store will stuff a pack with the equivalent of thirty pounds (fifteen kilograms) so you can see how that weight feels on your back.

It's important to remember that the bigger the backpack, the less likely you'll be able to carry it on an airplane. Most baggage sizes are 45 linear inches (22 x 14 x 9 in), or 115 centimeters (56 x 36 x 23 cm), including handles and wheels, so if you get a backpack with those dimensions, you'll be able to carry on. This is roughly 40–45 liters (depending on the brand and shape), so this is what to aim for if you want to fly carry-on only.

PRICING OUT A BACKPACK

Most backpacks cost between $99 and $300, while the medium-sized store-brand names generally cost around $199. Backpack prices depend a lot on size, fabric, and brand. Store brands are cheaper than big-name brands like The North Face, Osprey, and Gregory. I don't believe any backpack is worth $300, no matter how nice it is. These expensive backpacks tend to be large and have more bells and whistles, special padding, and material than you really need. I think any backpack under $200 (not including tax) is fine. That's the most I'd be willing to pay for something I was going to use for a long trip and could use for years to come. Everything a $300 backpack can do on the road, a $200 backpack can do just as well.

You'll find that most travel backpacks are also hiking backpacks that could be used for camping and multi-day treks in the woods. Buying a backpack that was meant to be used in the Rockies instead of the streets of New Zealand doesn't matter—backpacks are pretty interchangeable these days, and getting a backpack meant for the outdoors simply means you'll have a stronger and more durable pack.

One way to get backpacks cheaper than the listed price is to buy last year's models at a discounted price at an outlet store. An outlet store sells last year's products that brands got rid of to make room for the new models. REI (Recreational Equipment Incorporated) has a good outlet store (rei.com/outlet), and others include Backcountry (backcountry.com), Sierra Trading Post (sierratradingpost.com), and Campmor (campmor.com). All of these companies sell gear for about 30–50 percent less than the current model's price.

So what's on my back? I use an REI backpack. REI (rei.com) is a sporting and outdoors company in the United States that sells a wide variety of sporting, outdoors, and travel gear. I've had one of their backpacks since 2004. You know those advertisements where they try to destroy products to prove how good they are? Well, my life is that ad. I have put this backpack through the wringer. It's been crushed, thrown around, dropped, squeezed into tiny places, dragged, and kicked around. And it's held up well. I'm a huge fan.

Besides selling their own gear, REI sells gear from other quality manufacturers like The North Face, Eagle Creek, and Osprey. They are an excellent company, with locations around the United States that offer very good prices on backpacks and other travel gear. I find their customer service to be superb and their sales staff to be very helpful and knowledgeable.

Another option is EMS (Eastern Mountain Sports, ems.com), a US company similar to REI, while MEC (Mountain Equipment Company, mec.ca) is the Canadian equivalent. Moreover, any large sporting goods store will have a good selection of backpacks to choose from. Shop around for the best deal.

Buying a backpack for your trip is going to be a time-consuming process, so you'll need to try a lot on. If possible, head to your nearest outdoor store to try the bags on. You can get input and advice from the store's staff, who will be able to answer any and all questions you have about your backpack. They can walk you through the proper fitting process too.

Conversely, you can also just get a bunch sent to your house, load them with all your gear, and try them on to see which one feels right. That way you will know exactly how the bag fits when you have your gear in it, not padding in the store. Then return the others (but, of course, make sure to check the return policy before purchasing).

In the end, you have to try on a variety of backpacks to see which one is the perfect fit for you and which matches the needs of your trip. Just go with what literally feels right.

8

TRAVEL INSURANCE

've been a scuba diver ever since a fellow travel writer told me if I didn't stop being afraid of trying it, he would make fun of me to all the other travel writers out there. In the face of potential public embarrassment, I gave in . . . and I loved it. But a few years later, I joined some friends on a trip in Thailand, and I wasn't able to equalize the pressure in my ears properly on a dive. I popped my left eardrum, and though it was a minor injury (I can still hear), the hospital bill ended up costing me a couple of hundred dollars. However, because I had travel insurance, I was fully reimbursed.

You never know if an accident or illness will strike while you are traveling, and most regular health insurance plans don't cover you overseas. Purchasing good travel insurance in case you get sick is a smart move—you don't want to take risks with your health.

Many people think, "I don't need travel insurance—I'm healthy and I won't get sick." But they don't realize that travel insurance is much more than just medical protection. It also covers trip delays, cancellations, theft, lost gear, and so much more.

It was there for me when I lost my bag in South Africa. It

was there for my friend when he had to be helicoptered out of the Amazon after a bad fall. And it was there for my friend when she had to fly home because her father died. Travel insurance covered all those bills. With plans costing just a few dollars per day, in my view, it's foolish not to get it. I would rather hedge my bets and not get stuck with a giant hospital bill.

That said, getting good travel insurance is one of the most complex and confusing aspects of trip planning. With countless plans and companies available, it can be hard to decide which plan to get (which is why I'm devoting a whole chapter to it).

The most important part of travel insurance is medical coverage. If your current health plan doesn't cover you overseas, travel insurance is a must. It's the only way you will be able to get care on the road without paying a large hospital bill. Medical evacuations can cost hundreds of thousands of dollars. Over the years, I've seen far too many GoFundMe campaigns for travelers who got seriously injured but didn't have travel insurance trying to cover the cost of getting home.

When I'm shopping for travel insurance, I make sure my policy has two important medically-related features:

First, make sure they have a high coverage limit on your medical expenses. Most good travel insurance companies provide up to $100,000 in coverage, though more expensive policies will cover you for higher amounts. The maximum coverage limits you can find are usually around $2,000,000, which is likely more than you'll ever need. High coverage limits are important because if you need serious attention or long-term treatment overseas, you want to make sure your high hospital bills are covered. The worst thing you can do is go cheap and get a policy with a $20,000 coverage limit, suffer a major injury, and use that limit up in one emergency surgery. Don't be cheap with your health. I tend to go with policies that cover around $100,000 as I'm generally healthy and don't do a lot of extreme sports or activities. If you feel like you have more risk, you'll want a policy with a higher limit.

Second, make sure your insurance policy covers emergency evacuation. For example, if you are hiking out in the woods and break your leg, your travel insurance should cover your evacuation to a hospital. If a natural disaster happens and you need to be evacuated to safety, your insurance should also cover you. This protection usually covers an expense of up to $300,000.

Emergency evacuation also means transportation from the foreign hospital to your home country. Standard emergency evacuation usually includes this provision, but it's always important to double-check that your policy will cover the cost of your flight back home if needed.

Before you purchase travel insurance, be sure to check if your current medical coverage extends to overseas travelers. Generally, it doesn't, which is why the travel insurance industry is so big. I've yet to find a general health plan that covers people overseas unless they buy a separate policy, but with so many different insurers and policies around the country, it's simply smart to double-check.

Beyond covering medical emergencies (which is really the main reason to get travel insurance), travel insurance offers other benefits. It can cover lost or stolen property, provide other emergency services, and offer trip cancellation protection. Here are additional criteria to look for when choosing your insurance provider:

Coverage for travel to most countries in the world. Make sure the insurance provider covers all the countries you are visiting.

Insurance companies will have a list of the countries excluded from their policy (usually war zones and countries listed by the government as "not safe"). If you are traveling to those countries, your policy will not cover you while you are there.

Twenty-four-hour emergency services and assistance. After all, you don't want to get sick and find out you need to "call back during normal business hours" for help.

Coverage for lost, damaged, or stolen possessions. If your backpack gets stolen in Greece or falls off the back of a bus in Brazil, it's important to know that your travel insurance will give you money to buy new supplies so you aren't stuck with just the clothes on your back.

Cancellation protection and trip interruption. You want to make sure you have protection in case of delays or cancellations from airlines, hotels, cruises, or any travel-related company. That way you won't be out any money for rebooking a flight or having to get a last-minute hotel room.

Family emergency coverage. If an immediate family member suddenly gets ill or dies and you need to get home, you'll want to know that there is coverage available so the flight home will be paid for. As traveler Dawn Lynch states, "While we were in Thailand, my father passed away unexpectedly. I called my insurance carrier, World Nomads, before I bought my ticket home to the States. They told me to go ahead and buy the ticket, and we would sort out the details when I got home. Once things settled down at home, I called them and filled out a form online, and although it did take numerous phone calls, I did receive a check for my plane fare prior to my return to Thailand."

Financial protection. If the tour company or airline you're using goes bust, make sure you're covered up to $10,000 (which is likely more than you'll need unless you're doing a high-end adventure tour). This is a relatively new addition to some policies so you might have to shop around to find it.

Electronics coverage. Most travel insurance companies only cover a small amount, usually up to $500 as part of their basic coverage. You can often buy supplemental insurance for a higher amount. For instance, Clements Worldwide (clements.com) offers special coverage for your electronics. Prices vary depending on the country you visit (between $145 and $195), but they don't offer insurance for the whole world so you have to get coverage for your specific country. However, any non-travel and home insurance companies such as State Farm offer plans that can help you cover your electronics. If you already have homeowner's insurance, there is a possibility some of your gear is covered if it is already specified in your existing policy. If your travel insurance doesn't have a high coverage amount for electronics and you aren't covered via your homeowner's insurance, I'd consider buying supplemental insurance. After all, most of us travel with expensive electronics these days.

WHAT IS NOT COVERED

It's also important to know what is not covered by your plan. Travel insurance policies do not cover accidents sustained while participating in extreme adventure activities such as hang gliding, paragliding, or bungee jumping (unless you bought additional coverage for these activities).

Moreover, the vast majority of insurance companies won't cover you if you injure someone on the road (called third-party liability). If you are drunk and fall out of a window, most travel insurance companies won't cover you because you were drunk and that would be considered recklessness. As would being under the influence of drugs. All policies may become void if you are under the influence.

If you book a trip somewhere but then decide to cancel it because of war, suspected terrorism, or other kinds of conflict, your trip cancellation insurance won't cover you unless there has been a State Department warning that advises travelers to stay away. To put it another way, you will only be reimbursed if the US government tells you to stay away, not because *you* decided to stay away.

Knowing these exclusions will become very important when you decide to make a claim, so read your policy in depth and know all the exclusions. Most people go wrong when making a claim because they didn't know what was—or wasn't—covered.

COVID-19 AND OTHER PANDEMICS

As many travelers learned the hard way during COVID, most travel insurance policies do not cover pandemics. Prior to 2020, I never really gave the "pandemic clause" much thought when reading my insurance policies. However, now pandemic coverage is at the forefront of every traveler's mind (and rightly so).

Fortunately, travel insurance companies have adapted and most companies now provide limited coverage for COVID-19 (or other pandemics). This limited coverage usually includes trip cancellation or delay, though some also have medical coverage specifically for COVID.

Before you buy a plan, be sure to read the fine print regarding pandemics. Make sure you fully understand what is and is not included so you can take appropriate action should a situation arise. When in doubt, call the company and speak with a representative.

TRAVEL INSURANCE LOOPHOLES

Even the best travel insurance companies have their limits. Often, in the fine print, you'll find that plans aren't as good as you thought. The medical portion of travel insurance is more about emergency care than replacing your normal health care. A lot of people who purchase travel insurance are disappointed when they find out they can't get an annual physical with it.

One big complaint I hear a lot is about theft, as there's a lot of confusion over this. Let's say you are in New Zealand and someone snatches your bag at the train station. Will you get reimbursed? You might say the answer is an obvious yes but, to an insurance company, the answer is actually "maybe."

If your bag was on your person (i.e., you are physically holding it in some way), the answer is yes, you'll be covered. But if you left your bag unattended while you went to the bathroom, or even had it in the seat next to you on a bus, the answer is likely no. Most insurance companies would say you are at fault for not watching your bag or keeping it physically connected to your person. It's a sneaky loophole in 99 percent of plans, so be sure to read the exact wording on theft before purchasing a policy.

As for other common loopholes, insurance companies often apply the "reasonable person test" to claims. Would a reasonable person do an activity drunk? Leave their bag unattended? Forget to ask their doctor for forms? Probably not. And that's how the insurance company will judge your claim. (Which is why you always want to have tons of documentation when making a claim!)

In the end, you get what you pay for with insurance. Maybe two companies offer similar plans but one is really cheap. Usually the devil is in the details and one will have smaller payouts, take longer to process claims, deny more people, or have so many rules in the fine print that it turns out you aren't going to get paid when you think you are.

Know your policy in and out.

Remember, travel insurance is *accident* insurance. It is there to protect you in case of emergency and, if need be, get you home in a hurry. If you want a global health plan (because you're now an expat or digital nomad living abroad), you need a completely different type of plan from regular travel insurance.

Some of the most popular travel insurance companies include SafetyWing (safetywing.com), World Nomads (worldnomads. com), MedjetAssist (medjetassist.com), and IMG (imglobal.com).

Every insurance company is different, and you should look around to see what companies offer and which are best for your trip. I highly recommend the website InsureMyTrip (insuremytrip.com). They compare insurance policies for more than twenty insurance providers, and because they let you compare plans in a grid layout, it's easy to see exactly what each company covers. You'll be able to compare medical coverage limits, emergency evacuation coverage, trip cancellation coverage, dental coverage, disaster coverage, and everything else under the sun.

Generally, insurance will run you between $500 and $1,500 per year for a single person depending on the depth of coverage you get.

FREQUENTLY ASKED QUESTIONS

Over the years, people have emailed me asking advice on this topic. No matter how much I write on this subject, there are always questions, so before we end this chapter, I want to address some common ones.

Is travel insurance the same as health insurance? No. While there is a large medical component for sudden illnesses and accidental injuries, it can also cover you for trip cancellation, trip interruptions, loss or theft of your gear, and emergency transportation should you need to get to the nearest hospital fast.

Okay, but my travel plan has medical coverage. I can go see a doctor when I want? Travel insurance is there for unexpected emergencies. Break a leg? Pop an eardrum? Get food poisoning or dengue fever? Travel insurance has you covered. Want to go see a doctor for a physical or get a new crown on your tooth? You're on your own!

Can I get treated for an illness I already have? Most travel insurance plans don't cover preexisting conditions. If you need medication for an ongoing chronic disease or a medical condition you knew of before you bought the policy, you could be out of luck. Moreover, if you get sick under one policy and then you extend it or start a new policy, most insurers will consider your illness a preexisting condition and won't cover it under your new policy. There are some exceptions to this so always check in advance.

My credit card offers some protection. Isn't that good enough?

Credit cards, even the best, offer very limited insurance protections. Some offer coverage for lost or stolen items, medical expenses, and trip cancellation if you booked your trip with the card, but they may not cover your being airlifted home or a major accident. And, while I have never used it, many writer friends of mine have said the claims process was much more arduous than travel insurance companies and, while they were eventually made whole, it took a lot longer.

While it's nice to have this protection as a backup, I wouldn't rely on credit card insurance as my primary coverage when abroad.

How does insurance actually work? Do they mail me a card I can show the doctor?

If you experience a major medical emergency that requires surgery, overnight hospitalization, or emergency repatriation, then you or your doctor would contact your travel insurance company's emergency assistance team. They can help make arrangements and approve costs. Every insurance company has a twenty-four-hour contact number you can call for emergencies. I always suggest travelers save this number in their phone before departure just to be safe.

For all other situations, you'll likely need to claim reimbursement from your insurer. In these instances, you would pay out of pocket and then submit documentation to the insurance company after the fact. Be sure to keep all documentation, file any necessary police reports, and save all receipts. Companies don't reimburse you based on your word.

Also keep in mind that if you need to go home due to an injury, travel insurance will not cover your bills upon arrival back to your country of residency.

I read reviews online. Every company sucks. Most people don't read the fine print of their policy. (Have you ever read your iTunes agreement? No? Exactly.) People buy it, don't read their exact policy wording, and make assumptions about coverage. So, when something goes wrong, they scream bloody murder when something isn't covered and write a nasty review online.

So take online user reviews of insurance companies with a grain of salt. I've read them, and most of the time I think, "You didn't read your policy!" I'm by no means an ardent defender of the insurance industry, but if you're filing a claim with no documentation, no proof of ownership for what you lost, or making a claim for something that is specifically excluded by the policy, you should expect to get denied. Bad reviews don't necessarily correlate to bad insurance. It just means people don't follow instructions.

To ensure that you get fully paid for your claim, make sure you have all your receipts and necessary forms. Be sure to keep receipts for all the money you paid so you can have proper documentation. Police reports and official letters will also help make your claim go through a lot quicker.

When making a claim, keep a running journal of the dates/times you contacted someone, who you talked to (along with their employee ID), what was said on the call, and any other exchanges including emails and texts. This will help you counter any delays or miscommunications when problems arise.

WHEN SHOULD YOU BUY INSURANCE?

Even though you can wait until you leave to purchase a plan, I think it's best to get your travel insurance as soon as possible (since most plans usually take twenty-four to forty-eight hours to activate). You can't get travel insurance to cover you after something bad has happened. For instance, if a typhoon ruins your trip, your policy would only cover you if you bought it before the typhoon formed.

Don't wait to get insurance. The second you know you are going somewhere and have the dates, buy travel insurance! You can even buy travel insurance after you've booked your flight, so long as the policy is activated before you depart. And many companies allow you to buy plans abroad.

Picking your travel insurance is going to take some time, but it's worth it.

You don't want to end up like my friend in Peru who decided against coverage, only to break her arm and have to spend lots of money to get it fixed in Lima. It's always better to be safe than sorry.

9

WHAT TO DO WITH YOUR STUFF

Before you leave for your trip, you'll find yourself walking through your house or apartment and wondering what to do with all your possessions. You can't take it all with you. If you are going on a long trip of a year or more, you can store your things in a storage unit, but that costs money.

I've found the best solution is simply to sell everything you own. While I know that seems like a huge undertaking, you'll see in this chapter that there are many ways to get rid of your stuff and lighten your load. It simply takes time.

When you come back, you'll find you have a newfound appreciation for simplicity, and you'll be amazed at how much stuff you had that you didn't really need—so sell everything. I used to have so much stuff, but now every time I return home, I find myself needing even less stuff than before. You just learn to live without. That might not work for everyone, but at the very least, selling your stuff provides you with money for your trip.

There are many websites that can help you sell your stuff.

In the United States, the best and most famous site is probably Craigslist (craigslist.com). You can buy and sell anything there, and I used it to get rid of my stuff before I traveled.

Today, Facebook Marketplace (which I have already mentioned a bunch) is also an easy way to get rid of your belongings. When I recently moved out of my apartment, I listed everything on Facebook Marketplace and it was gone within a day. People are also less likely to try to bargain you down, and you can see people's profiles so you know they aren't scammers.

In the UK and Australia, the equivalent site is Gumtree (gumtree.com), while the Craigslist equivalent in New Zealand is trademe.co.nz.

To sell your old clothes, check out the websites Vinted.com, ThredUp.com, and Poshmark.com. Moreover, you can always sell things on eBay (ebay.com) or have an actual garage sale. For an "online garage sale" feel, try VarageSale (varagesale.com) or OfferUp (offerup.com, only available in the US). To get rid of your old electronics, use sites like Swappa.com, Gazelle.com, or decluttr.com.

There are *a lot* of ways to get rid of your belongings these days (and what you can't sell, you can always donate).

If, however, you want to keep your stuff and can't store it at someone else's home, a storage unit is always an option (though, again, this costs money). Storage companies like Public Storage (publicstorage.com) and Extra Space Storage (extraspace.com) generally start at $35 per month, although prices vary depending on the size and location of the unit.

If you are only going away for a short period of time and you don't want to sell your stuff or put it in storage, consider getting a short-term renter for your place. You can use a local rental company or a website like Airbnb (airbnb.com) or Vrbo (vrbo. com). I know many people who use this option when they have permanent homes they plan to come back to.

Whatever your choice, try to downsize as much as possible before your trip. This not only reduces the amount of stuff you have to store, but it frees your mind to focus on your experiences. No one wants to be worrying about a TV or computer or paying that storage bill while hiking through the mountains of Nepal.

WHAT TO DO WITH BILLS AND MAIL

Sometimes we can't get rid of all our bills. When we go on the road long-term, we ideally lose lots of bills—car payments, insurance, rent, cell phone, cable, and so on. However, there might be loans or debt you have to pay off that you just can't get away from. Heck, I am still paying off my student loans for that MBA I got in 2006! Even if we can't get rid of our bills, we can still make our life easier using automatic bill pay. With the prevalence of electronic banking these days, you'd be hard-pressed to find a company that wouldn't let you set up automatic payments.

Moreover, I only use one credit card on the road. By tying everything to one card, you'll make it much easier to remember to pay your bill while lying on the beaches of Thailand.

As for your physical mail, chances are you won't get much after you automate all your bills and sign up for paperless statements. These days it's very easy to get ebills so you don't get any paper mail. I hardly ever get paper mail these days unless it's related to my health insurance, which is required by law to send printed material to you.

If you really do need your mail or are getting physical mail that can't be turned into an electronic statement, sign up for Anytime Mailbox (anytimemailbox.com), which starts at $5.99 and has international locations. They'll collect and scan any mail you have and send it to you. They will even hold it if you ask.

Bills and mail should be the least of your problems when planning your trip. In our modern electronic era, it is very easy to automate your bills and get rid of your mail.

PART TWO

ON-THE-ROAD EXPENSES

Saving money on the road requires breaking away from the conventional mindset that travel is expensive. It's about looking for alternatives to mainstream accommodations, transportation, and tours.

While everyone wants to "travel like a local," the real way to save money on the road is to travel like you live. When we are home, we live within our means. We spend less money than we earn because we know the consequences of not doing so.

So why shouldn't we do the same when we travel?

People in the destinations you visit live a day-to-day lifestyle similar to yours back home. Folks in Paris aren't staying in hotels, paying for lots of tours, taking taxis everywhere, or eating five-star meals every night. They shop at markets and cook dinner. They take the bus, ride the metro, look for deals, and try to find free activities to fill their days.

Once you're on the road, you're going to have *a lot* of opportunities to spend money. If you aren't careful, you'll quickly find that you've busted your budget. Travel is filled with temptation. There's always some activity to enjoy, some new restaurant to try, or someone looking to drag you to the nearest bar. Travel can suck your money out of your wallet like a vacuum cleaner.

Making your money last is as much about knowing how you spend as it is about knowing how to find good travel deals. The way to be smart and realistic about how you spend money is by creating a budget. (This will also help you come up with a personalized amount you need.)

When I travel, I don't budget a lot of money for accommodations or transportation. I find the cheapest accommodation and I walk almost everywhere. I'm that friend that says, "It's not that far, we can walk it," even when the walk is like an hour! However, I always budget a lot of money for food and drinks because that's what I want to enjoy the most. I didn't spend every night at home so I could avoid the nightlife in Australia or eat pasta in my hostel in France. No, not me. I came to live. I came to eat and drink in the culture. I have no problem sleeping on someone's floor if it means I can have a nice meal.

I know what I like, what I want, and how I spend. Because of that, I can set realistic spending goals for my trip. Sure, there will always be something you didn't predict. I didn't predict having to buy a new camera after falling into the ocean or taking a last-minute flight to Fiji from New Zealand to meet up with some friends. I didn't expect to learn how to scuba dive in Fiji. Stuff happens on the road. That's just the way it is. (And it's why you should always budget in a cushion, which we'll talk about in the last chapter of this book.)

However, you *can* anticipate a lot of your costs if you know what you want to spend money on. Too often I hear: "Wow! That tour is so expensive. I blew my budget." Or, "I didn't expect to drink so much!" Or, "This place is more expensive than I thought." My response to these statements is, "Well, what did you expect to do on the road?" If you do your research, you will know exactly how much things cost and you can plan your budget accordingly. And if you know yourself well, you will know how you will spend your money.

I can't emphasize enough how important this is: *You'll never be able to properly budget if you don't know where your money is going.*

I write down in a journal everything I spend money on. This way I can keep track of what I am spending so I know when I am getting close to my budget and when I need to cut back.

Personally, I use a Moleskine notebook—but you can use whatever works best, like an Excel spreadsheet or an app to track your expenses. Two free apps I like at the time of writing are TravelSpend (travel-spend.com) and Trabee Pocket (trabeepocket.com).

The people who have to go home early are always the ones who have no idea what they are spending their money on.

Part Two of this book teaches you the general tricks and tips needed to get into the savings mindset and save money on the road. Once you know a few basic tips, finding deals—no matter where you go—will come easily to you. Moreover, while a lot of this book is about taking an extended break around the world, the tips in the upcoming chapters are universal—it doesn't matter if you are taking a two-week trip to Spain or a two-month trip through South America.

10

TIPS FOR SAVING MONEY ON ACCOMMODATIONS

Accommodations are one of the biggest day-to-day expenses, so cutting that cost can have the greatest impact on your budget. To save money, you can always spend a night on the train, stay in dorms, find a campsite, sleep in monasteries, or stay with your grandmother's friend's cousin.

I've stayed in a ton of different kinds of accommodations during my years traveling the world, and below are the major types you'll likely encounter, how they work, and their pros and cons.

APARTMENT RENTALS

One option for group travelers, families, and couples (or even solo travelers not interested in hostels) is apartment rentals.

Apartment rental websites allow people to rent out their extra individual room, a couch, or, more commonly these days, their entire apartment.

These spaces have boomed in the last decade. They went from a thing homeowners did to earn extra money to a big business where people own multiple properties and entire companies exist solely for furnished rentals. You'll even find hotels and traditional bed-and-breakfasts on many of these websites. Before 2016, you might have associated a company like Airbnb with "someone renting out extra space"; now we think of all these companies as simply "vacation rentals." The expectation is that you're getting a place someone likely doesn't live in.

There are many companies in the world that offer these services (region-specific ones are listed in the destination chapters in Part Three), but the two big global companies are:

Airbnb (airbnb.com): The largest apartment rental website out there with a strong inventory around the world, especially in cities. Not only do they have apartments and homes to rent; Airbnb also offers tree houses in the jungle, tiny houses, mansions, and more. You will find a lot of unique properties here (and you can still also find people renting out individual rooms in their houses).

Vrbo (vrbo.com): Vacation Rentals by Owner, or now just Vrbo, is an online marketplace for vacation rentals that focuses more on homes in tourist destinations rather than apartments or quirky rentals. Think of it like renting a beach house for your family trip or a cabin in the woods for a romantic getaway.

These two global companies control the majority of the rental market, but there are a number of smaller players out there too. Some companies, like Fairbnb (fairbnb.coop), try to combine the profit motive of Airbnb with the ethos of hospitality networks. However, as much as I like that idea in spirit, the reality is that at the time of writing they don't have large user bases and simply aren't that good.

If you want to camp on people's property (via a tent or RV), check out Campspace (campspace.com). This website features home campsites around the world and connects people who will let travelers camp in their backyards for a small fee.

Apartment rental prices depend on several factors: distance from the city center, competition on the site (lots of choices equals better prices), size, and amenities.

As a solo traveler, I am not a fan of apartment rentals. When I travel, I like to meet people and I find apartment rentals a little too removed for that. I also don't love them for short-term stays as the fees can often make a short stay more expensive than a hotel or hostel.

If you are traveling as a big group or a family, an apartment rental is probably a much better option. Squeezing a bunch of people into these apartments will be much cheaper per person than booking a room in a hostel or hotel, and you'll get to be together in a shared space.

When searching for places to rent, I have certain criteria to ensure I'm getting a great place:

Is the calendar updated? While listings show up in a search only if they are available, hosts don't always update their calendar. If someone hasn't updated their calendar in thirty days, I tend to skip it. There's nothing worse than going to book a place only for them to cancel and say, "Whoops, sorry, it's not available!"

Do hosts reply often? You don't want your inquiry to go unanswered. These sites show the percentage of messages hosts reply to. The higher, the better.

Are hosts active users? Active users are good users, so look to see when they last logged on. If it's been a while, your query might go unanswered.

Are hosts verified? Verified accounts are less likely to be people of suspicious quality, as the listing site has found at least some background information on them.

Do hosts have good photos? Any listing that doesn't include a lot of photos of the place is probably lying about its quality.

Do properties have reviews? If other people stayed there, had a good time, and found the apartment as advertised, you probably will too. Additionally, I like to make sure properties have reviews within the last six months to ensure the listing is still active.

Have hosts been someone else's guest before? If they were someone's guest and that went well, it's likely they aren't going to be crazy. To check, go to the host's profile and it will list reviews from people they have stayed with.

These rules are helpful guidelines, but at the end of the day, you have to go with your gut.

Before you book, make sure you compare the prices since every website has a different inventory. The inventory on these sites consists of what people decide to put up and, as such, there is no real uniformity among these services like the uniformity often found among hotel booking websites.

Apartment rentals come with a lot of pros, but they have a lot of cons too. Airbnb and Vrbo aren't the same "using a person's place while they are gone" websites they used to be. They are platforms for big property rental companies and landlords that buy up entire apartment buildings to rent out to travelers. As these websites have grown, they have taken a lot of housing stock off the market, especially in big cities. They have driven rents up, and many destinations around the world have put restrictions on these services to limit their local impact.

If you're going to use these services, please take into consideration local laws and the sentiment around them. Be sure to search blogs and news websites to see if there are any reports or information on how locals feel about these services. We want to be good travelers and leave places as we found them. Destinations are not Disneyland. People live there and are just trying to go about their lives. Always remember that.

If you're going to stay in an apartment in a large city as a solo traveler or couple, please try to rent a room from someone who lives there or, if it's an entire apartment, make sure it's lived in and not run by a large property management company (you can usually tell from the photos if a place is truly lived in). This way you don't contribute to overtourism and the pricing out of locals. I'll discuss this in the destination-specific chapters in Part Three.

FARM WORK

World Wide Opportunities on Organic Farms (wwoof.net), or WWOOF for short, is a service that matches people looking for work on farms with farmers who are looking for labor. It's more a loose affiliation of like-minded groups using the same name rather than one large international organization. There are currently over 130 countries that participate in the WWOOFing program worldwide, but there is no central database on the number of farms, as each country maintains its own list.

In order to become a WWOOFer, you will need to sign up for the national organization in the country where you will be traveling. By visiting the website of the umbrella organization, you can get access to the national chapter you need. There is no international WWOOF membership, so you'll have to buy a membership from each country's organization (which can get pricey if you are planning to do this in a lot of destinations). Annual membership usually costs around $30 per country.

Generally, you have to be at least eighteen years old to join, but each country sets their own rules. For example, Germany, the UK, Portugal, and Italy take WWOOFers under eighteen but you may need a letter of consent from your parent or legal guardian. WWOOF Switzerland has a minimum age of sixteen while you have to be twenty years old to WWOOF in Turkey.

After you fill out the online membership form and pay your fee, you'll be sent a list of participating farms in your country of choice and can decide which ones to contact. All you have to do is contact the farms that interest you, talk with the host, and make arrangements for your arrival and duration of stay. There is no formal contract involved and you are free to leave anytime you want.

You don't need any previous experience in farming to participate—just a desire to work. Traveler Bethany Salvon spent time WWOOFing in Serbia and Italy and says: "We did not have any experience on farms or as WWOOF volunteers before our first farm in Italy. Most WWOOFers we have met have no experience at all— they are simply interested in learning more about organic farming and they have a desire to help out local farmers."

Moreover, you don't just get your hands dirty on the farm. You do a number of chores. As Nora Dunn of theprofessionalhobo.com describes her experience, "Although the WWOOF acronym implies work on organic farms, the opportunities and responsibilities vary well beyond gardening at many places. Where I volunteered for over six months, I did everything from cooking for large groups of people, to cleaning lodges, to promotional work, and only occasionally did I get my hands dirty in the garden or tend to the expansive nature trails."

If you don't want to join WWOOFing but still want to work on a farm, the best way around the membership fee is to simply show up in an area you want to work in, find a hostel, and ask about nearby farms that take volunteers. Since most WWOOFers are travelers, hostels in regions popular with WWOOFing keep track of which farms take volunteers. Ask them where you should go. Dunn used this method successfully in New Zealand when she didn't want to pay the membership fee but still wanted to work on a farm. Additionally, the websites Workaway (workaway.info) and HelpX (helpx.net) both have a good number of volunteer listings.

HOSPITALITY EXCHANGE

The best way to save on accommodations is to not have to pay for accommodations—and a hospitality exchange does exactly that. Hospitality exchange services connect travelers with locals who offer a free place to stay with no strings attached. Sometimes it's a bed, sometimes it's a couch, and sometimes it's literally just space on the floor.

The major hospitality exchange organizations are:

Couchsurfing (couchsurfing.com). Founded in January 2004, this is the largest hospitality network, with more than twelve million members in two hundred thousand cities. Membership used to be mostly free (you paid for some services) but, during COVID, they paywalled the entire site with a small membership fee. It now costs $2.99 per month or $14.99 per year. While usage of the website declined after they started charging for membership, it still remains the largest network and its user base consists of people of all ages.

Servas International (servas.org). This is the oldest hospitality exchange in the world. Servas was created in 1949 and is actually recognized by the United Nations. Participation in Servas requires two letters of reference, a membership fee, and a personal interview with a local Servas coordinator. After the interview, the traveler gets a "letter of introduction" that's good for one year of travel, and a list of hosts in the country where the traveler is visiting. There are about 15,000 members in Servas, who are primarily baby boomers and senior travelers.

Facebook Groups. You don't naturally think of Facebook as a place to find traveling partners but, in the last few years, there have been a number of good and verified Facebook communities that connect travelers with each other. You can find places to stay, travel partners, and people to do things with. In my opinion, people have moved back to Facebook because you can look at people's profiles as well as Instagram accounts. While popular groups are always changing, at the time of publication, ones that I like are Girls LOVE Travel, Find a Travel Buddy, and Solo Trips & Travelers.

Warm Showers (warmshowers.org). This hospitality exchange was founded in 1993 and is dedicated to people on bike trips. It has about 185,000 users spread out across the world. There is a onetime $30 fee when signing up that goes to support the website infrastructure, but it's free to use after that.

BeWelcome (bewelcome.org). This website was founded in 2013 as Couchsurfing started charging for services. It was founded by ex-Couchsurfing members who felt that charging money went against the service's ethos. It's free to use and has over two hundred thousand members in pretty much every country in the world.

Travel Ladies (travelladies.app). This app was founded in 2019 for solo female travelers and connects travelers with locals. They also connect people looking for travel buddies and have a lot of safety tips and information.

These sites work by having users sign up, create profiles, and connect with one another with the expectation that one day, those who will be hosted will pay it forward and host someone else. You don't necessarily have to host anyone in the future, but most people find the experience of being hosted rewarding and decide to host someone else in return.

The largest and most active website used to be Couchsurfing. It was hugely popular and offered a ton of meet-up capabilities, events, and an astounding app that let you see which travelers were in the same vicinity as you. However, since they paywalled the service, usage has dropped off significantly. A search in February 2024 for London showed 229,457 total hosts but only 896 active hosts in the last six months and only 496 active within the last month. That's a big, *big* difference. Similar searches in other cities reveal that same trend.

In fact, *all* of the websites listed above aren't as popular as they were during their peak in the late 2000s and early 2010s. Changing tastes and travel styles, membership fees, bad design and user experience, and growth in other ways to meet people and find accommodation has led travelers, especially Gen Z travelers, to avoid most of these platforms (with the exception of Facebook Groups, which has seen a surge in usage in the last few years).

While travelers don't use them as much as they used to, these sites and apps still remain a wonderful source for connecting with locals and getting free accommodations, and I think you, dear reader, should try doing it on your trip.

People are often scared to use these services because they are concerned about safety. I understand that concern. There you are, in a new city, with all your stuff—in a stranger's home. What if they try to murder you in your sleep? What if they steal your stuff? What if they are rude or smell? These are all valid concerns. However, I've found that people who are willing to open their homes to strangers tend to be very open-minded and friendly people who are also usually former travelers themselves. They know what you are going through. They want to help. They want to show you their city and what makes it special. Besides, you never really know who has the key to your room in a hotel or hostel. You are always trusting a stranger. I figure, why not trust a stranger who thinks the way I do?

So, how do you find great people who will agree to host you but aren't total creeps? Here are my criteria on what to look for in a potential host:

Always check to see that they have multiple (and current) profile pictures. This shows you that they're a real person. See if they've included pictures of themselves with their friends, from their travels, and having fun. This shows that they care and have a social life. Moreover, make sure that their photos match their age. If their profile says that they're thirty and their photos look as if they were taken ten years ago, that's a bit weird. This is all advice that you should apply to your own profile as well. When hosts are looking at your profile, they also want to make sure you're not a creep.

Have recommendations and reviews. Both hosts and travelers can accrue recommendations from other hosts, friends, and guests. As always, the more positive reviews, the better. If you see that other people have stayed with the host and had a fun and safe experience, you probably will too. You might not get along with the host in the end, but at least you know they aren't a creep and won't steal your stuff.

The same works for you, the potential guest. Hosts want to

see that you aren't a creep too. However, if you are new to the service and don't have any reviews, ask your friends who use the service to write you a review and describe you as a person.

Be a host first. One way to earn reviews is to host people first. Being a host isn't always about having people stay with you; sometimes it's just being a tour guide. I've had amazing hosts who just showed me their town—from the girl in Ukraine who brought me to a university party, to the guy in Oxford who took me rowing, to the friends in Munich who took me to an amazing rock concert. None of them hosted me in their homes but they took the time to show me around their city.

So if you don't want to have people in your home, offer to take people out and show them around your city. If people have spent time with you—even if they haven't stayed at your place—you'll increase the likelihood that people will consent to have you at their house.

Fill out your profile in detail. If you've taken the time to fill out your profile, it probably means you are serious about the service. It will give people a chance to learn what kind of person you are instead of taking a guess based on the one email you wrote them and that ten-year-old photo you quickly put up. Profiles with forethought and detail get a lot more responses. People want to know about the stranger they are going to have in their home, and your thorough and complete profile lets them do that.

Write a captivating and personal email. Write a personalized email about why you want to stay with someone. Talk about what you liked about their profile, why you would be a good fit, your habits, what you want to get out of it, and even what you can offer the host. Be interesting and be personal.

The reason most people fail when using these websites is because they send out boring, generic, cut-and-paste emails. Here is an example:

Hi Matt,

I'm coming to Austin next week for three days. Can I stay with you?

Sam

I would ignore or respond "no" to that email. It doesn't tell me anything about the person. I have to do the extra work to go to the person's profile, click around, and figure out if the person is normal or not. A much better email would be:

Hi Matt,

How are you? I'm coming to Austin next week for three days and saw your host page. Like you, I'm also a big fan of sci-fi, Scotch, and Thai food. It would be awesome to have a host who could show me those things around Austin. I've heard lots of wonderful things about the city and am looking to get outdoors and explore. I also love to cook and would like to cook you a meal from my country, France! I'm quiet, clean, and won't be in your way if you need to work or something.

Sam

That's the kind of email that would get a response from me! Don't be self-centered. It's obvious you are looking for a free place to stay, so be sure to offer something so the host doesn't just feel like they are being used. Let hosts know what you can do for them and why it's going to be a fun experience.

No matter what, you need to use your own judgment when picking a host from a hospitality exchange. You can talk with hosts over email to get a feel for them and their expectations. If it doesn't seem right, don't do it! Once you use a hospitality exchange, you'll see that there was really nothing to fear after all—and you'll learn why travelers love these services.

HOUSE-SITTING

House-sitting is exactly like it sounds—while someone else is on holiday, you watch their house and take care of any pets (or plants) while they are gone. These services are great for travelers who may be a little older, more settled, and want to stay in a place longer-term.

The biggest house-sitting websites are:

House Carers (housecarers.com). One of the largest of these sites with a strong inventory in Australia and New Zealand. They've been around for more than ten years. Membership fee is $50.

MindMyHouse (mindmyhouse.com). A smaller site with a better user interface and lower annual membership fee ($29), this site has been around since 2005 and has a strong inventory in Europe, the United States, and Australia.

Nomador (nomador.com). Nomador is mainly focused on Europe (especially France), though it is growing worldwide. Its unique "trust profiles" help lay a foundation of trust between homeowners and house sitters. Annual memberships range from $99–$199.

TrustedHousesitters (trustedhousesitters.com). This is the largest organization out there with 180,000 members. Founded in 2010, house sitters pay a $20–$50 registration fee and create a profile and fill in security information. You're then able to search for houses in your destination and contact the owners. This website also focuses on pet-sitting if you want a shorter arrangement.

In addition to the above websites that cover multiple countries, there are also country-specific ones such as House Sitters America, House Sitters UK, House Sitters Canada, and so on. All you need to do to find them is google "house-sitting [destination name]." If you're only interested in house-sitting in a particular locale, these websites usually have way less competition than the bigger players, making it easier to get your first gig. They also have lower annual membership costs.

House-sitting websites work similarly to hospitality networks. You will sign up and create a profile where you will include your photos, personal information, experiences, and any skills or references you may have. You'll also want to be quick as a lot of house-sitting gigs get applications very quickly, especially in major markets and big cities.

Before you agree to house-sit, I recommend having a Zoom call with the hosts so you can see how your personalities match up. Take the time to ask questions and make sure you are a good fit. Additionally, you should ask to be connected with any previous house sitter so you know what you can expect from the home and homeowner. In many ways, house-sitting is like a job, and you want your employer to be pleasant and not a jerk.

After you and an owner have come to an agreement, you sign a legal form via the platform with the terms and conditions you both agree to. (This form protects all parties in case something goes wrong.)

House-sitting commitments tend to be long-term (that is, a month or more) and are suited for travelers who want to stay a longer time in one specific place. Nora Dunn (theprofessionalhobo.com) uses house-sitting regularly to save money: "One of my specialties is house-sitting around the world, and I have done it in six countries on three continents—and counting. In exchange for free accommodation, you are charged with keeping an eye on the house in the homeowners' absence, and sometimes caring for pets, gardens, farm animals, or performing other chores."

If you are going to house-sit, it is important to do your research to ensure the home is in the location you want and that your responsibilities are clearly spelled out. Nora advises you to "be sure to determine exactly what your responsibilities will be before you agree. In one case, I was charged with the care of three big dogs and a large house and garden, and although I loved the position, it was a lot of work; in retrospect, I should have been paid a stipend, given my daily time commitment and the money the homeowners were saving by not having to put their dogs into a kennel and hire a gardener." That is why the legal contract is so important—it spells out your responsibilities.

Of her experience, Nora says, "House-sitting is a fabulous

way to experience the comforts of 'home' on the road, often for extended periods of time."

HOSTELS

Hostels are one of the cheapest forms of accommodation in the world. Hostels are places that offer shared (and sometimes private) rooms for travelers. They are a rite of passage for backpackers and long-term travelers. I love them and they are my favorite form of accommodation. Some of my favorite travel memories involve hostels and I'm still friends with people I met in hostels decades ago.

Hostels still have a bad reputation in the United States (though less so these days thanks to social media). We think of them as being filled with dirty, stinky rooms with uncomfortable mattresses and no security. Or we think of them as places from movies like *Hostel* where we are going to get kidnapped and end up in some sick, twisted medical experiment.

One of my favorite travel movies is *A Map for Saturday*. When the star and director, Brook Silva-Braga, reaches Europe, his friends come to visit. In an interview, one of his friends asks, "Why would you want to stay at a hostel? You have to worry about your stuff all the time." Brook responds that hostels have lockers, and his friend admits he didn't know that. I think that is emblematic of people's perception of hostels. In the United States, we just don't know a lot about hostels. We don't have a big backpacking culture—instead of cheap hostels, we have Motel 6. Thus, what we think about hostels comes from what our parents told us when they traveled in the 1960s or what we see in movies.

It's true that hostels are mostly composed of dorm rooms with minimal furnishing, but the beds can often be quite comfortable. And in hostels you will find Wi-Fi, free breakfast, hot showers, common areas, bars, kitchens, individual lockers for your stuff (don't have a lock? You can rent one from the hostel!), and bed lights to read at night. They also help you book and organize tours. It's also very common for hostels to have curtains in the shared dorm rooms for extra privacy.

Sure, there are dirty hostels out there, just like there are dirty hotels. You get what you pay for, after all. But so long as you are staying at a highly rated hostel, it's doubtful there are going to be any issues.

Here's my advice to avoid the bad, dirty hostels and find those wonderful, clean hostels where you can make the best of friends:

Cheaper is not better. Budget travelers have a natural inclination to go with the cheapest option around. However, don't try to save a buck just to save a buck. Super-cheap hostels are often unclean, the beds are uncomfortable, the showers are dirty, and the pillows are thinner than a supermodel. Pay a bit more if you can. Your body will thank you.

Location, location, location. Where a hostel is located will have a huge effect on your experience. If you have to spend an hour on public transportation just getting to and from your hostel, you'll end up wasting a lot of your time. The best hostels are close to the action, where you can step out your door and into an adventure. (The exception is if the hostels are so remote that just staying there is an experience in and of itself.)

Before you book, check out the address on Google Maps and

see where it is in relation to the things you want to see and do. You didn't travel around the world to spend your time commuting!

Go with a late checkout. Never stay at a hostel with a checkout time before 10 AM. The really good hostels have 11 AM checkout times, and the best ones let you check out at noon. Sleep is valuable on the road because you'll rarely get enough of it. Hostels with late checkout times understand this and are often more relaxed environments. There's just something wrong about a hostel asking you to be packed and out so early in the morning.

Knowledgeable staff. Employees make any business, and the best hostels have staff that are helpful, knowledgeable, and friendly. A hostel is like a home, and you want the people there to welcome you like a long-lost family member. I never understood why hostels don't recognize that being a hostel is not about being a cheap place to stay; it's about creating a warm environment.

Look for a bar. Bars are not deal-breakers and there are a lot of wonderful hostels without them, but they make for a great place to socialize with other hostel guests. Usually if a hostel has a bar, they put a strong emphasis on making sure the people staying there are having fun, interacting, and being festive.

Look for a common room. If a hostel doesn't have a bar, it should have a big common area. The best hostels are the ones that give travelers a place to hang out and socialize with one another. Common areas facilitate interaction and make it easier for solo travelers to meet people. The best hostels I've ever stayed at always had an amazing common area.

Look for organized activities. Really good hostels also organize activities such as walking tours, bar crawls, BBQs, or anything else that gets people together.

Make sure there is breakfast. Look for a place with a decent breakfast (i.e., more than bread and cheese) or at least one that begins and ends when people are actually awake (i.e., something like 7–10 AM instead of 6–9 AM). (Breakfast is also a great way to load up on snacks for the day, which helps cut down on your food budget.)

Make sure there are lockers. It's surprising, but I've actually been in hostels that don't provide lockers (or will charge you for them). In this day and age, lockers should be standard and you should never pay for security. This is a deal-breaker for me, especially since I travel with electronics.

Make sure there is a kitchen. Prioritize hostels with kitchens so you can lower your food budget by cooking your own—and sharing meals with other guests. Nothing binds people closer together than a shared meal (and a few glasses of wine). It's a good way to meet other people in your hostel.

I don't need a hostel to have all the things on this list, but a truly wonderful hostel that understands what travelers are looking for has *most* of these things.

Additionally, as more and more people shift to remote work, hostels have started to accommodate long-term travelers who work on their laptops. If you're a remote worker, these hostels are great places to stay as they have fast Wi-Fi and make it easy to connect and network with other digital nomads. However, if you're not working online while traveling, avoid these hostels since most people will just be on their laptops and that's kind of boring if you're not doing it too. Instead, stay at a hostel that caters to backpackers. It will be much more enjoyable and you'll have an easier time meeting people.

In the end, what really makes a good hostel are the people—and even the worst hostels will be great if you meet good people. But removing the people from the equation, I look for hostels that have most of the amenities noted earlier. Good hostels are not simply there to take your money in exchange for a bed—they are there to enhance your experience as a traveler. In my experience, I would always prefer to stay at a place that is looking to make sure I have a good time.

One other final point about hostels is that prices for them have risen a lot post-COVID, and many have adopted a dynamic pricing method similar to what airlines use. Most hostel owners took on a lot of debt to stay in business during the pandemic and have raised rates in response. Additionally, many hostels around the world have been bought up by large chains and are no longer the small mom-and-pop operations they used to be. They are big businesses with yield managers who are focused more on the bottom line than the guest. As one hostel owner explained, the big chains amass treasure chests for the off-season so they can make improvements to get more customers, while smaller hostels barely get by out of principle.

Hostels are simply not the "dirt cheap" places they used to be, but they are still often the cheapest option, especially if you are traveling solo. (As I mentioned earlier, if you're part of a group, it may be cheaper to look at a hotel or apartment rental.)

The website Hostelworld (hostelworld.com) has the largest inventory of hostels and is the de facto leader in the industry. Workaway (workaway.info), Worldpackers (worldpackers.com), and HelpX (helpx.net) can help you find jobs in hostels where you can work a couple hours a day (e.g., cleaning) in exchange for free accommodations.

HOTELS

Everyone thinks hotels are expensive and, for the most part, they are! However, there's never been more ways to get cheap hotels and you can find some really good deals out there. The best way to get a cheap room is to use a last-minute booking website like LateRooms (laterooms.com), Last Minute (lastminute.com), HotelTonight (hoteltonight.com), Priceline (priceline.com), or Hotwire (hotwire.com).

I find Priceline and Hotwire to be the best, as they have the largest inventories and the lowest prices, but you should always leave no stone unturned. Both websites (Priceline's Express Deals and Hotwire's Hot Deals) let you book unknown hotels for really low rates. All you know is the class of hotel and the location. Despite the risks associated with booking an unknown hotel, I've never had a problem (like getting stuck with a bedbug-ridden flea trap) and I quite like getting hotels up to 50 percent off their listed price.

Besides trying to find a last-minute or discounted hotel, some other tricks to use when looking for a hotel are the following:

Use discount rates like AAA or AARP. If you are part of the AARP (American Association of Retired Persons) or AAA (American Automobile Association), you can get special rates on hotel rooms around the world. (Fun fact: Anyone can join the AARP. I'm a member. You don't need to be retired or old.) Both organizations have amazing travel benefits and most hotel chains give you discounts as a member. It's well worth the membership.

Use Mr. Rebates or Rakuten. If the lowest rate is through a major booking site like Booking.com, Expedia.com, or Hotels.com, go through Mr. Rebates or Rakuten. By using their links, you'll get 1–10 percent back. As I mentioned in chapter three, I always use these websites when shopping online. Getting up to 10 percent off your hotel is a HUGE deal.

Get discounted gift cards. You can book major hotel chains with hotel gift cards. Check out a website like Giftcardgranny.com for discounted gift cards and use it to book your hotel. (You can also stack this with Rakuten for added savings.) For example, say a hotel room is $100. After you buy the gift card for $90, you book via Rakuten, which is also offering 5 percent off Marriott hotels. Then you use the gift card at checkout for a total savings of 15 percent. That's not bad for just a few extra clicks!

Buy someone else's reservation with Roomer. Often people can't go on a trip and can't cancel the reservation, so rather than lose the money, hotels put these rooms on Roomer, where they sell it at a discount to earn some money back. I've never used this website, but I've heard good things about it.

Use Google. My favorite hotel booking site is Google. Why? Because if you search for hotels on their platform, they will show all the booking sites so you can compare them all at once to see who has the lowest rates and book it right there. Beyond Google, I find the best hotel booking sites to be Booking.com, Hotels.com, and Agoda.com.

11

TIPS FOR SAVING MONEY ON FOOD AND BEVERAGES

After accommodations, food is going to be your next largest day-to-day expense. Saving money on food when you travel is about eating like you do when you're at home. You don't eat expensive meals all the time when you are home, and you don't need to when you're on the road. My philosophy on eating while traveling is to pretend that expensive food doesn't exist and to eat like I would back home: cooking a few meals, eating at local markets, and having the occasional "fancy" meal.

It's all about balance. After all, you didn't save money and live like a pauper to cook pasta in a hostel every day.

Here's how to save money on food.

COOK YOUR MEALS

Everyone knows a week's worth of groceries is cheaper than a week's worth of restaurant meals. I generally find that, when traveling, I spend about $80–$100 per week on groceries (depending on the destination) as opposed to $20–$50 per day at restaurants (sometimes even more). Following these rough numbers, if I cooked all my own food while traveling, that would be roughly a 73 percent reduction in my food expenses! While it's unrealistic to avoid restaurant entirely while traveling, it just goes to show you the power of cooking your meals!

Even if you are simply going away for a two-week vacation, consider cooking some of your meals. Food costs add up quick—a snack here and a dinner there and you'll be wasting a lot of money on food. The majority of hostels, guesthouses, and shared apartments have full kitchens where you can cook your meals. (They provide pots, pans, and utensils too!)

While we all love to travel to try new food, you don't always need to eat at a restaurant to do so. Supermarkets are a good place to learn about the food of a culture. How people eat, what they eat, and what they don't eat can tell us much about how they view food, life, and health. You see a lot of fish in Scandinavia, lots of meat in Austria, packed shelves of wine in France, and a wide selection of vegetables and cured meats in Italy. In Bangkok, you see a lot of prepared meals. In Australia, it's skewers ready to be thrown on the BBQ. The emphasis on food is different all around the world, and roaming local markets will help you understand the culture as much as it will help you save money.

Every country has grocery stores but, since some are more

high-end than others, always be sure to ask the staff at your accommodation for the cheapest stores to shop at.

EAT WITH LOCALS

Just like with hospitality networks, the internet has allowed people to open their homes for individuals looking for a culinary delight. Many websites have sprouted up that connect travelers with locals looking to host a dinner party or have people over for a home-cooked meal. Each host sets their own price, and you can pick from a variety of cuisines (depending on what the host wants to cook).

The biggest player in the space is Eatwith (eatwith.com) with over 5,000 hosts in over 130 countries. Other websites include WithLocals (withlocals.com), Traveling Spoon (travelingspoon .com), and Airbnb Experiences (airbnb.com/experiences).

As most of these websites are by request only (except for Airbnb Experiences), I suggest booking these experiences well in advance to give the host enough time to respond and prepare. These experiences are not something to book last-minute.

While the costs are often higher than cooking your own food (or sometimes even eating at a restaurant), I love that you get to go into a local's home and share a meal. There are often other people there, too, so you'll be able to make new friends. It's like going to a friend's place for a dinner party. Frankly, it's a much more interesting way to eat. In Lyon, my host turned out to be a jazz musician who invited me and my friend to a jazz club, which we would never have found without him. In Paris, I got to hang out with a couple who shared my love of Thailand and we talked until the wee hours of the morning. I've absolutely loved these experiences and can't recommend these services enough.

FOLLOW THE FIVE BLOCK RULE

I live by what I call "The Five Block Rule." I don't eat within five blocks of a major tourist attraction or area. I simply walk in any direction for five blocks and then look for a place to eat. There's an invisible line at this area that tourists don't go past. All of a sudden, you notice that the crowds are gone, and that's when you want to start looking. Sure, you might find a good meal in a tourist area, but you'll find a better, cheaper meal outside it. Go where the menus aren't in multiple languages. Go to those tiny hole-in-the-wall places that you are unsure about. The meal might not always knock your socks off, but it will be a memorable and more local experience.

While in Barcelona, my friends and I wandered away from the touristy La Rambla neighborhood and found a local tapas restaurant. We filled our stomachs for $12 each, while on a busy tourist street a single dish can cost $20 all by itself!

If you are unsure of where to eat (and don't like the idea of randomly wandering into restaurants), try apps like Yelp (yelp.com), Urbanspoon (urbanspoon.com), OpenRice (openrice.com), and TheFork (thefork.com). For vegan and vegetarian recommendations, check out HappyCow (happycow.net). I use them often to find recommendations for food in the cities and towns I visit. You can also ask the tourist office or the staff at your hostel or hotel, or you can ask taxi drivers, who tend to eat at cheaper local food stalls. After all, the local staff isn't going to eat in the tourist area.

Furthermore, ask locals the question, "Where do you eat?"

not, "Where should I eat?" If you ask people the second question, most people will send you to the popular restaurants that tourists visit. They'll think, "Hmmm, where do visitors go and what's popular in town?" However, by asking where *they* eat, you will get recommendations for local restaurants and hole-in-the-wall spots where locals eat on a day-to-day basis. It's a small change in wording that leads to big results.

EAT THE LUNCH SPECIALS

In many parts of the world, you can dine on dinner menus at lunch-special prices. The "plate of the day" is the best bargain in the world. For example, while I was in Barcelona, I went to a seafood restaurant near the beach where dinner would have cost about $50. But because I was there at midday, the lunch special allowed me to get the same meal for only $20. Another destination that comes to mind for this is Singapore. Singapore is a very expensive place by Asian standards—food there can cost as much as it does in the United States—but restaurants have fixed menus for lunch that cost between $10 and $15 as opposed to $25 for dinner.

You will find this in so many destinations around the world that I couldn't possibly list them here, but trust me when I say it's very common.

Sadly, there is no one website where you can find all the restaurants in the world that offer lunch specials. They vary from city to city and region to region. What you can do (other than wander aimlessly around the city in hopes of finding a place, which I have done many times) is ask the tourist office or the staff at your hostel/hotel if they know where to find lunch specials.

Moreover, the websites listed on page 120 under "The Five Block Rule" can help you find lunch deals too.

Since most hostels and hotels provide breakfast, I try to eat out during lunch to capture these specials, and then cook dinner back at my accommodation. To me, this combination ensures I save money on food but still get to enjoy the local cuisine.

GET A FILTERED WATER BOTTLE

Everyone always wonders if the tap water is safe to drink. The answer is usually yes. The water in every modern country is safe for consumption. From Singapore to Australia to Japan to Greece, the water is safe to drink. Heck, you can even drink the tap water in Costa Rica. The United States doesn't have a monopoly on safe tap water. (But you should always double-check to make sure.)

You need to stay hydrated when traveling, and buying water every day costs money. Even if a bottle of water only costs $1, assume that you'll buy two per day and suddenly that becomes $60 per month for something you can get from the tap for free.

If the tap water in your part of the world is not drinkable, you can use Steripen (steripen.com) to purify your water, save money, and reduce your plastic waste. These products use ultraviolet light to purify water and are small enough to be carried in your pocket.

Additionally, the LifeStraw (lifestraw.com) and Grayl (thegrayl.com) water bottles come with attached filters, and these products are what I use when I travel. All you do is fill the bottle and the filter does the rest! If you are traveling to parts of the world with a lot of unsafe drinking water, I advise getting one of these devices.

12

TIPS FOR SAVING MONEY ON TRANSPORTATION

The methods to save money on transportation will vary a lot from region to region (see destination chapters in Part Three for specifics), but the general advice in this chapter can be applied to anywhere in the world.

To begin, let me say my view on transportation is like my view on food: stay local. Take as much public transportation as possible, get transportation passes when you can, and avoid taxis like the plague. If you follow that simple ethos, you'll save yourself a lot of money trying to get from point A to point B.

TAKE LOCAL PUBLIC TRANSPORTATION

Forget the private coaches, taxis, and tourist buses—do what the locals do and take buses or trains. It may be easier to get in that tourist bus, as companies will pick you up from your hotel or hostel and take care of the logistics for you, but it's more fun to figure out the local transportation system—and you'll save lots of money by doing so. Even in hyper-expensive countries like Norway or Sweden, public transportation is rarely ever more than $4. It may take some time to figure out the map and where you need to go, but learning the way is half the fun of traveling, right?

Hostels and hotels have maps and timetables for public transportation. When you arrive at the airport, the information booth will also have timetables for you. They can also tell you if there is an app to download for maps, routes, timetables, and tickets. (And, these days, there almost always is—and a lot of public transit systems let you just tap your credit card for the fare.)

Even if you don't speak the local language, the signs and timetables at the bus stop usually have a price listed. If the price isn't listed, I've never found a bus driver who didn't understand "how much?" At the very least, they have always understood the confused look on my face while holding a bill out in front of me! (Additionally, you can ask staff at your accommodation to write down your destination in the local language.)

Google Maps also provides information to many destinations on how to navigate local transportation and schedules. It's an invaluable resource to help you get around.

BUY METRO CARDS

City metro cards provide a considerable discount over single-use tickets. Even if you are going to be in a city only for a few days, you can usually buy a set number of tickets for a cheaper price.

For example, in Paris, you can buy a carnet (card with ten prepaid rides) for about $19, which is $8 less than paying for trips individually. In New York City, the metro is $2.90 per ride, but a seven-day unlimited-ride pass is only $34, which means if you use the subway at least twelve times, you come out ahead.

If I plan to be in a city for more than two days, I go to the closest metro station and ask what options are available, then I select the pass that meets my needs. Never assume that these cards are just for commuters—even if you're only going to be in the city for a few days, there is likely an option that will save you money!

GET TRAIN PASSES

Train passes are offered in many regions of the world and can represent a 50 percent savings on the price of train tickets. These passes will either allow you a set number of train rides or unlimited rides for the duration of the pass. This option is particularly popular in Europe, as we will discuss in chapter seventeen. Nowadays you can book trains and order passes online to lock in cheap prices, so there's no need to wait until you get to your destination. If you plan on using the train system often, you should definitely consider a rail pass. Country- and region-specific passes are discussed in Part Three.

SHARE A RIDE

Need a ride between cities? Get one with a local! The rise of the sharing economy has made it easier for locals to offer to drive visitors around their city as well as post rideshare opportunities between cities. There are a ton of reputable websites that help make this possible:

- Liftshare (liftshare.com/uk) in the UK
- Gumtree (gumtree.com) in the UK, Australia, and New Zealand
- Kangaride (kangaride.com) in Canada
- BlaBlaCar (blablacar.com) in Europe, Mexico, Brazil, and a few other places
- Jayride (jayride.com.au) in Australia
- Coseats (coseats.co.nz) in New Zealand

These websites work by connecting drivers with riders to split the cost of the ride. Drivers have to be verified and submit their ID, license, and registration information. Websites let you rate drivers too. These sites work best closer to departure as that's when most drivers post their rides (after all, think about your own trips: you don't always know what time you are leaving until right before you're going).

I've used these services in Europe and have found them to be a safe and fun way to get to know locals. The one downside is that people's plans often change and sometimes your ride gets canceled last minute. This happens only about 20 percent of the time, but it's something to be aware of. Drivers also set their own prices so just make sure the bus isn't cheaper if you are using these services solely based on price. (While they often aren't cheaper than long-distance buses and trains, I think the ability to ride with a local adds a lot of value and is something worth factoring in.)

Additionally, there are a lot of Facebook Groups you can check out if you type in your destination name and the word *ride-sharing* into Facebook's search bar.

AVOID TAXIS

Taxis are a waste of money. Do not use them unless absolutely necessary. If you're arriving at a destination at night, they can assuage your nerves about taking a bus to your hostel. That's about the only time I think they are worth it.

Check out Lyft (lyft.com), Grab (grab.com), DiDi (web .didiglobal.com), or Uber (uber.com). These companies offer "ridesharing" services that are like a taxi but work via an app over your phone. They are well-used services. Lyft is only in the United States, while Uber is global, and Grab and DiDi operate primarily in Southeast Asia and Latin America. Using these services also means that you won't get ripped off negotiating a rate with a taxi driver who doesn't want to turn on their meter because rates are set in the app. You can visit their websites or simply download the apps in the Apple or Google Play store.

13

TIPS FOR SAVING MONEY ON ACTIVITIES

N
o one wants to spend twenty bucks every time they enter a museum or pay full price for a tour. At those prices, pretty soon all you can afford is to see the museums from the outside. And all those walking and food tours can really add up. Luckily, there are tons of ways to see attractions and fill your day with activities without busting your budget.

VISIT THE LOCAL TOURISM OFFICE

One thing I can't stress enough is that you should always visit the local tourism office. It's always the first thing I do in any city because it's their job to have up-to-date information on what is going on around town: free events, festivals, concerts, and so on.

If you are ever in need of free or cheap activities, be sure to go to the local office and just ask.

Tourism offices also have deals and discounts that are not offered elsewhere. When I was visiting chateaus in the Loire Valley, the tourism office offered $2 off entrance tickets—which was a deal I couldn't find anywhere else. This is something that happens all the time. Furthermore, while at the tourist office, take some of those advertisement brochures that offer discounts. Most of them (especially the maps) contain ads for discounted tours and meals.

Local tourist offices are often found at airports, main train stations, or in the city center where the main tourist attractions are found. Be sure to head to one when you get to a new city to see what discounts they offer and any other information they have for you.

Plus, these offices are staffed by people who live locally so they can tell you how to navigate life in the destination, delicious eateries, cheap grocery stores, beautiful parks, and everything in between! Don't miss them.

GET CITY TOURISM CARDS

I love these cards and can't recommend them enough. In fact, I'm always surprised how most travelers avoid these cards! Local tourism offices (think London Tourism, Paris Tourism, New York Tourism, etc.) issue cards for all their attractions, tours, and restaurants. These cards (which you will have to pay a onetime fee for) give you free entry and substantial discounts on many of the attractions and tours in a city, free local public transportation (a huge plus), and occasionally discounts at restaurants and stores.

The cards are typically valid for one, three, five, or seven days. The first day begins when you first use your card, whether at a museum or on the train.

Years ago, I used the London Pass. This tourist card cost me at the time $95 for two days of sightseeing. With the pass, I saw the following paid sites:

- Westminster Abbey
- Tower of London
- St. Paul's Cathedral
- Ben Franklin House
- Britain at War Museum
- Shakespeare's Globe Museum
- London Tombs

Without this pass, these attractions would have cost me $170! I saved 45 percent just by using the London Pass, and I didn't even use it for everything it offers. And the math on this pass still works because, even though the price of the pass has gone up, so has the price of the included attractions!

I could fill an entire book with the number of times I've gotten city tourism passes that have saved me money (but I won't because this book is long enough as it is).

Most travelers never think of these passes because they aren't very well advertised or promoted. I hardly used them during my first trip around the world, and it was only when I got into travel writing that I learned about them. In fact, I don't think I've ever met a backpacker who has gone out and gotten these. Now, if I know someone is going to do a lot of sightseeing, I shake them and say, "Save money; buy a tourist card!" They are the single best way to save money if you plan to do a lot of sightseeing so be sure to check if the destination you are visiting offers one of these passes.

Will these cards always save you money? No. In places where attractions are really cheap, they aren't always a good deal because, in the end, it's all about the math. The only way to determine if the pass is a good deal is to add up the cost of what you (roughly) want to do, and then compare the combined price of admission against the cost of the pass. If the pass saves you even $1, buy it! Otherwise, skip it.

I'll go more into this in the destination-specific chapters in Part Three.

FIND FREE MUSEUM DAYS

Most museums have special discounted hours or free nights, even famous museums like the Louvre or the Guggenheim. If I don't have a tourism card that offers free entrance into the museum I want, I look up the museum on the internet to find out which days and times it offers free entrance. While not every museum offers it, enough do that it's worth checking. Tourism offices also maintain a list of free days and times for museums in the area. Just remember that you won't be the only one who had this idea and should expect the biggest crowds on these days!

USE GOOGLE

My favorite thing to search? "Free things to do in (X city or Y region)." There is so much information available online these days that you can easily find cheap or free activities, attractions, quirky museums, and the like that sometimes not even the local tourism board knows about. Don't skip this search!

TAKE FREE WALKING TOURS

Free walking tours are one of my favorite things to do in a new city. Not only do they orientate you but you get to spend a few hours learning about the history of the spot you are visiting. And, when you're done, you can ask the tour guide for tourist-free places to eat and drink.

Free walking tours used to be only found in Europe, but they have since made their way all around the world and most cities now have companies offering them. They typically last two or three hours and give you an overview of the central historic areas of a destination. Depending on the size of the city, there might be other free walking tours covering different neighborhoods and topics. At the end of the tour, you tip your guide (that's how they make money) whatever amount you feel is appropriate. I typically give about $10. In theory you could give nothing, but I don't think that's very cool and think you should always pay something.

Appendix A has a list of some of my favorite companies around the world but be sure to ask your hostel or local tourism board for an up-to-date list of companies, dates, and times.

Additionally, there is the International Greeter Association (internationalgreeter.org) located in 150 destinations around the world. This program pairs you with a local who will show you around their city (for free) and tell you about life in it. It's a really wonderful (and underutilized) service, so don't miss out on it.

You'll learn a lot and get an insider's look at the place you are visiting. Greeters need to be requested in advance as they are arranged on an as-needed basis, so reach out at least two weeks in advance.

TAKE AN AIRBNB EXPERIENCE

I think Airbnb Experiences (airbnb.com/experiences) are one of the greatest things to do when you travel. You get unique experiences run by passionate locals who can tell you inside info about the city or region. From wine tastings to street art tours to hikes to tea ceremonies, an Airbnb Experience is a tour run by someone who just wants to share their passion with you (so you often find very quirky and unique tours). I always meet interesting people and "get off the tourist trail" when I take them. While there's still a cost to them (prices vary a lot depending on the type of tour), they are often cheaper than organized tours because an individual running a tour has less overhead than a professional tour company with lots of staff. Be sure to look them up when you travel.

GET A TRAVEL DISCOUNT CARD

Travel discount cards can save you money on hostels, airfare, transportation, and tours. Sadly, these cards skew a lot toward students and youth travelers. Pre-COVID, there used to be a lot more discount cards but many of the companies offering them went under during the pandemic. As such, there are only three big cards left:

ISIC (International Student Identity Card). This student-only card provides discounts on activities, accommodation, and transportation. It can be purchased through their website (isic.org) for $20. There is no upper age limit on the card, so you can get one as long as you are a full-time student; it doesn't matter if you are twenty-one or fifty-one. Part-time students aren't allowed to get this card (unless you're thirty years old or younger).

There's also a youth version for those under thirty and a teacher version available on the same website.

Hostelling International (HI). Hostelling International is an international hostel chain with locations in more than eighty countries. HI members get discounts at hostels as well as discounts on tours, gear, and more. The price for an individual annual membership varies based on where you live but expect to pay around $15 for a membership.

Youth Hostels Association (YHA). The YHA is an affiliate organization of Hostelling International located in sixty-two countries that offers 10 percent off locations as well as other travel-related discounts with their membership card.

PART THREE

BREAKING IT DOWN BY REGION

While there are general travel tips and rules that can apply to every region in the world, there are many tips and tricks that are specific to individual destinations. While the internet and social media are great resources for finding deals, sometimes the best advice can only be learned from on-the-ground experience.

The following chapters break down cost-saving strategies for some of the most common destinations in the world with long-term travelers. Most travelers don't spend much time touring the countries of Africa, traversing across the 'Stans, roaming Mongolia, or lounging in Oman. It would be hard to provide information on all 196 countries in the world, so I had to make some trade-offs and omit the lesser-visited countries and regions in favor of the regions that see the highest volume of long-term travelers. Every place in the world is worth a visit and these omissions don't reflect any bias. Trade-offs had to be made or you'd be reading a seven-thousand-page book!

It is important to keep in mind that each person has a different style of travel, and therefore traveling will not cost the same for everyone. Though some might not prefer the life of a budget traveler, long-term travel requires us to always save money where we can. The cost-saving tips that follow are not set in stone, and some may not apply to you. Some people can travel on a few dollars a day and some need a few hundred. The tips and tricks in the sections here represent a framework to start with, but the exact amount you spend in each destination will depend on you.

Appendix A has a complete list of booking websites and tour companies for everything mentioned in the following chapters. If you want to book a hostel in New Zealand or a tour in Thailand or a bed-and-breakfast in Chile, all that information is easily accessible there.

14

AUSTRALIA

Growing up, I always thought Australia was a cheap destination (where this assumption came from, I do not know). But once I traveled there, I found it to be even *more* expensive than most of Europe. I was totally blown away by the high cost of food, transportation, and activities. Could you travel Australia on $75 a day? Yes. Is it likely? Probably not.

You can come close if you limit most of your adventure activities, but Australia is made for people who want to get outside, and all those wonderful activities like camping in the outback, sailing the Whitsunday Islands, and diving the Great Barrier Reef eat into people's budgets very quickly.

However, Australia does offer a lot of opportunities to save money. The country was made for the classic road trip, and it has a lot of hostels and jobs available for travelers. After all, it's remained one of the top backpacking destinations in the world despite its costs for a reason! Add in friendly, helpful people eager to show visitors their country and a diverse and beautiful landscape, and you'll understand why everyone who comes here leaves wanting more.

ACCOMMODATIONS
Hostels

Hostels in Australia are incredible. Many have pools, bars that serve food, extensive kitchens, comfortable beds, BBQ pits, large common rooms, tour desks, and a growing number have pod-style dorms with curtains for privacy. They offer a wonderful community atmosphere, and many go out of their way to host events and dinners so travelers can meet each other. Australia has a real travel culture (almost every Australian goes backpacking at some point in their lives!) and they bring that ethos to the hostels they run.

Hostels generally cost $25–$35 per night for a dorm room, while private rooms run $75–$110 per night. Hostels in the major cities on the east coast (that is, on the popular backpacker trail) tend to be more expensive than on the west coast due to higher demand. Sydney and Melbourne, the two most popular cities in the country, will be on the higher range (and the more popular hostels in those cities about 20 percent above that), while second-tier cities like Brisbane, Perth, and Cairns will be more in the middle.

At the time of writing, the Nomads Hostel (nomadsworld.com) group offers a bundle package called Bed Hopper, which allows you to pre-buy stays at a discount starting from ten nights for $300 (i.e., $30 per night). This pass works well if you're traveling during high season when the average price of the room can be a lot more than $30 per night. The price per night drops to $27 if you buy the sixty-day bundle, but that's a lot of time in a Nomads Hostel and, with many amazing hostels in Australia to experience, I wouldn't get that pass.

Budget Hotels

Budget hotels (two-star hotels) usually cost around $100 for a double room, private bathroom, TV, and breakfast. Budget hotels in Australia are pretty standard affairs and have all your typical hotel amenities. In smaller towns or more rural destinations, expect more B&B-style hotels in quirky homes and a more personal experience. Owners tend to be very friendly, welcoming, and helpful.

Personally, I think you get more value from a private hostel room over a hotel, especially in big cities, given all the added amenities in hostels as well as the social atmosphere they provide. Prices aren't that different, so unless you are really against hostels, I would choose a private room in a nice hostel over a budget hotel.

Apartment Rentals

Like the rest of the world, apartment rentals are incredibly popular in Australia. They are an especially good option in smaller towns where hostel and hotel choices are limited. A room in someone's home costs $35–$70 per night while an entire apartment can be as low as $70 to as high as $250, depending on size and location (Sydney would be on the higher end).

As apartments aren't that much more expensive than hotels (on average), I like using them over renting a hotel because I have access to a kitchen, allowing me to cook and keep my food costs down. This is my preferred method of travel in Australia if I'll be in a city for a while or traveling with friends, especially since Australia doesn't suffer the overtourism issues that other parts of the world do (as we discussed back in chapter ten).

The best website for apartment rentals is Airbnb as it's the most commonly used website in the country. For large vacation homes, Vrbo also has a large presence in Australia, especially for rentals in beach destinations. If you want to use a local company and you're in New South Wales, check out Holiday Rental Specialists (holidayrentalspecialists.com.au).

Camping

Camping is the most popular way to save money in Australia as there are *many* car parks and campgrounds. Australians love the countryside and you're never more than a couple of hours from a campsite. The road-trip/van-life lifestyle is huge in this country, especially with seniors who retire, rent an RV, and spend years driving around (sort of like in the United States).

Campsites cost $10–$30 per night for a spot that can be for either a car or a tent. At a minimum, they have toilet facilities and electricity. On the upper end, they can have pools, kitchen facilities, Wi-Fi, and cabins for rent.

Laurence Norah from the website FindingtheUniverse.com spent a year camping around Australia and never once had a problem locating an affordable place. As he states, "Campsites are easy to find, everywhere you go. They range from expensive to free. The closer you are to cities or popular destinations, such as most of the east coast, the harder it gets to find cheap sites. Good options are national parks, where there may be a nominal fee, or rest stops, which are free and legal to camp in, unless indicated otherwise."

Camps Australia Wide (campsaustraliawide.com) produces a book that lists all the free and nearly free campsites around Australia (14,000-plus at last count). It's comprehensive and a good resource, but if you don't want to pay for the book (it costs $110), they have a free app with all their listings. Hostel and hotel booking sites list campgrounds, too, but they don't always have as many options.

Hospitality Exchanges

Years ago, I used Couchsurfing while I was in Broome, Australia, a small town on Australia's west coast. I had a great experience, and since a national election was occurring at the time, I learned a lot about Australian politics.

While Couchsurfing isn't as popular as it was before, there are still a number of active hosts in the country (though, at the time of writing, Sydney only had 136 active hosts accepting guests out of 7,000 profiles). Servas (servas.org), Travel Ladies (travelladies.app), and BeWelcome (bewelcome.org) also have a large number of members in Australia. Between these sites and Facebook Groups, you're likely to find a host if you want one.

House-Sitting

There are lots of house-sitting opportunities in Australia. For example, TrustedHousesitters has 845 open listings as of this writing! Because Australians do so much long-term travel, there's always a good number of listings. According to Nora Dunn, "Because Australia is geographically so far from most of the rest of the world, many Australians choose to take extended leaves of absence from work and go away for up to months at a time. This means they like to have somebody to keep an eye on things at home, which gives house sitters a chance to sample a slice of local Aussie life."

That being said, because this is such a sought-after country, expect a lot of competition for sits and, as such, be sure to have good references and request sits far in advance.

While all the websites listed in chapter ten have hosts, one additional Australia-specific site is Aussie House Sitters (aussie-housesitters.com.au).

WWOOF

Australia is one of the most popular destinations in the world for farm work. It has a large agricultural and cattle industry that re-lies heavily on the influx of young people who come to Australia to work and travel, especially because working on a farm extends the entry visa. It's very easy to find a job even if you don't have any farm or agriculture experience. The work isn't great—you'll be picking fruit most of the time—but you'll get free room and board. Jobs are so abundant in Australia that you are pretty much guaranteed to find a spot.

However, WWOOFing doesn't exist in Australia (at least not officially), so you'll need to use the websites Workaway, World-packers, and HelpX to find farm work opportunities. Hostels can also help. Many of these opportunities may require you to have a working holiday visa though.

FOOD

Australia is a remarkable country for food. The climate is very conducive to a wide variety of fresh produce, meats, cheeses, fish, and a ton of world-class wine. Australians love healthy food and you can find some really good cafés throughout the country. Australia might not have the long food tradition of China, Japan, France, or Mexico, but it certainly has lots of quality cuisine. However, dining out in Australia isn't cheap—most meals at sit-down restaurants with table service cost $30 or more. When I first encountered these prices, I thought I was doing something wrong by spending so much, but as a plethora of Australian friends told me, "We just get screwed here."

An average no-frills meal in Australia will run you $10–$20. This includes pub food, fish-and-chip shops, cafés, Chinese or Indian takeaways, and quick lunch shops. In general, expect to pay $10–$12 for fish and chips (French fries), $13–$15 for avocado toast with poached eggs on top, and a burger might be around $15. There are plenty of small sandwich shops where the price for a sandwich is $8–$10. A pint of beer or a glass of wine will cost between $8 and $10.

A meal at a nice, sit-down restaurant costs around $35–$50 for a starter, entrée, and drink. Prices will be slightly higher in the big cities where entrées cost about $20 per plate.

If you cook your meals, expect to pay $60–$100 per week. For that price, your groceries will include pasta, vegetables, chicken, and some other basic foodstuffs. Kangaroo meat (it's abundant and common) is very cheap, lean, and delicious, and can be a good alternative to more expensive steaks. Campsites, hostels, apartments, and even some budget hotels will usually have kitchen facilities for you to use, which makes cooking very easy to do.

There are unfortunately few ways to save money on food in this country outside of just cooking your meals. If you want to eat out, you are going to spend a lot of money, especially if you want to avoid a diet of fish and chips, burgers, or other cheap pub food.

TRANSPORTATION

You'll find that medium to large towns have extensive bus systems that cost around $2–$4. In the largest cities in Australia, you will also find a commuter rail and tram system that extends into the nearby suburbs. These train rides cost $2–$5 depending on distance traveled. Prepaid day and weekly passes that reduce the rate of the daily fare are available.

Moreover, almost every major city in Australia has free bus or tram service in their downtown areas (called the Central Business District, or CBD) so it's easy to get around without spending money.

Trains

Australia's train system mainly covers the east coast, and you'll find a lot of interstate trains between Queensland, New South Wales, and Victoria. The country's rail system is split up among a few carriers.

While all the cities have commuter rail networks, Queensland and New South Wales have extensive intrastate rail networks:

- TrainLink (transportnsw.info/regional) covers New South Wales.
- Queensland Rail (queenslandrailtravel.com.au) covers Queensland's coast from Brisbane to Cairns with only a few interior routes.

Then there are six scenic train routes:

- The Ghan runs from Adelaide to Darwin in the middle of the country.

- The Indian Pacific runs from Sydney in the east to Perth on the west coast.
- The Overland runs from Melbourne to Adelaide.
- The Great Southern runs from Adelaide to Brisbane.
- Spirit of the Outback runs from Brisbane to Longreach.
- Spirit of Queensland runs from Brisbane to Cairns.

Journey Beyond Rail (journeybeyondrail.com.au) is the official provider for The Ghan, Indian Pacific, Overland, and Great Southern. Queensland Rail (queenslandrailtravel.com.au) runs both the Spirit of the Outback and the Spirit of Queensland.

However, one problem with the Australian rail network is that trains are infrequent (sometimes only one per week) and regional lines are not connected for seamless train travel between different parts of the country. Australia also lacks high-speed trains so train travel is slower than other transportation. For example, the trip from Sydney to Melbourne takes about eleven hours, while you can drive it in just under nine hours.

Between frequency, speed, and cost (the bus is cheaper), I would skip taking the train as your primary means of transportation.

That said, the scenic multi-day train journeys are phenomenal luxury train experiences and an incredible way to see the countryside. Fares for these cost from $1,400 all the way up to $4,000! But they are truly once-in-a-lifetime experiences. If you have the money, take them. The basic fares do not include meals, though they are available to purchase on the train. Higher service tickets (gold and platinum) will include food.

With the exception of the Overland (which is just a day trip), these train rides last a couple of days depending on the route you take. Keep in mind that these journeys need to be booked far in advance as they are very popular.

Buses

The easiest way to see Australia is via Greyhound Australia (greyhound.com.au). While there are smaller regional providers in each state, Greyhound has the largest and most extensive network throughout the country. However, outside of Broome, it doesn't really operate in Western Australia. For buses there, check out Transwa (transwa.wa.gov.au).

Greyhound offers two passes for travelers: National Whimit Pass, which covers the entire country, and East Coast Whimit Pass, which covers only the east coast.

Both passes work similarly. The National Whimit Pass allows you to travel any route, in any direction, for as many days as your pass allows, making as many stops as you want. At the time of writing, they had five versions that cost $264 for 15 days, $334 for 30 days, $377 for 60 days, $476 for 90 days, and $562 for 120 days. You can also create your own pass from between 7 and 60 days with prices starting at $218. The days are consecutive and you can travel as often as you want. You can see the route network at greyhound.com.au.

The East Coast Whimit Pass only allows you to travel from Cairns to Melbourne on any stops along the coast. They have three versions: $191 for 7 days, $244 for 15 days, and $297 for 30 days (though you can create your own pass for a maximum of 60 days). You can see the route network at greyhound.com.au.

These passes are a great deal and will save you a lot of money. For example, if you were traveling the east coast and got the 30-day pass, that works out to around $10 per day. But you aren't likely to travel every day. Realistically, even if you rush around, you are probably moving around every three days, which means you would take about ten bus trips in a month at a cost of around $30 per trip.

That still works out to be cheaper than buying individual tickets! For example, the twelve-hour bus from Sydney to Melbourne starts at $90, while the one-day bus from Cairns to Brisbane starts at $186. The shorter six-hour bus from Cairns to Townsville starts at $45, and Canberra to Melbourne takes eight hours and starts at $72. Even the short three-and-a-half-hour trip from Sydney to Canberra starts at $34.

All in all, a bus pass is the best option if you are taking multiple journeys because the price will always average out cheaper than individual tickets. So, unless you are only doing one or two trips, get the pass.

Flying

Australia is a big country and the quickest way to get around is to fly. However, there is *very* limited air competition in Australia, so while flying is the quickest, it can sometimes be some of the most expensive. In fact, Australians regularly complain that they can fly to Asia cheaper than they can fly across the country. While flights between major cities can be as little as $50, flights into the outback are hundreds of dollars and not very economical.

Australia has three major airlines:

- Qantas: qantas.com
- Jetstar (a subsidiary of Qantas): jetstar.com
- Virgin Australia: virginaustralia.com

There are also some very small regional airlines in Western Australia that fly routes between Perth and a few outback destinations but are mainly used by mining companies to shuttle employees around. But, for the most part, flights (especially those going across the country or into remote areas) are prohibitively expensive and should be avoided.

Camper Vans

The most popular and cheapest way to travel around Australia is to drive around yourself. Camper vans do two things: First, they lower your transportation costs because van rentals are really cheap, and driving yourself is cheaper than taking the bus or flying (especially if you team up with other travelers to split the gas). Second, they also double as a bedroom, so you can save on accommodation by sleeping in the van instead of a hostel.

As mentioned before, campsites dot the country and are generally 50 percent less expensive than a hostel dorm bed. A lot of travelers—young and old—use this method to get around Australia as it's the most economical way to explore the country.

The major companies for camper van rentals are:

- Spaceships: spaceshipsrentals.com.au
- Travellers Autobarn: travellers-autobarn.com.au (Note the UK spelling.)
- Wicked Campers: wickedcampers.com.au

Rentals start as low as $45 per day. The website CamperDays (camperdays.com) is a good website to use to compare prices.

While there are many opportunities to buy new vans, renting

or buying a used van is far more economical. Once people stop traveling, they sell their van to the next traveler. You can find a lot of rentals on the website Gumtree (gumtree.com.au) or on hostel message boards (a lot of hostels in Australia have boards for ride-shares). The Facebook Group Backpacker Campervans for Sale Australia (facebook.com/groups/525139527623724) is an active marketplace at the time of writing.

The best part? When the journey is over, you can just sell your van to a new group of travelers as a way for you to recover some of your up-front costs.

Hitchhiking

Hitchhiking is fairly common in Australia, especially among travelers. You see a lot of travelers do it and it is generally safe. Hitchwiki (hitchwiki.org/en/Australia) is the best resource for up-to-date tips and information.

Ridesharing

Ridesharing is very popular among travelers in Australia. You'll find a lot of people posting on hostel message boards, Gumtree, and in Facebook Groups that they are looking for passengers.

All you have to do is split the cost of gas, which is why I highly recommend traveling this way. It will lower your travel expenses and make the trip more enjoyable as you make new friends along the way!

While websites mentioned in chapter twelve are good resources, be sure to check out Coseats (coseats.com) and Bushride (bushride.com) for Australia-specific rides.

Attractions and Activities

When talking about what to do in Australia, you're really talking about what you're going to do outdoors. Australians love to get outdoors, and with such a beautiful and diverse countryside, you will too. Like everything else in this country, tours are expensive and there are few ways to lower the costs.

Most outdoor activities in Australia take up a whole day, though larger trips into the outback generally last at least one night.

Multi-day activities are expensive, generally costing $300–$400 while day trips will cost $100–$170. For example, a one-day trip to the Great Barrier Reef can cost $170, while two nights sailing the Whitsunday Islands can cost upward of $300–$400. A three-day trip to Uluru from Alice Springs is around $400–$550. (These prices reflect the average among companies aimed at budget travelers. Luxury and more all-inclusive tours cost more.) Entry into most national parks in Australia costs between $5 and $8 but can be up to as much as $19 for the most popular parks. Some regions offer an all-park pass for a onetime fee. In New South Wales, for example, it costs $43. In Queensland, all national parks are free of charge to visit, but you have to make a reservation and pay a fee if you want to camp overnight.

Buying tours together can also help save money. Many tour desks in hostels (as well as throughout the country) offer bundle discounts, and you can usually get around 10 percent off the tours.

Australia is also a "young" country. I remember visiting a town in Western Australia that was considered "old." Then the guide said it was founded in 1948, making it younger than my dad! Because of that, Australia lacks the sorts of historical sites you find in other parts of the world. There's an old house here or there, but most of the activities will focus on nature as opposed to visiting historic ruins, old religious sites, or castles. Most of the museums are history or art museums located in big cities, and admission fees are around $15 (many are free though).

At the time of writing, there is no single tourist card for Australia, nor do any of the city tourism boards offer one. The only option for savings is via a company called iVenture (iventurecard.com), which offers a tourist card for Sydney and Melbourne. Two-day passes begin at $130 and cover most of the museums and major attractions in each city. However, the pass only saves you money if you do at least half of the attractions and excursions included in the pass, which will mean that you'll be extremely busy during your visit. A better option is their flexible pass, which allows you to pick the activities you want to do and save 40 percent off normal entrance.

In the larger cities, you'll find a number of free walking tour companies, which is a good way to explore neighborhoods and fill a few hours. My favorites are listed in Appendix A.

HOW MUCH MONEY DO YOU NEED?

On a very tight budget, I think a traveler could get by in Australia on $60 per day. It would entail Couchsurfing or house-sitting, cooking almost all your meals, limiting your partying, and spending most of your money on transportation and just a handful of activities. While it's not impossible, it would require you to constantly watch your pennies. But some travelers do it, and you could probably do it too.

However, I think if you were to budget $130 per day, you would be able to travel around the country without compromising too many experiences. For example, if you did Melbourne to Cairns, which is the popular east coast route that most travelers take, your approximate costs for one month would be $900 for hostels (average price of $30 per night), $1,000 for food (mixing cooking and eating out), $150 for drinks, $1,500 for tours and activities (assuming three big activities and a couple smaller tours), and $300 for your Greyhound bus ticket.

Most backpackers stay in dorms, do a lot of famous activities, get bus passes, and try to balance eating out and cooking. A lot of them kill their budgets by drinking so if you limit that (or add in more cooking and fewer meals out), you might be able to get your budget closer to $100 a day.

Additionally, using a camper van for accommodations and getting around on your own, you could lower your daily average even further.

Conversely, if you're staying in budget hotels, private apartments, or hostel private rooms, you'd have to add at least $40 per day or more to your daily budget, so you'd average about $170 or more per day, which is a lot if you're traveling long-term.

Australia isn't a cheap destination, but like any place, if done smartly and skillfully using the budget tips mentioned in this section, it doesn't need to be overbearingly expensive. While a trip there won't be as cheap as a trip to Costa Rica or Thailand, you can still find ways to save money and reduce your costs.

15

CENTRAL AMERICA

Belize, Costa Rica, El Salvador, Guatemala, Honduras, Nicaragua, Panama

Central America gets a bad rap in mainstream media and many people think it's a "violent" place. While there are generally more safety concerns here than other parts of the world, the region is not as unsafe as the media makes it out to be. As they say, if it bleeds it leads, and most stories we hear about this region involve drugs, gangs, and corruption.

While those problems do exist and travelers have to be more vigilant here in regard to safety (especially in bigger cities), this is a region full of welcoming people, lush landscapes, and rich history. I've been to this region many times, and it remains one of my favorites in the world. I love the relaxed lifestyle, the beautiful beaches, the azure-blue water, the warm weather, the jungle treks, the friendly locals, and the flavorful food.

The region is also an incredible bargain for travelers. It's cheap to eat, stay, and get around, and your dollar goes very far in these countries. While the rise of digital nomad hubs in the region has made it slightly more expensive than in the past, it's still a deal compared to other regions of the world.

ACCOMMODATIONS

Hostels

While hostels are abundant in Central America, most hostels (especially in small towns) tend to be pretty basic, offering few of the amenities you find in other parts of the world. Not many have kitchens or common rooms, offer tours, or have bars. That said, the rise of digital nomads post-COVID has turned many destinations (mostly beach towns) into "nomad hubs" that are filled with many upscale hostels. In these places, free breakfast is common, there are bars, pools, discounts on tours, and even pod-style beds. (I hope, by the time you read this, that trend has continued.)

A night in a hostel in Central America ranges between $10 and $25 for a dorm room. In Costa Rica, Belize, or Panama, you will pay on the higher end of that range as these places are the most expensive in the region. A private room will cost you $30–$45 for a double bed and a shared bathroom, with Costa Rica, Belize, or Panama on the higher end of that range or slightly more. If you want a private room with your own bathroom, expect to pay between $50 and $70 (or more).

In major touristy beach areas in Panama, Belize, or Costa Rica, you'll likely spend about 10–20 percent more, especially during peak season.

Budget Hotels

Small, family-owned guesthouses or hotels will be the most affordable accommodation option in the region besides hostels. I love these mom-and-pop spots as they often have beautiful rooms, unique decorations, large breakfasts, and are safe and clean. Plus, your money stays within the community instead of going to some corporate hotel's headquarters.

These hotels usually cost between $25 and $35 per night for a private room with an en suite bathroom, and most come with breakfast. In cheaper countries like El Salvador, a private room can be as low as $20 per night, while in more expensive destinations, you can expect to pay around $40–$60 per night.

Just remember many of these accommodations are the "you get what you pay for" kind of places. The cheaper you go, the fewer the frills.

If you want something a little nicer, comfier, and with AC, I'd budget at least $40 per night and closer to $65 per night in more developed and touristy destinations.

Apartment Rentals

Apartment rentals have become very widespread throughout the region, especially in bigger cities where you can find an abundance of options. For example, Panama City has over one thousand apartment rentals, which is double what it was when I wrote the last edition of this book. As more digital nomads have moved to the region after COVID, there has been a lot more demand for this kind of accommodation.

Generally speaking, private rooms in someone's home cost between $20 and $40 per night, while entire apartments will cost $55–$65 per night. If you're visiting one of the popular digital nomad destinations, expect to add another 20–30 percent on top of that. As an example, on the small island of Caye Caulker, Belize, you'll find private rooms starting at $60 per night and entire apartments for about $90 per night. In Antigua, Guatemala, another hot spot but with more accommodation options, expect to pay around $35 per night for a private room and at least $65 per night for an entire apartment.

Airbnb has the largest inventory in the region, while Vrbo has a lot of beach destination options. At the time of writing, there was no "local" country-specific version of either company anywhere in the region.

Camping

Camping can be done easily at hostels and in national parks. Most hostels have space where you can pitch a tent or string up a hammock for $2–$5 per night, while national parks require camping fees that vary from country to country. Some hostels will provide a tent or hammock for you, but if you have one with you, almost any hostel outside of the big cities (there's not a lot of room in buildings in San Salvador or San José!) will let you pitch your own.

Hospitality Exchanges

While you'll be able to find hosts in most major cities, the pool of available hosts in Central America is often very limited. You can try to find a host on Couchsurfing, Travel Ladies, or BeWelcome, but you should not count on this method as you can in other parts of the world. Servas has an extensive network in this area of the world and is often a better choice here in terms of availability.

House-Sitting

House-sitting is not widely used in Central America. Panama and Costa Rica are the most active destinations, but even there, you rarely find more than a handful of opportunities at any given time. Generally speaking, house-sitting in the region tends to happen through word of mouth, personal connections, and location-specific Facebook Groups within expat communities. Since house-sitting opportunities are so rare, be sure to plan far in advance for any sits.

WWOOF

WWOOFing is available throughout Central America, but there aren't many hosts (at the time of writing, Costa Rica had the most with ten opportunities) so you'll want to make sure you organize everything well in advance to guarantee a spot. Most openings are for small farms, though you can find unique opportunities such as working on coffee plantations or making chocolate.

Similarly, Worldpackers, HelpX, and Workaway all have limited options.

In short, while you might get lucky, this isn't an option I would count on.

Homestays

Another popular option in this region are homestays. Homestays pair you with families for language exchange. In exchange for a small fee, you will get room and board with a local family who will help you learn Spanish (and, in exchange, you might also help them with their English). Accommodations are usually basic, but if you want to learn the language and get immersed in the culture, this is your best choice in the region. Prices vary wildly but expect to spend around $100 per week.

Worldpackers and Workaway have a lot of opportunities available. Additionally, many language schools in the region can also help you find a host. Combining a multi-day language course with a homestay experience is an excellent way to really dive deep into learning Spanish.

FOOD

The cheapest places to eat are the roadside restaurants that dot this region. These restaurants tend to be small family establishments and tend to only sell whatever the main type of local dish is. At these *"comidas"* (as they are called locally), you can expect to pay around $6 for a two-course meal that consists of chicken, rice, and beans.

If you want really cheap food, you can find empanadas (fried pastries filled with meat, cheese, or potatoes) for $1. Not only are they cheap, but they are tasty—they were a staple on my trip throughout Costa Rica. Additionally, premade plates of food (usually chicken or beef, rice, and tortillas) are often sold on local buses during stops on longer trips for about $3–$5.

If you are looking to sit down at a restaurant that is slightly more upscale than the local *comidas*, you can expect to pay at least 25 percent more money. A typical meal in a restaurant with table service costs $6–$12 for a main dish and a drink. In a major tourist area, you're likely looking at $15 and up, regardless of the country.

If you are looking for Western food, you are going to pay for it (at least by local standards). That burger, pasta, or pizza will cost about three times as much as the local dishes. If you are craving a burger or pizza, expect to pay around $15 for a meal with a drink (even higher in tourist areas). Since the local cuisine here is so delicious and filling, it's not worth spending the money on a bad and expensive version of what you can get back home.

If you want to cook your own food, you can head down to the local market and pick up enough fruit, vegetables, meats, and dairy for around $30 per week. That said, I wouldn't buy groceries in this region. Central American food vendors and markets are inexpensive enough and, outside of Airbnb-style apartment rentals, there are few places that have kitchens. I love buying fruits and snacks at the local markets, but I rarely buy groceries when I travel here and would not recommend it.

TRANSPORTATION

In the cities, public buses are the cheapest and most convenient way to get around. Fares are usually less than a dollar everywhere within the city limits.

Trains

Trains are not an available method of travel in Central America. Though there are some freight trains that move cargo in the region, you won't find a passenger train network in any country (Belize doesn't even have a train line of *any* kind). If there are trains, they usually run from the capital to one other major city and are generally commuter trains.

Buses

Countrywide and intercountry buses are the most widespread and easiest way to travel the region. You can catch most buses for $10. Longer bus rides and overnight trips are generally around $30. This is the most common way for people to travel—locals and tourists alike. Buses in Central America (often called "chicken buses" due to the abundance of chickens and rice transported on them) are slow, operators try to squeeze as many people on as possible, and they stop frequently to let people on and off.

But drawbacks aside, riding on these buses is an unforgettable experience. You're cramped, you feel a bit lost, everyone is looking at you like "Who's the gringo who didn't take the tourist bus?" (If you're tall, the seats are going to feel quite small.) But that's what makes these buses so fun. You meet a lot of interesting people and can get a really good sense of how the locals travel. To me, they are often a highlight of my trips because people take interest in you, you get to talk to them, and you get to learn about local life.

Buses can simply be booked at the station or flagged down from the side of the road. In Central America, there's no real need to book in advance (and most online booking websites are only in

Spanish). Tourist offices and the registration desk at your hostel/ hotel can give you up-to-date information about bus times and pickup locations during your visit.

Another option is to take a private tourist bus. These buses are quicker, have nicer seats, and go from point A to point B relatively quickly. Unlike local buses, they won't stop twenty times to pick people up until they are full, but they are generally double to triple the cost. You pay more and the bus will only be filled with other tourists, but sometimes you just need to move a little quicker (and that's OK!). These can be booked from your hostel/hotel or the company's website.

All in all, booking a bus in Central America is simple: all you do is show up and buy a ticket. There is always a bus and, normally, always a spot. It's the only real way to get around anyway.

Hitchhiking

This region, though serviced heavily by bus, relies a lot on hitchhiking. Buses can be late, sporadic, and sometimes extremely full. Many locals also simply can't afford the bus and you'll find hitchhiking to be widespread and relatively safe. It is not uncommon to see single women, families, children, and old grandmothers on the side of the road looking for a ride. I've done this in Belize, Costa Rica, and Panama.

That said, use caution when entering someone's car, especially if you are a solo female traveler. I wouldn't hitchhike in El Salvador or Honduras because, in my opinion, the countries aren't very safe. Use your judgment and, if something feels off, wait for the next car. Hitchwiki (hitchwiki.org/en/Central_America) is again the best resource for more information.

Flying

There is a limited regional air network in this region. The biggest operator is Copa Airlines (copaair.com/en/web/us), which is based out of Panama. The Colombian airline Avianca offers some direct flights between big cities in Central America, and the Guatemala-based TAG flies directly to a few other destinations in the region.

Outside of the capital cities and any international airports, the airports tend to be very small and only accommodate small propeller planes. Most of those small airlines have dubious safety records and I try to avoid them as much as possible.

Furthermore, flights are overly expensive. A flight from Guatemala City to Belize City is typically as much as $250, whereas the bus is only about $75 (though of course the trip is a lot longer by bus). This type of vast price difference is typical of the region. The bus rides may be longer, but if you are trying to see this region on a budget, you should not fly.

ACTIVITIES AND ATTRACTIONS

There isn't a huge selection of museums in Central America, and most of them only have signs and descriptions in Spanish. While in Panama, I went to the Panama Canal Museum (a popular tourist attraction) only to find a few very abridged descriptions in English. Most museums in this region tend to be small and focused on their colonial and indigenous history. Admission generally costs about $2–$5, and you can get discounts on museums in the region with the student or youth discount cards discussed in chapter thirteen. These are generally 50 percent off the adult price.

Entrance to national parks is typically inexpensive, only costing around $10. Archeological ruins cost between $5 and $15 for small ones while larger ones like Tikal in Guatemala can cost around $20.

Adventure activities like diving, zip-lining, ATV tours, canopy tours, and the like tend to be expensive, costing between $60 and $120. The coasts of Honduras and Belize are the two biggest dive hot spots in the region.

It isn't easy to save money on popular activities here. Tourism boards don't offer tourism cards like you see elsewhere in the world. Sometimes local museums will sell combination passes that might save a dollar or two, but that's rare. In general, the listed price is the listed price.

HOW MUCH MONEY DO YOU NEED?

Central America is very affordable. Outside of Panama, Belize, and Costa Rica, you can travel this region for around $50 per day without skimping too much. This would entail hostel dorms, eating at local markets and inexpensive restaurants, bus travel, a few activities, and limited drinking. In other words, the typical "backpacker budget." Costa Rica, Belize, and Panama are more expensive and require around $70 per day, especially if you're staying in popular beach destinations.

If you were looking to do more adventure activities or stay in private rooms, I would add $20 per day to your budget. Conversely, if you were to hitchhike, stay in only the cheapest accommodations, eat only local market food, or follow the other tips in this section, you could reduce your costs by $5–10 per day.

The biggest "budget busters" in this region are private accommodations, adventure activities, and drinking, so as long as you keep those three in check and stick to local cuisines and restaurants (again, there's no need to have a terrible pizza), you should be fine.

While the region isn't as affordable as it used to be, it's still relatively cheap by global travel standards and one of the best for travelers on a tight budget.

16

CHINA

C hina has fascinated travelers ever since Marco Polo traversed the Silk Road in 1271. As China's prominence and economic might in the world continue to grow, more and more people flock there seeking to explore and understand the country like the explorers of yore. This gigantic and diverse place can be a culture shock for many travelers—there's a strong language barrier, it's chaotic, crowded, the food is "weird" to Westerners—but travelers are richly rewarded with friendly people, delicious cuisine, a country in constant flux, a rich history, and incredible landscapes.

Post-COVID, tourism is finally returning as China relaxes its travel restrictions. While the days of China being a super-cheap destination are long gone, the country remains a budget destination with many opportunities for savings, especially when you get out of the major cities and into the countryside.

One thing to note is that China is fast becoming a cashless society and, by the time you read this, it may be even more cashless. You'll want to download a payment app like Alipay, WeChat, or whatever else exists at the time you read this as it is nearly impossible to pay for something without one of these apps.

ACCOMMODATIONS
Hostels

Despite the size of most cities in China, there is a relative lack of hostels throughout the country. In Beijing, a city of millions, there are just under ten hostels listed on Hostelworld at the time of writing, and Shanghai, another city of millions, only has eight hostels. (However, Hong Kong, which has a long backpacker tradition, has forty-one!)

While scarce, hostels in China are a great value for the money and include a lot of amenities. Guests typically get free drinking water, Wi-Fi, and heated blankets (those winters are cold!). Hostels also have large common rooms and lockers. In short, they have everything a traveler could need and are similar to hostels in the West. Some hostels in remote locations may have squat toilets in lieu of Western toilets, so bring your own toilet paper! (I would bring flip-flops for the showers too.)

Outside of the big cities, a dorm bed will cost between $10 and $15, while private twin or double rooms will cost between $25 and $45. However, prices in the large cities can cost double that. For example, dorms in Beijing and Shanghai begin around $20 and go as high as $35; while in Chengdu, they cost around $10–$15, and in Kunming, they begin around $8–$10. Private rooms are around $30–$45 a night and go between $65 and $90 in the megacities of Hong Kong, Beijing, and Shanghai depending if you get a single bed private room (which is very common in

China) or a double bed private room. (Single beds will be on the lower end of the price range.)

Budget Hotels

Budget hotels begin around $20 for a twin room in the country-side and start at $40–$50 per night in larger cities like Shanghai, Beijing, and Hong Kong. In these cheap hotels, you'll find basic accommodations—a heated blanket, air conditioning and/or heat, a water kettle, and quite often a television set (but with only Chinese-speaking channels). Accommodations can get kind of spartan when you get into the countryside and, in China, you truly get what you pay for, so don't expect a lot of comfort and amenities if you're staying on the cheaper side of hotels.

In Hong Kong, hotel prices will be much higher than mainland China. A single room in a hotel starts around $40 and goes as high as $90 per night.

Another thing to keep in mind is that hotels advertising breakfast rarely serve a Western-style or continental breakfast. You should expect dumplings, steamed bread, various vegetables, rice, congee, and warm water.

Given the spartan nature of budget hotels in China, I would consider spending a few extra dollars per night for something a little comfier and cleaner.

Apartment Rentals

Because of the abundance of cheap accommodations throughout mainland China and Hong Kong, you won't find many people listing rooms or apartments. If you do happen to find one for rent, it likely won't be a great deal because it will be meant for Western visitors—and the locals know Westerners can pay more money so they charge high rates.

At the time of writing, Airbnb no longer operates in China (though it still operates in Hong Kong). Vrbo operates in China but there are minimal listings for big cities and the properties are not particularly affordable, so I would skip them.

While there are a few Chinese versions of Airbnb and Vrbo, their websites are only in Chinese and not very useful to foreign travelers. At the time of writing, I would recommend travelers avoid apartment rentals as an accommodation option.

Hospitality Exchanges

Hospitality exchanges are not big in China. Beijing, a city of 21.5 million people, had only 106 Couchsurfing hosts who had logged in the last six months at the time of writing. Hong Kong, the most "Western" city in the country, only had 158. BeWelcome had fewer than 20. The numbers drop exponentially once you get out of those cities, and there are many places in China with no active hosts.

In short, while there are active hosts in larger cities, there are so few that I wouldn't count on this option while you are traveling the country. You may luck out and find a host but travel here without counting on it.

House-Sitting

At the time of writing, house-sitting is also not a viable option in China.

WWOOF

There is no official WWOOFing in China and the only organization that shows up when you search is not affiliated with the official WWOOF organization. Similarly, Worldpackers, HelpX, and Workaway have fewer than a handful of listings at the time of writing. I wouldn't count on any volunteer opportunities while in the country.

FOOD

Food in China isn't the same "Chinese food" that we eat in the West. There's no sesame chicken, crab Rangoon, fortune cookies, or General Tso's chicken. In China, food is less fried, contains more parts of the animal (there's a good chance your chicken soup will have an entire chicken in it!), and is often a lot spicier. (There's a tremendous amount of regional variety, too, so be prepared to encounter a lot of dishes you've never heard of before!)

The food in China is its own kind of delicious. For breakfast, locals tend to eat either a noodle soup, a thin rice porridge, a Chinese pancake with egg in it, fried savory puff pastry with meat, or steamed dough. Except for when people are on their lunch break alone, lunches and dinners consist of shared plates with everyone getting their own bowl of rice and using chopsticks to eat off the same plates. (FYI: This is generally how food is eaten throughout Asia. The idea of the individual meal is not common in this region. Everyone shares a bunch of dishes and then splits the bill.)

A meal from a street vendor usually goes for $1–$2. For this you might get noodles, Xinjiang BBQ, rice, pork buns, or a soup.

A full meal in a sit-down restaurant will cost between $3.50 and $8. If you stick to the local food, you'll never go broke. You could spend less than $10 for an entire day's worth of food. Always go to the busy places where you see lots of people to get the best stuff.

In western China, southwestern China, and the interior, food is much cheaper than in the big metropolises (Beijing, Shanghai, etc.), and you can eat for under $5 per day (about half the costs of the big cities).

For Western-style food (French, Italian, burgers, etc.), you can expect to pay much higher prices for food that will be a disappointment compared to home (though larger cities like Hong Kong and Shanghai have very high quality and high-end Western cuisine). A Western-style sandwich can run about $6–$8, and a cup of coffee can be similarly priced as back home. Meals at Western-style restaurants can be as high as $30 and above in bigger cities.

But again, what's the point of traveling overseas to eat bad versions of what you can get at home? While I'm guilty of sneaking Western food when I crave something familiar, the Western food in China (especially on the budget end) is just generally not good. And, once you get out of the major cities, Chinese food will pretty much be your only choice, except for an occasional McDonald's or KFC.

Since food is so inexpensive, there's no need to self-cater or cook your own meals. You are better off eating the street food and at the restaurants. Moreover, most hostels don't have kitchen facilities for you to use even if you did go grocery shopping. Therefore, cooking is not something I recommend. The food is cheaper and better than what you can make anyway.

TRANSPORTATION

Local transport within a city or area costs about thirty to forty cents per subway ride or fifteen to thirty cents per bus ride. Taxis charge around $1.50 to start and fifty cents per mile if they're willing to run their meter, which is sometimes a battle. Keep in mind that it is rare to find a taxi driver who knows enough English for you to explain where to go. Have your destination written out in Chinese whenever possible.

Two indispensable ridesharing apps are DiDi (web.didiglobal.com) and Hello Ride (helloride-global.com). To use both, you'll need to download Alipay, one of the most used mobile wallets.

Buses are the most common means of getting around in the cities. Service in the major cities is fairly extensive and fares are inexpensive, but expect buses to always be packed. Traffic is also really bad in big cities in China so don't be in a rush as you're not going anywhere quickly.

Major cities in China have underground metro systems. The price of a typical subway ticket is less than $1 depending on distance; in Hong Kong, it is between sixty cents and $3.50, also depending on the distance. As of May 2024, there are metro systems in operation in fifty-five cities across mainland China including, but not limited to, Beijing, Shanghai, Guangzhou, Shenzhen, Tianjin, Wuhan, Chengdu, Hangzhou, Zhengzhou, and nearly all major economic and tourist centers.

Trains

Although crowded, trains are the best way to travel in China as they are fast and comfortable. At any given time, over ten million people are traveling by rail. Moreover, China has been upgrading their very old trains to modern ones similar to those in Europe or Japan. The new fleet is cleaner, comfier, and has air-conditioning.

Ticket prices are calculated according to distance traveled and, on some longer routes, by class. Third-class seats (which tend to be hard and uncomfortable) are the cheapest and therefore most packed, as those tickets are the only ones most rural Chinese can afford. In this class, you'll get a ticket with an assigned seat number. If seats are sold out, you can opt for a standing ticket, which will at least get you on the train.

Trains in China are designated by a letter to show their category and speed. G trains are the fastest, D trains are high-speed trains that run a little slower, and K trains run at 75 mph. The slow "fast" trains are designated with the letters Z and T. Non-high-speed trains are the slowest and cheapest, running at 62 mph. These trains simply are designated by number.

The G train from Beijing to Shanghai takes around five hours and is around $77–$93 for second class, $129–$141 for first class, and $260–$324 for a VIP seat. By comparison, the non-high-speed train takes a whopping nineteen hours but costs just $25 for a hard seat or standing ticket, $43 for a hard sleeper, and $66 for a soft sleeper. D and T trains are your middle-of-the-road option, taking (only) twelve to fourteen hours and costing between $44 and $77.

"Hard" sleeper cars are doorless compartments with bunks on three levels and come with sheets, pillows, and blankets. Lower bunks are less expensive than top bunks and lights and speakers go out at around 10 PM. The soft sleeper is the top level of service on trains. They consist of four very comfortable bunks in a closed compartment, with lace curtains, teacups, clean washrooms, carpets, and air-conditioning.

Another example is the popular Shanghai to Xi'an route. The fastest G train takes just 5.5 hours and costs about $100 for a second-class seat, $160 for a first-class seat, and $300 for a VIP or business-class seat. K trains take 21.5 hours and tickets for a hard sleeper are $46–$60, a soft sleeper is between $70–$116, while hard seats or standing tickets are just $25.

If the fares for fast trains seem high compared to everything else mentioned in this section, that's because they are! The Chinese government has been raising train fares on their high-speed lines to help cover the debt they took on for these massive projects, and this is still the case as of May 2024. (Hopefully, by the time you read this, they will have stopped raising them.)

The slow trains are obviously the most affordable but significantly slower. I would opt for the high-speed trains rather than the numbered slow trains unless you can break up the journey into segments. Nineteen hours is a long time to be on a train!

Some large stations have special ticket offices for foreigners; otherwise, there is always someone around with basic English skills—although it's a good idea to have a translator app on hand in your phone. It should also be noted that foreigners need to present their passports when buying tickets. One helpful trick is to get the person at your hostel to write out in Chinese which ticket you want to buy so you can just show it to the ticket agents at the station.

Scalpers (also called "touts") swarm around train stations selling black-market tickets; this can be a way of getting scarce tickets, but foreigners frequently get ripped off so I recommend avoiding this.

As trains sell out in advance, especially around Chinese holidays, it's often a good idea to book trains in advance when you can. Three reputable websites are China Highlights (chinahighlights.com/china-trains), Trip.com (trip.com/trains/china), and China Ticket Online (chinaticketonline.com).

Long-Distance Buses

Long-distance bus service is very common. Thankfully, main roads are rapidly improving and the number of highways is increasing. Buses are generally cheaper than trains. For example, the nine-hour bus from Beijing to Anshan is $29, while the train can be as much as $56. The two-hour bus from Beijing to Tianjin is $4–$6, while the high-speed train is around $8–$13.

On the other hand, if you are traveling on slower trains (and in the cheap hard seats), you will often find them to be a less-expensive alternative to buses, so be sure to check the prices of both before you book. Additionally, China is investing heavily in rail infrastructure and, since the central government controls the prices, train travel has become a lot more affordable—and faster—in recent years. Even if the train costs a couple of dollars more, it might be worth it for the hours of saved time.

ETrip (etripchina.com/bus) is a good China-specific resource to look up buses online.

Flying

Although traveling around China in buses or trains is the best way to see the country's vast and lush countryside, sometimes it's more efficient to fly given the country's size. If you don't have the time or inclination for a long overland trip (and getting around China does take a while), flying is your most efficient option. China has numerous airlines, and major ones include:

- Air China: airchina.com.cn
- China Eastern Airlines: ceair.com or us.ceair.com/en
- China Southern Airlines: csair.com/en
- Spring Airlines: en.ch.com
- Cathay Pacific: cathaypacific.com
- HK Express: hkexpress.com/en-hk/
- Sichuan Airlines: global.sichuanair.com
- Hainan Airlines: hainanairlines.com

Additionally, nearly every province of China has regional carriers that operate close to their main hub, such as Hainan Airlines, Shanghai Airlines, and dozens of smaller regional carriers.

Fares for major routes between large cities (like Beijing to Hong Kong) start around $90 when booked in advance. Refer back to chapter six for tips on finding a cheap flight as these methods apply to flights in China as well.

ATTRACTION AND ACTIVITIES

Sights and activities are inexpensive in China—even the popular attractions such as the Great Wall and Forbidden City are under $10. While the Great Wall never kept out invaders, it's beautiful and is about $6 to visit at Badaling, Mutianyu, and Simatai. Smaller temples, activities, and sights around the country are even more reasonably priced and cost around $2. Cable car tickets are $12–$16.

If you want to see giant pandas, the breeding facility in Chengdu costs around $9. In Qufu, the hometown of Confucius (one of the most famous philosophers in Chinese history), you will find tickets for the Confucius Temple, Confucius's home, and the Confucius Mausoleum for between $11 and $22. Seeing the famous terra-cotta army in Xi'an will only set you back about $16. No matter how you slice it, attractions in China are reasonably priced.

Prices for hikes and outdoor activities start around $30. For example, a trip to the Jade Dragon Snow Mountain (Yulong Xueshan) costs around $33 for a guided hike, a visit to the Jiuzhai Valley (Jiuzhaigou) can be as high as $30 depending on the season, and a three-day pass to the Wuyi Mountains (Wuyishan) in Fujian Province is $35. You'll pay between $20 and $26 to visit the Yellow Mountain (Huangshan) in Anhui Province.

In Hong Kong, activities and attractions are much costlier than in mainland China. Most museums begin around $10, and observation decks and activities are between $20 and $30.

While Hong Kong has a city tourist card run by a third party, cities in mainland China do not. You simply won't find discount cards and offers like you can in other parts of the world. However, if you are a student and have an ISIC card, you can get discounts to most of the national parks and UNESCO World Heritage sites.

There are free (e.g., tip-based) walking tours in many of China's biggest cities, but outside the main tourist areas you won't find many that are run in English. They are listed in Appendix A.

At the time of writing, there are no Airbnb Experiences in China.

HOW MUCH MONEY DO YOU NEED?

China isn't as affordable as it used to be but it's still a great budget travel destination. If you're staying in hostel dorms, traveling cities by bus or bicycle rather than by taxi, eating from street stalls or small restaurants, taking a mix of high-speed trains, slow trains, and buses, and resisting the urge to splurge, you'll be able to travel around the country for around $60 per day.

That may seem like a lot, but as we've already covered, the high-speed trains are really expensive and can eat into your budget. Depending on how long you spend in the country, you could lower your day budget to between $40–$50 per day by traveling only on buses or slower trains.

If you were to only stay in hotels or hostel private rooms, take only high-speed trains, and splurge once in a while on a few high-end meals, you'd likely spend around $100 per day.

China can be done cheaply if you stick to the traditional backpacker style of travel or have a lot of time that lets you take slower trains or buses. Outside of the major cities and high-speed train travel, everything else in the country is very inexpensive so there's plenty of ways to keep your costs low.

17

EUROPE

Europe is not the monolithic destination most travelers consider it to be. Prices vary greatly depending how far north, east, south, or west you go. You could fork out $125 per day in one place, switch countries, and then spend just $50 per day.

By balancing expensive countries like France and England with cheaper destinations like Poland, Romania, and even Greece, you can keep your daily average low. I spent more than $100 per day while visiting friends in Sweden (mostly because they kept taking me to restaurants and clubs), but while exploring Eastern Europe, my daily average was closer to $30.

When talking about Europe, I think it is best to break it up into four zones: Western Europe, Central Europe, Eastern Europe, and Scandinavia, as the countries that are included in each "zone" tend to be similar in price and methods of saving money.

WESTERN EUROPE

Belgium, France, Germany, Greece, Ireland, Italy, Portugal, Scotland, Spain, Switzerland, the Netherlands, United Kingdom

Western Europe is expensive. High taxes, high prices, and high-valued currencies (euro, Swiss franc, British pound) are a deadly combination for the budget traveler. Post-COVID, prices have risen a lot as travel to the region has skyrocketed. Be prepared to spend more here than in other parts of Europe, especially if you're visiting during the peak summer months.

ACCOMMODATIONS
Hostels

Hostels in Europe contain a wide range of amenities—free breakfast, Wi-Fi, kitchens, common rooms, bars, outdoor patios, pools, and tour desks. In my opinion, European hostels are some of the best in the world. They foster a great sense of community, go out of their way to organize activities, and are often just really lovely.

And Western Europe has some of the cream of the crop.

Outside of peak season, hostel dorm rooms in the region cost between $29 and $45 per night, depending on the room's size and hostel's popularity and location. (The bigger the city, the higher the rate.) In large, heavily visited cities like Paris, Barcelona, Amsterdam, or London, dorm beds can be as much as $75 per night during the peak summer months thanks to the dynamic pricing I talked about in chapter ten. Meanwhile, in a smaller city like Athens, in "cheaper" countries like Portugal, or in rural areas of the more popular countries, peak summer prices might only get as high as $55.

The majority of hostels in this region also have private rooms with en suite bathrooms. Private rooms usually average $100–$150 per night in popular destinations, while smaller cities and destinations will average between $80 and $100 per night. However, during peak summer months, private rooms can be as high as $300 per night in some of the larger cities!

While these rooms are cheaper than staying at a large brand hotel (think Hilton), I don't recommend them unless you are specifically looking for the hostel vibe as most small, budget hotels offer private rooms at cheaper prices.

HostelPass (hostelpass.co) offers discounts of up to 20 percent off many hostels throughout Europe as well as discounts on tours. The pass costs $29.99 per year, so if you're staying in a lot of hostels, this pass will pay for itself in no time. I highly recommend it.

Budget Hotels

Moving up from hostels, you'll find "pensions," which are small, family-owned budget hotels. They are those indeterminate places you see as you walk around the streets of Europe that make you go, "I wonder how good that place is."

Pensions are quaint, cozy, and intimate. Rooms typically come with a double bed, a private bathroom, heat/air-conditioning, and occasionally a TV. They are no-frills establishments, and you aren't going to find twenty-four-hour room service. But they will provide a decent bed, privacy, and often a small breakfast.

You're probably asking, "OK, so what's the difference between a pension and a budget hotel?" Honestly, nothing. Pensions are just the old name for small budget hotels before the rise of websites like Booking.com. They used to be more B&B-style accommodations that also offered meals, but nowadays, pensions in the traditional sense of the word tend to be only located in smaller, rural towns. In big cities, you get the modern budget hotel experience (think two-to-three-star bare-bones hotel) even if they call themselves a pension.

Rooms in two-star, no-frills hotels typically cost between $50 and $140 per night. A room in Paris will cost at the higher end while a room in Athens will cost at the lower end. You'll get the basics—decent bed, shower, maybe air-conditioning, and clean space but nothing more. During the peak summer season, prices could be about 50 percent higher, especially in prime destinations like Rome, Paris, Barcelona, Ibiza, or Amsterdam.

Apartment Rentals

If you are looking for the comforts of home, apartment rentals are very common throughout Western Europe. Whole apartments usually cost between $50 and $200, depending on how many people you have as well as the size and location of the apartment. The closer to the city center, the more expensive. The more rural the destination, the lower the price. In major cities like Paris, Amsterdam, London, and Madrid, the costs will be on the upper end of that range, and likely even higher during peak season.

But if you are traveling in a large group, the cost of an apartment rental will be cheaper on a per-person basis than a hotel or hostel.

Private rooms in someone's home usually start from $50 per night (or about $70 in larger cities for something central). Prices are pretty uniform throughout the region.

However, as apartment rental options have greatly expanded in Europe, there's been a lot of backlash against them over the past few years. European cities are small, lack high-rises, and don't have a lot of housing stock. As more and more owners put units on these websites instead of renting them out to residents, locals have pushed back as they have gotten priced out of their neighborhoods.

But since the money is so good, many residents, especially the older ones, turn their old apartments into vacation rentals to help pay the bills, which makes their neighbors do the same. The added tourists then continue to raise the cost of living, which only pushes people to rent their places. It creates a vicious cycle.

Because of this, many cities have put restrictions on these services (Barcelona, Venice, and Amsterdam usually get the most press). You'll see lots of "Airbnb go home" graffiti in cities across Europe. Locals are generally not a fan of these companies.

Because of all the overtourism issues mentioned in chapter ten, I do NOT recommend renting apartments in cities in Western Europe unless you can be sure that it is really a home someone lives in and not an apartment used solely for vacation rentals. If you are going to use these services, try to only rent a room in someone's home. It will be cheaper and you'll get to interact with a local. It's a more fun and sustainable tourism experience. (In the countryside, where hotels are limited, whole apartment rentals are OK with me!)

Camping

Camping is very easy to do in this region. You can find campgrounds and RV parks dotting the edges of cities throughout

Europe. Campsites cost between $10 and $45 per night per person for a tented space.

If you are traveling by RV or car, expect to pay double that per night. These sites provide toilets, showers, kitchen facilities, and places for your tent (or RV). Some even provide internet access. You can rent tents at most campsites for around $10 per night.

If you don't have a tent (or don't want to camp), many campsites have dorm rooms and lodges on their grounds. Dorm rooms tend to cost around $25 per night, which is still cheaper than a dorm in the city center.

One thing to remember is that most campsites are often far from the city center, so if you want to see the sights, you'll have to pay for transportation to and from the city each day. Make sure these campsites are near a bus or train route so you can conveniently get to where you want to go. Moreover, many campsites are closed during the winter months, so be aware.

You can find campsites listed on most hotel bookings websites, Hostelworld (hostelworld.com), Campspace (campspace. com), and Camping.info (camping.info).

Hospitality Exchanges

Hospitality exchanges are still incredibly popular in Western Europe with a large pool of active hosts. For example, on Couchsurfing, London still had 448 hosts active in the last month, while Amsterdam had 309. Even tiny Zurich had 176 hosts. During the summer months, hosts get inundated with thousands of requests because of the influx of travelers to Europe, so to be successful, put in your requests far before you need the accommodation to give the potential host enough time to plan for your visit. Don't be afraid to follow up, either.

Couchsurfing is the largest network but Servas, BeWelcome, and Travel Ladies all have a big user base in Western Europe too.

House-Sitting

Western Europe has a lot of opportunities available for people who are interested in house-sitting. However, it is also the most competitive part of the world, so you'll likely need some experience and reviews before you snag an opportunity. The more popular the destination, the more competition there is to sit there.

Long-term house sitter Sam Anthony says, "There are tons of house-sits in Western Europe, especially the United Kingdom, where I easily lined up a summer's worth of house-sits around London, Brighton, and Glasgow. The UK is a great place for even newer house sitters to get started as there are so many opportunities available, though competition can be high for more popular locations (such as London)."

Be sure to check out the websites listed in chapter ten as they all have hosts throughout the region.

WWOOF

WWOOFing is very popular in this part of Europe, especially in the large agriculture areas of Germany (500+ farms), Italy (800+ farms), France (2,000+ farms), and Spain (300+ farms). At any given time there can be hundreds of listings throughout the region, so you'll have no problem finding opportunities. Just make sure you put your requests in early, especially during the popular summer tourist season when demand is at its peak. Worldpackers, HelpX, and Workaway all have a lot of volunteer farm listings you can search too.

FOOD

Europeans don't eat out like we do in the United States. We are very much a grab-and-go, quick-meal culture. Europeans tend to cook more of their own meals and shop at outdoor food markets. The mega-food stores you see around America are a rarity in Europe, especially Western Europe. Buying your groceries at markets, cooking your own dinners, and making your own sandwiches are the most inexpensive ways to eat.

I love wandering the local markets, tasting the local food, and having the finer points of French cheese or Italian Balsamic vinaigrette explained to me by local shop owners. Shopping at an outdoor market in Paris and then picnicking in front of the Eiffel Tower sounds much better to me than spending $30 at a restaurant.

You can cook your own food for around $100 per week. (This number is, of course, variable and depends highly on your eating needs.) You'll be able to feed yourself pretty well if you shop at grocery stores and buy food at the local farmers markets. The cheap grocery stores in this region are Profi, Lidl, Aldi, and Penny Market.

If you're looking to eat on the cheap anywhere in Western Europe, you can find small shops to get sandwiches, slices of pizza, or sausages / hot dogs for between $5 and $8. You'll often find these shops in train stations, bus stations, and main pedestrian areas. European eatery chains like Maoz (falafel) and Wok to Walk (noodle shop) are also inexpensive, offering meals between $8 and $13.

Additionally, in Germany and Austria you will find street vendors selling hot dogs, currywurst (sausages covered in curry powder and ketchup), and other sausages for around $3. These are quite popular because they are filling, cheap, and delicious!

Eating this way will cost between $25 and $35 per day (especially if you stay in a hostel with free breakfast). You won't be eating fabulous meals, but you'll be saving a lot of money. If your goal is to stretch your dollars as far as possible, this is the best way to do that (besides cooking for yourself).

Sit-down restaurants with simple menus and table service typically cost $15–$25 for a main dish. These are no-frills places. Picture your neighborhood Italian restaurant. It's delicious, it's satisfying, but it's nothing super fancy. Indian, Asian, or Middle Eastern food is also widely available and an affordable way to eat out, costing between $10 and $15 for a meal.

It's also common for restaurants to have a "plate of the day" served at lunchtime. This is a set menu that includes a few dishes at a price cheaper than what you would find for dinner. You can get a large meal for $10–$15 (often with a drink included) for a substantially reduced price. In Spain, for example, look for the "menu del dia" at restaurants at lunchtime—often a three-course meal and drink for a very low price. This is one of my favorite ways to sample local cuisine while traveling in Western Europe.

The city tourism cards discussed in chapter thirteen also offer discounts on food and beverages. While the restaurants that participate in tourism card discounts tend to be more expensive than grab-and-go places, the discounts given (up to 20 percent) can make them very affordable.

Specific to the United Kingdom, check out the Tastecard (tastecard.co.uk), which offers up to 50 percent off (as well as two-for-one deals) at more than one thousand restaurants. You don't need to be a United Kingdom resident to get the card. Membership costs about $10 per month and you can cancel your membership whenever you want to avoid being charged in the future. The website will ask for a local address during the booking process, and I simply use the address of the place where I am staying while in the UK.

TRANSPORTATION

Transportation around most European cities typically costs between $2 and $3 for a one-way ticket by tram, subway, or bus. Europe has a large and well-funded public transportation system that makes getting around cities very convenient for travelers. (City tourism cards usually provide free public transportation, which is another reason to get them.)

Trains

Trains are my favorite form of transportation in Europe. Traveling by train allows you to see the countryside as you speed from city to city. They are spacious so you can walk around and stretch your legs, and many of them have dedicated dining cars.

Train companies have moved to a similar dynamic pricing model as airlines (though not as extreme), so you can often save up to 30–50 percent off by booking tickets a week or more in advance. Prices are higher on weekends and peak travel time, so always be sure to get your tickets as soon as you can.

For example, a high-speed train from Berlin to Munich costs between $45 and $75 and takes under four hours, Bordeaux to Paris is between $60 and $110 and takes two hours, and Madrid to Barcelona starts between $30 and $95 and takes two hours and thirty minutes. And the Eurostar from London to Paris can start as low as $60 and go as high as $300 for a second-class ticket!

That's a huge range, so booking as early as you can—especially on high-speed, high-traffic routes—will save you the most money. Generally, you're going to pay at least $60 for a train ticket, and the longer the ride, the more you'll spend.

Non-high-speed trains are a lot cheaper, with short distances (one to two hours) costing $15–$30 and longer journeys (three to five hours) costing around $50. Train prices vary a lot, but generally speaking, the slow, short journeys cost about 40–50 percent of the price for high-speed trains.

However, outside of small countries like the Netherlands, Belgium, or Switzerland, most train travel is now "high speed." You still may find yourself on commuter lines for short distances into smaller towns near large cities but, if you're going between major cities, your train is 90 percent likely to be a high-speed train. When I started traveling Europe in the mid-2000s, the journey from Nice to Paris took an entire day and made frequent stops, but with the new high-speed line, the journey is only 5.5 hours with usually only one or two stops. That said, you'll still find slower trains with more stops on late evening or overnight routes.

In the United Kingdom, the National Rail service (nationalrail.co.uk) is always expensive, no matter how long your trip is.

It's one thing citizens in this part of the world love to complain about. Bring up the National Rail to Brits and just see how long they'll carry on complaining about it. A journey from London to Liverpool can cost as little as $50 or it can cost as much as $200 during peak hours (midday).

To avoid that, booking your ticket with National Rail more than a week in advance and traveling during off-peak hours can secure you tickets for as little as $20. These saver seats are often available in very limited numbers, which is why you need to book early.

To save money on trains, be on the lookout for deals from the national rail companies. Germany's Deutsche Bahn offers special "super saver" fares that give discounts to travelers under twenty-seven and over sixty-five, as does France's rail network, SNCF. Spain's Renfe railway network offers a 30 percent discount to travelers under twenty-five and a 40 percent discount to those over sixty. In Italy, Trenitalia offers discounts for travelers under thirty and over sixty as well as family fares. Beyond age-based discounts, they often have flash sales and unlimited train travel specials (Germany, for example, often offers unlimited train travel passes). Be sure to always check your options online before you walk into the train station to purchase a ticket.

Rail Passes

Eurail passes are one of the most popular travel products in the world, and few travelers making their way across Europe go without one. These train passes give you a set number of stops in a set time period. You can get continent-wide passes, country-specific passes, or regional passes. Just as there are trains that go everywhere in Europe, there is a pass for everyone. Passes come in two varieties: first class (valid for first- and second-class cars) and second class (valid for only second-class cars).

Rail passes are sold via Rail Europe (raileurope.com), which is a United States–based seller. You can also find passes on the main Eurail website (eurail.com). There's no difference between the two—Eurail is the pass issuer and Rail Europe is the reseller. Europeans need to use the site Interrail (interrail.eu).

Most travelers use the popular Global Flexi Pass. A two-month, fifteen-day (that's fifteen days of travel) second-class ticket costs about $608 for adults and $457 for travelers twenty-seven years and under (a value of $41 per trip for adults and $31 for youths). A first-class adult ticket costs about $772 (a value of $52 per trip), and twenty-seven and under costs $580 (a value of $38 per trip). A "flexi" pass allows you to use your days anytime during the two-month period, unlike consecutive day passes, which have to be used day after day. Consecutive day passes can be bought for up to three months. These passes cost up to $1,135 for a three-month pass and are not worth the price because every day you don't use the pass, your money is wasted (so don't get them).

You buy your pass before you go, and it becomes active the first time you use it on a train. You don't need to buy a ticket ahead of time—you can simply show up at the train, present the conductor with your pass, and continue on your journey. That said, some countries require you to book a seat ahead of time and place limits on which trains you can use. When you receive your rail pass, you'll get a small book that tells you the specific reservation rules for each country covered by the pass.

So, are Eurail passes worth purchasing? Maybe.

Rail passes are all about money. If it doesn't save you a dollar, it's not worth getting. That means you have to do a lot of math to figure out if a pass is right or not. It can be a time-consuming process but is certainly worth it in the end.

As mentioned before, train prices are now variable and no longer fixed. If you are willing to prebook months in advance, you'll easily find some unbeatable bargain deals such as Paris to Amsterdam for $40, Rome to Venice for $25, or Amsterdam to Berlin for $45. Because rail passes cost roughly $52 per trip, you can't beat booking individual tickets far in advance.

But who prebooks a multi-month trip to Europe? That defeats the free-spirited nature of long-term travel.

So, without going through a ton of math and boring you with price tables and spreadsheets, here are some general guidelines to determine if you should get the Eurail pass or not:

- If you have fixed dates and can book months in advance, a rail pass is likely not for you as those early-bird tickets are pretty cheap.
- If you are taking a lot of short trips (two to three hours or less), a pass won't save you money.
- If you are taking a lot of high-speed, long-haul trains, a pass is likely to save you money.
- If you are traveling around Europe with no fixed plans, rail passes may work out to be a better value than buying same-day point-to-point tickets.

To me, the pass is about flexibility and being able to hop on and hop off trains when I want. If you are traveling long-term, you likely aren't going to schedule your travel months in advance.

You are going to want the ability to go with the flow, which using a pass will give you.

There have been many times I've said or heard other people say, "I'm going to Paris tomorrow," only to then leave three days later. Eurail passes are much better than buying the tickets the day of—and they retain that same "today, I'm going here" flexibility.

Getting the wrong pass, however, will definitely cost more than buying individual tickets. If you buy a Global Pass and then visit one to three countries in relative proximity to one another, you're definitely going to lose money. A large, multi-country pass will only work when you travel to many countries and over long distances.

You also need to read the fine print. As I mentioned, some countries require you to pay reservation fees to secure your seat, while others do not. France and Italy, for example, charge reservation fees of up to $12. (The book you'll receive when you buy the pass will contain all the fees you may incur with it.)

You will also have to make reservations for overnight trains and pay a reservation fee (anywhere between $7 and $70 depending on the country and the type of accommodation booked) in addition to what you paid for your pass. Rail passes reduce the cost of sleeper trains, but unlike for day trains, they don't eliminate it.

In the end, a train pass isn't right for all trips, but for most people who will be spending a long time in Europe and traveling vast distances, having a pass will save them money.

The best way to figure out if a pass is right for you is to look up train prices for the routes you'll likely be on and add them up. If the total amount is close to or more than the cost of a rail pass, get the rail pass so you have the added flexibility.

Buses

In the UK, the cheapest way to travel around is via the Megabus (uk.megabus.com), where fares can cost as little as $2.50. You'll need to book at least a month in advance on popular routes to get the special fare. However, even if you don't get the cheap fare, you can find regular fares for around $25, which is still considerably lower than day-of buses on National Express Coach (coach.nationalexpress.com), which cost around $37. For me, Megabus is the only way to go when in the United Kingdom. Moreover, they now serve Paris, Amsterdam, and Brussels for around $20 for a one-way ticket.

The main bus company in Europe is called FlixBus (flixbus.com). Fares often start as low as $6. Their buses include Wi-Fi, electrical outlets, free baggage (one carry-on and one stored under the bus), and comfy seats. They go all over the continent and are often the de facto intercity bus company in many countries. You can find their route map at global.flixbus.com/bus-routes

If you have the time, FlixBus will be cheaper than the train, even if you are going long distances. For example, Berlin to Paris is about $60 for a last-minute bus ticket, while a last-minute train is as high as $185 (booking in advance will get the price down to around $90 but that's still more expensive than the bus). The downside to bus travel is that, instead of being able to get up and walk around the train, you are cramped on a tiny bus. What you save in money, you lose in comfort. However, I think the savings are worth it, especially when you are on a tight budget.

Personally, I love the bus for short journeys of two to three hours, especially when I am on a tighter budget. The fares can't be beat. However, for long-distance journeys, I'd rather take the slightly more expensive train so that I can spread out and move around.

While FlixBus dominates the region (and is the *only* bus company in many countries like Germany), there are still a lot of country-specific carriers (all of which have similar fares to FlixBus). To find fares and companies, Busbud (busbud.com) and GetByBus (getbybus.com) are the two best websites to use.

Flying

The rise of the budget airlines discussed in chapter six has made flying around Europe quite inexpensive. European budget airlines often have deals with fares as low as $15 (though there are a lot of added baggage fees). Generally, you can find most flights for $50 (including fees) if you book at least a month in advance. If I need to get somewhere in a hurry or far away, I'll fly because fares are cheap.

The most popular budget airlines in Europe are:

- easyJet: easyjet.com
- Ryanair: ryanair.com
- Transavia: transavia.com
- Vueling: vueling.com
- Wizz Air: wizzair.com

These airlines are just "buses in the sky" and do not offer a luxurious travel experience, but they will get you safely from point A to point B in a timely manner. One thing to note is that these airlines often fly into smaller, out-of-the-way airports, so be sure to look up how far the airport is from the city center.

You can refer back to chapter six for further information on how to find cheap flights.

Ridesharing

Ridesharing is a great way to get between cities in Europe. The ridesharing website BlaBlaCar (blablacar.com) is hugely popular. I've used it to get around Switzerland and France and I absolutely love it. Though not cheaper than the bus, I find ridesharing a fun way to get around, meet locals, and learn about the culture. You're doing this for the experience.

Most drivers post their trips a few days out so this option is best to book within the week of travel.

Hitchhiking

Hitchhiking isn't super common in the region. Some people have had some success, but they often have to wait a long time for someone to pick them up. It's not a transportation method I would recommend or rely on, but if you want to do it, check out Hitchwiki (hitchwiki.org) for country-specific information.

ATTRACTIONS AND ACTIVITIES

One thing I love about Western Europe is the uniformity of activity costs. Museums, day trips, attractions, guided tours, pub crawls—there's not a lot of variation in prices. The Louvre in Paris is $24, the Prado in Spain is $17, the Acropolis in Athens is $24, and the Van Gogh Museum in Amsterdam is $24. See? All relatively the same price. In general, prices are between $20 and $25 for the large, ultra-famous, everyone's-heard-of-them museums. Smaller, not-so-well-known museums typically cost a few dollars less. In the United Kingdom, all public museums are free (which is something every country should do) so you won't have to worry about costs there.

Full-day tours vary in price depending on the type of tour as well as the location. For example, a full-day wine tour in Tuscany is around $140 while a similar tour in Bordeaux is around $75. All in all, if you're doing full-day tours related to food, wine, history, and the like, expect to pay between $60 and $150.

Airbnb Experiences is wonderful for offbeat and unique tours. There are a lot of hosts and activities and incredible variety in this region of the world. Prices vary a lot (expect to pay at least $35 for a half-day tour) but I *love* using this platform for activities and the chance to meet locals. Don't skip using them.

Pub crawls, if that is your thing, can be found in every large city in Europe. Most are run by the local hostels, but some are run by major companies like Ultimate Party (joinultimateparty.com) or 1 Big Night Out (1bignightout.com). They cost between $20 and $40 and include free entrance, free beer, and free shots. They are a fun way to meet other travelers.

The two best ways to save money on activities in Western Europe are by taking free tours and by getting city tourism cards. In the vast majority of Western European cities, you can find free walking tours. They are a perfect way to familiarize yourself with city attractions, learn some history, and get your bearings in a new environment (so when you walk around alone, you know where you are). They typically last two to three hours. Appendix A lists more of my favorite walking tour experiences.

Next, get a city tourist card as I mentioned in chapter thirteen. Attraction and museum prices can really add up in most countries in Western Europe, so the math on these passes usually works in your favor if you're doing a lot of sightseeing. When I plan to do a lot of sightseeing in any Western European city, I tend to get these cards because they save me money and come with free public transportation. Win-win.

CENTRAL EUROPE
Austria, Czechia, Hungary, Poland, Slovakia, Slovenia

When I first started visiting back in the mid-2000s, this region still had a rough-and-tumble, off-the-beaten-path feel to it. I love the historic cities, the lovely mountains and rivers, incredible wine, and hearty food. However, over the years, this region has developed significantly and tourism is now gigantic here. Just try to visit Prague in the summer—it's you and a million of your closest friends. Even the shoulder season is crowded now. However, when you get out of the larger cities, you still can find some beautiful towns without the crowds.

ACCOMMODATIONS
Hostels

Like their Western brethren, hostels in this region are filled with lots of amenities and offerings. Dorm rooms in the region cost between $29 and $45 per night, depending on the room's size and the popularity of the hostel. Popular cities like Prague or Budapest or Vienna will be on the higher end, especially if you are traveling during peak season. For a private room in a hostel, you'll pay between $55 and $70 per night, though during peak summer season the range is between $100 and $150.

HostelPass, which I mentioned in the last section, has a lot of inventory in the region and is a good way to save money on hostels.

Budget Hotels

Pensions and budget hotel rooms typically cost $40–$70 per night depending on your location, though expect higher prices in larger, more popular cities like Vienna, Salzburg, or Prague. For example, a room in the center of Prague costs around $100 per night, but if you're willing to stay just outside of the city center, the average price drops to around $60. Smaller "secondary" cities are also cheaper. In Brno, you can nab a room for around $65, while in Bratislava you'll pay about $55. Prices will be about 30–50 percent higher in most popular cities during peak season.

In the countryside and mountain towns, you'll find fewer city-style budget hotels and more pensions with a homier, B&B vibe to them.

It's not luxury at these prices, but it's a roof over your head and a clean bed to sleep in. All of these hotels will have your standard amenities, but since the prices are usually similar to a private room in a hostel, I generally will choose the hostel because it's easier to meet people.

Apartment Rentals

Apartment rentals are very common throughout this region of Europe. Whole apartments usually cost between $40 and $100, depending on how many people you are traveling with, as well as the size and location (as usual, the closer to the city center, the more expensive). For example, prices start at $60 in Prague, $75 in Warsaw, and $60 in Vienna. Prices jump at least 30 percent during peak season. A private room in someone's home is cheaper and is usually between $25 and $45 per night.

However, just like in Western Europe, there are lots of problems with overtourism and apartment rentals, especially in cities like Prague, Krakow, Vienna, and Budapest. I again would advise against using apartment rental services in major cities unless you are renting a private room, and only use these services in the countryside where there are limited hotel options.

Camping

Campsites cost between $10 and $30 per night per person for a tented space. If you are traveling by RV or car, expect to pay double that per night. These sites provide toilets, showers, kitchen facilities, and places for your tent or RV. Some even provide internet access. You can rent tents at most campsite parks for around $8 per night.

If you don't have a tent or don't want to camp, many campsites have dorm rooms and lodges on their grounds. Dorm rooms tend to cost around $17 per night, which is still cheaper than a dorm in the city center.

Hospitality Exchanges

Hospitality networks aren't as popular here as they are in Western Europe and they are very hit or miss. For example, at the time of writing, Couchsurfing had only 25 active hosts accepting guests in Vienna who had logged in the past 30 days (1,000 if you expand your search to "maybe accepting guests," but that usually means no). However, BeWelcome had 126 hosts accepting guests. In Krakow, on the other hand, Couchsurfing had 165 hosts compared to BeWelcome's 44.

There's always the possibility of finding a host; you'll just need to look at a few websites.

Travel Ladies has a wide user base in the region, so be sure to check them out if you're a solo female traveler.

House-Sitting

House-sitting in Central Europe is not nearly as popular as it is in Western Europe. You may find some house-sits in the larger capital cities (such as Budapest, Warsaw, and Vienna), but it's not a reliable means of finding accommodation in this region. It's still worth a look on house-sitting websites if you are already a member, as house-sits do pop up now and then and competition isn't as fierce as in other areas of the world.

WWOOF

WWOOFing opportunities can be found all over this region, but outside of Austria (over three hundred farms), most countries only have between twenty and fifty farms so there aren't a ton of options. Another thing to note is that the farms in the region tend to be smaller and only take a couple of WWOOFers at a time. Similarly, Worldpackers, HelpX, and Workaway also have very few opportunities listed on their websites.

FOOD

Food in this region is often hearty. Since most of Central Europe was part of the Austro-Hungarian Empire for centuries, you'll find a lot of similarities between the food in each country. For example, most traditional pubs and restaurants will have goulash on the menu (though the style will vary slightly). Wherever you are in Central Europe, expect to see a lot of pork and pork by-products on menus (who knew there were so many different types of sausages!). You'll also find a lot of heavy meats, stews, and slaws in this region of the world.

Meals at a hole-in-the-wall restaurant with table service typically cost $15–$30 for a main dish that consists of pork, chicken, or a hearty beef dish. (The upper end of that range is going to be some sort of giant pork leg or something similar.)

In Central Europe, some of the most affordable food can be found at pubs with stick-to-your-ribs fare involving pork or some sort of fried food. It's not healthy, but it's filling (and really good!). Expect these meals to cost between $15 and $20.

You will find a lot of street sausage options throughout the region, often costing around $5. If you eat meat, they are a great way to get a cheap, filling meal.

Indian, Asian, or Middle Eastern food is also cheap throughout the region. Most full menu items are between $10 and $15, and you can usually snag a Turkish döner kebab for about $4.

Beer is also super cheap in the region, with most pints costing between $2 and $3 at a bar.

If you're looking to cook your own food, expect to spend around $60 per week for your basic staples. The cheap grocery stores in this region are Profi, Lidl, Aldi, Billa, SPAR, and Penny Market.

TRANSPORTATION

Transportation around most Central European cities by local tram, subway, or bus is typically between $1 and $3 for a single-journey ticket.

Trains

Trains are a great way to travel the countries in the region and my preferred method. Because the countries are smaller, the train rides are a lot shorter and smoother than the bus. Fares are relatively inexpensive too. A train journey from Prague to Vienna costs about $20. Prague to Krakow is an eight-hour journey and costs about $25. The two-and-a-half-hour train ride from Vienna to Budapest costs about $25, and Budapest to Krakow is an eight-hour train ride and costs about $60.

In short, trains in this region are very affordable!

Rail Passes

The rail passes mentioned in the last section cover the entire area and the same guidelines listed apply. However, if you are *only* visiting countries in Central Europe, a rail pass is not worth getting because the distances aren't as vast and the prices for trains aren't as expensive as Western Europe.

Buses

The main bus company in this region is FlixBus (flixbus.com), though there are some country-specific operators. Most bus fares in the region cost about $15 for something under three hours, while longer journeys (four hours or more) start at $25 and can go up to $50 depending on the length of the journey.

Bus prices in the region are the cheapest when you book two weeks or more in advance. You can often find rates 50 percent cheaper than last-minute prices.

Busbud (busbud.com) and GetByBus (getbybus.com) are the two best websites for finding routes, fares, and companies.

Flying

Countries in this region are so close together that I would avoid flying unless you are going from "one end to the other," like Vienna to Warsaw or Prague to Budapest. While the flight from Vienna to Prague is only fifty minutes, between getting to and from the airports, getting there early, and possible delays, it's not that much shorter than the four-hour train ride. Generally, I wouldn't recommend flying around the region.

Ridesharing

BlaBlaCar (blablacar.com) only operates in Hungary, Czech Republic, and Slovakia. Rides are pretty frequent between major cities, so definitely consider using the company if you are in those countries. At the time of writing, there weren't any other apps to choose from.

ATTRACTIONS AND ACTIVITIES

Prices for activities and attractions vary considerably from the expensive (hello Austria!) to the inexpensive (hello Poland!). A lot of this is based on the fact that there are several different currencies used in the region (euro in Austria, Slovakia, and Slovenia, koruna in Czechia, złoty in Poland, and forint in Hungary), so there's a lot of variation based on the country exchange. Generally, you can expect to pay $15–$20 for a museum in Prague, Salzburg, and Vienna, and around $6–$12 in cities like Budapest, Krakow, and Warsaw. In the countryside, prices will be on the lower end of the range. Full-day tours cost between $40 and $60.

Unlike in Western Europe, I have not found tourism cards to be an exceptionally great value in this region. The only exception to that rule is in Austria where the high cost of museums and activities makes the city tourism cards worth it. Otherwise I would skip them because attractions are inexpensive—and you're not likely to use all the museums and amenities included in the passes anyway.

The number of free walking tours in the region has ballooned since 2020, especially in smaller, second-tier cities (think Linz or Brno instead of Vienna or Prague). As such, you should be able to find a free walking tour wherever you are in the region. In smaller cities, tours might not run as frequently, but in all the capital cities you'll find many free walking tour companies that often run multiple tours per day.

Airbnb Experiences are also widespread. I've shared my love of them many times throughout the book, so all I will add here is that they are a really good option in this region for last-minute tours. If you wake up and decide you want to do an evening food tour, you can have a lot of luck with these tours versus more traditional tour companies.

EASTERN EUROPE

Albania, Bosnia and Herzegovina, Bulgaria, Croatia, Estonia, Kosovo, Latvia, Lithuania, Moldova, Montenegro, North Macedonia, Romania, Serbia, Slovenia, Ukraine

When most Americans go to Europe, they envision Paris and Rome and London and skip over Eastern Europe (and a lot of Central Europe too). I think that is a real shame. To me, this region (and it's a big region, I know) offers some of the best value travel in Europe. Plus, there are fewer tourists so you don't feel like you are visiting Disneyland during school break. Now, of course, there are caveats. I lump a lot of countries into this part of Europe. Croatia is way more developed and touristy than Romania, which is a little busier than Moldova, the least visited country in Europe. Estonia sees more visitors than Latvia but not as many as Montenegro. Plus, some countries here are on the euro, while others are not. Costs aren't as uniform here, but I've tried to give the best ranges possible. Keep that in mind as you plan your trip.

ACCOMMODATIONS
Hostels

Hostels in Eastern Europe are a bit more basic than other parts of Europe. The farther east you go, the less likely you are to get free breakfast, pod-style accommodation, and nicer digs. The majority of hostels, however, will still have free Wi-Fi, common rooms, and kitchens.

For dorm rooms, you'll pay between $10 and $30 per night depending on the size of the dorm room and the popularity of the hostel. As a rule of thumb, the farther east you go, the cheaper it gets. For example, in Bucharest you'll pay about $20, while busy and expensive Dubrovnik will cost about double that. Little Plovdiv in Romania will cost only $15 per night, but busier Kotor in Montenegro will cost about $30 per night.

A private room in a hostel will cost you $25–$70 per night for a double bed with a shared bathroom. I love getting private hostel rooms when I'm in this region because I find them full of value. I get all the benefits of a hostel (Wi-Fi, the occasional free breakfast, a kitchen, and people to socialize with) with all the benefits of a hotel (a private, secure room) at an affordable rate.

While summertime drives prices higher everywhere, expect about 30 percent higher prices in Croatia's coastal hot spots over anywhere else in the region.

Budget Hotels

Budget hotels start at $30 for a two-star hotel with breakfast, private bathroom, Wi-Fi, and a double bed. If you want a hotel with a really comfortable bed, big breakfast spread, nicer decor, and more amenities, expect hotels to start at $55 per night. Summer prices, especially in Croatia, Bulgaria's coast, Montenegro, and Estonia, will be from $75 or more per night. Croatia's Dalmatian coast will be even *more* expensive than that during the summer, with prices for hotels starting at $125.

Apartment Rentals

You tend to find the biggest selection of apartment rentals in capital cities. In the countryside and mountain towns, you'll find a lot of vacation home rentals via websites like Vrbo. Prices for private rooms in a home begin around $20 per night in smaller, less popular destinations and go as high as $60 in more popular spots like Kotor or Dubrovnik. Whole apartments begin at $50 and go as high as $200.

Like the rest of Europe, overtourism is a problem here, especially in cities like Dubrovnik and Split. As a result, I really don't recommend using apartment rental services in touristy destinations.

Camping

Camping is less common in Eastern Europe and exists only around a few major cities like Sarajevo ($15 per night) and along the Dalmatian coast ($15–$20 per night). Furthermore, many campsites only open during the summer. You'll find an especially short camping season in countries up north, where winter comes early. Camping costs there are around $8 but can be as high as $12–$20 if you need to rent a tent. If you have your own tent, you can find campsites for around $7. If you have your own tent, many hostels will let you camp on their grounds for a little less than the cost of a dorm room.

Hospitality Exchanges

Couchsurfing is still very popular in Eastern Europe as many locals use it as a way to practice English. BeWelcome is also popular here, but Servas doesn't have as many users. In this region, hosts tend to be younger and are often students.

House-Sitting

House-sitting is even less common in Eastern Europe than in Central Europe. You may find some house-sits in the larger cities (such as Zagreb or Tallinn), but it's not a reliable means of finding accommodation. That said, it's still worth a look on house-sitting websites if you are already a member, as house-sits do pop up now and then and competition isn't as fierce as in other areas of the world.

WWOOF

WWOOFing in Eastern Europe is relatively small, with most countries having only a few dozen opportunities. It's best to inquire about openings far in advance but I wouldn't expect a lot of results.

Conversely, Worldpackers, HelpX, and Workaway all have a good number of opportunities listed on their websites so you are likely to have better luck using those websites.

FOOD

Food is much cheaper in the east than in other parts of Europe. Like in Central Europe, you'll find food to be hearty, heavy, and meat-based. Staples like potatoes, cabbage, and various meats are commonly used in popular dishes such as pierogi, borscht, and goulash. You'll also find a lot of fish and salted food in the Baltics, and a strong Italian influence in countries lining the Adriatic like Croatia.

In every country you'll find cheap outdoor food stalls selling fast meals (like pizza, sandwiches, kebabs, or sausages) that cost between $1.50 and $4. Just as in Western Europe, these meals present a quick and cheap way to eat. In Bulgaria, I practically lived off this little kebab and salad place near my hostel.

Moving up the food chain (pun intended), you'll find a lot of inexpensive eateries. One thing I really love about this part of the world is that, unlike Western Europe where getting a crepe in Paris or a plate of pasta in Italy is still expensive, the local food here is super cheap. You can expect a meal at a small corner shop to be between $4 and $7. To find these places, you just need to ask the manager of your hotel/hostel, as he or she will know the local spots.

If you are looking for something nicer, there's a wide selection of international food available in this region. A nice sit-down restaurant with a drink and a main meal will cost $15 and up.

If you decide to buy your groceries, you'll average about $45 per week. This will get you everything you need for large dinners, hearty meals, pasta, and some sandwiches.

TRANSPORTATION

Transportation is inexpensive in this region of the world. Public transportation, buses, trams, and trains in the cities cost between $1 and $2.

Train

Intercountry trains usually cost between $50 and $80, even when the ticket is booked last-minute. Short train rides of two to three hours cost about $30.

Eurail passes also work in all the countries in the region but, since trains are so cheap, I wouldn't get the pass unless you are going to other regions in Europe too.

When booking tickets, get someone to write the specifics down in the local language as English isn't always well-spoken in this part of Europe. In Ukraine, I had to ask my hostel receptionist to write the date and time I needed because of the lack of English proficiency in the country.

That said, I hardly ever take the train in this region of the world. Most countries don't have robust train systems, trains are often very old and slow, and countries are not well connected due to different track gauges. For example, if you want to go from Bucharest to Belgrade by train, it will involve a very indirect twenty-four-hour trip with lots of changes—and a final leg that can only be taken by bus. However, the direct bus takes just four hours.

While I've taken intra-country trains just to experience them, I much prefer bus travel in the region because it's cheaper and often faster due to more direct routes.

Buses

Buses are simply a much better option for travel in this region. Typical bus fares are $10–$25. For example, the bus between Belgrade and Zagreb takes five and a half hours and costs about $20. The four-hour ride between Split and Dubrovnik is only $17. Up in the Baltic nations, Vilnius to Riga takes four hours and costs as low as $10 on FlixBus (flixbus.com). The four-and-a-half-hour ride from Riga to Tallinn costs about $12.

In Eastern Europe, there are two major international bus companies: FlixBus and Ecolines (ecolines.net), which primarily serves Central Europe, the Baltics, and other Eastern European countries (except the Balkans).

In the Balkans, all countries have their own national bus service, which also serve neighboring countries. For example, buses in Bulgaria will go to Romania, Greece, Macedonia, and Turkey, but you can't get a local bus from Bulgaria to Estonia, which is where Ecolines or FlixBus comes in.

A helpful website for finding routes and prices is GetByBus (getbybus.com), which I find to be the best resource for this region.

Flying

In addition to the carriers mentioned previously, you will also find that Wizz Air (wizzair.com) and Air Baltic (airbaltic.com) all have extensive routes here. Relative to the cost of buses and trains, flying is less of a good deal than in Western Europe, since flights tend to be more expensive than buses or trains. I would travel the region by bus and only fly when traveling large distances (i.e., Romania to Estonia or Bulgaria to Serbia).

Refer to chapter six for advice on how to find cheap flights.

Hitchhiking

Hitchhiking is also a popular method of travel in this region, especially in the Balkans. When I was in Bulgaria with friends, we hitchhiked one day to a neighboring town. It took us a while to find someone to pick us up (we were a group of three), but eventually someone came by and gave us a ride. Use your common sense when hitchhiking with strangers. You can always say no if you feel the situation is unsafe, especially if you are traveling alone.

The website Hitchwiki can provide country-specific information and safety tips.

Ridesharing

Ridesharing isn't as popular in this region, but BlaBlaCar is available in Croatia, Serbia, and Romania. At the time of writing, there are no other ridesharing apps in the region.

ACTIVITIES AND ATTRACTIONS

In Eastern Europe, you'll find that activities cost much less than in other parts of the world. Prices are a little less uniform than in other parts of Europe in part because most countries are on different currencies (too many to list here!). However, the variation is only about $1–$2, and generally museums, churches, and attractions in this region cost $5–$10.

There are a lot of good day trips to old monasteries, castles, lakes, and parks in Eastern Europe. Most day trips cost $25–$50. For example, a day trip to the famous Rila Monastery in Bulgaria is around $25, while a day trip from Dubrovnik to the enchanting Bosnian town of Mostar is about $60. A day trip from Skopje, the capital of North Macedonia, to beautiful Lake Ohrid is about $70. While you're in Bucharest, if you want to spend the day at Bran Castle (aka Dracula's castle) in Transylvania, it will cost you about $25 for the trip.

Using your ISIC, YHA, or youth card will get you a discount on public attractions like churches and museums. These passes are widely accepted throughout this region and usually offer a 50 percent discount off the standard adult price for museums. They won't get you a discount on day tours and trips organized by tour operators though.

Free walking tours have exploded in popularity in recent years, and you can find them all over this region. More and more free tours sprout up every year so ask the staff at your hotel/hostel or visit the local tourism board. Keep in mind that sometimes people don't know about these tours and the only way to find them is via Google.

Many Eastern European cities offer tourism cards. However, I don't use them very often and I find the math rarely works out because attractions are already quite inexpensive. Unless you are visiting a lot of attractions (again, do the math), I wouldn't go out of my way to get these.

SCANDINAVIA

Denmark, Finland, Sweden, Norway

The Scandinavian countries are the most expensive in Europe. While this region is one of my favorite places to visit, it is by no means a good budget destination. It takes a lot more work here to save money, and even then, you still will spend a lot compared to elsewhere in Europe. Most travelers pass through here quickly because of the high costs, but if you have the time and money, stay here longer as it is one of the most beautiful regions in the world. There's just so much pristine nature here alongside some quintessential European cities. (Plus, during the winter, you get so many stunning chances to see the northern lights.)

ACCOMMODATIONS

Hostels

I'll be honest, I think hostels in this region are kind of bland. Most hostels in the world have big common rooms, bars, and kitchens, and they try to organize activities. In this region, hostels have kitchens and other basic amenities, but they don't often organize activities and social gatherings. Sure, I've stayed at some that were fun (City Backpackers in Stockholm is very good), but overall, they lack the charm and charisma you find elsewhere in Europe.

Hostel prices range from $30–$60 for a dorm room, while private double rooms with a shared bathroom cost $80–$120 per night. Norway is the most expensive country in the region and hostels here will cost the most.

Furthermore, hostels in this region don't offer free breakfast like their counterparts in the rest of Europe, though all the ones I've stayed at have a large kitchen to compensate.

In Sweden, you will need to pay extra for sheets (yeah, I hate it too), as they aren't provided free by hostels. They usually cost $3–$8 per night.

Budget Hotels

Budget hotel prices are on par with a private room in a hostel. You get a little more for your money—a private bathroom, breakfast, and a TV. Rooms generally start at $90 and go up from there. For example, in Copenhagen and Oslo, you can expect to pay around $140 per night, while in Stockholm and Helsinki the average is closer to $90.

I find budget hotels a lovely experience in this region. I love the aesthetic of Scandinavian architecture, and I've always found these hotels to be clean and comfy. Most hotels usually have a light breakfast. While I often prefer hostels for the social atmosphere, I prefer hotels in this region as they are generally a little nicer.

Apartment Rentals

Apartment rentals cost $100–$150 per night for an entire place, making them just slightly more expensive than hotels. If you are just looking for a room in someone's apartment, you can find them for as little as $40. I think this is a better option than hotels if you are looking to have your own room or accommodation.

Airbnb is the largest operator in the region and you'll find a lot of options in and out of cities.

That said, overtourism in the capital cities is a very big problem as there is a severe housing shortage. I would refrain from using any apartment rental service in major cities unless you are certain someone actually lives there rather than it belonging to a big property management company.

Camping

Camping is the cheapest option in the region, but because of the long winter, campsites are generally open only from April to October.

Campsites cost between $15 and $30 per night. To stay at any campsite in the region, you will need the Camping Key Europe card (campingkeyeurope.com), which costs $20 and is valid for twelve months. You can buy the card online or at the first campsite you get to in Scandinavia. This card is good for all campsites in Norway, Sweden, Denmark, and Finland, as well as at more than three thousand other campsites throughout Europe.

Camping sites require you to have your own tent, as they don't rent them out. If you don't have your own tent, you can stay in a cottage fitted as a dormitory, where a bed is the same price as a hostel.

In expensive Scandinavia, camping is one of the cheapest ways to lower your accommodation costs. It's an option that should be used often, especially in Norway where everything costs an arm and a leg!

You can also wild camp throughout the region (except in Denmark), which means you can camp in the countryside. Each country in Scandinavia has their own public access laws. In Sweden, for example, you're allowed to wild camp in the countryside for one to three nights, provided you do not disturb any of the local folk. In Norway, you can wild camp as long as you're at least 150 meters (or about 500 feet) from a residence and follow the "leave no trace" rule. Wild camping is also allowed in Finland but you must follow a set of rules similar to Norway.

Hospitality Exchanges

If you truly want to save the most money possible in Scandinavia, hospitality clubs are the way to go. However, because Scandinavia is so expensive, travelers rely heavily on hospitality exchanges to save money, and most hosts get inundated with requests. The response rate is very low here.

Moreover, these networks just aren't as popular in this region as they used to be. On Couchsurfing, Stockholm, the city with the largest number of hosts, only had 194 hosts who were accepting guests (341 if you change the parameters to active within six months). Helsinki only had 4 and 12, respectively, while Oslo had 82 and 136. BeWelcome had half those numbers. Once you get into smaller cities, the numbers drop even more.

That isn't to say you won't find a host. You might. It's just no longer as easy as it used to be given the limited number of hosts so you need to plan a lot further in advance.

House-Sitting

House-sitting is more popular in Scandinavia than in Eastern and Central Europe, though much less so than Western Europe. Sweden, Norway, and Denmark usually have house-sits available at any given time, though there may only be a few spread across the entire country (normally in the major cities). If you have a membership through the websites mentioned in chapter ten, it's worth taking a look to see what's available, but house-sitting in Scandinavia still isn't the kind of activity where you can line up house-sits back-to-back like in Western Europe.

WWOOF

WWOOFing is widespread in the region and you'll find more than one hundred farms in Sweden and Norway looking for workers, while Denmark has just under one hundred. Finland only has a handful of opportunities. Keep in mind that the climate makes for a short growing season so you'll want to apply early. Worldpackers, HelpX, and Workaway have a similar number of opportunities so be sure to check them out too.

FOOD

In Norway, food, including groceries, will be the most expensive in the region. I bought two days' worth of groceries for pasta and sandwiches and it cost me $36. To keep costs down, avoid fresh vegetables and chicken filets, which cost a lot of money here because they tend to be imported—a lesson I learned after my first food-shopping experience. If you cut those out of your groceries and stick to pasta, breads, deli meats, cheese, and a few cheap vegetables, you are looking to spend about $110 per week. If you really want discount chicken or beef, do what the locals do: buy them on their expiration date. Due to strict food laws, most meats "expire" well before they actually go bad and their prices are often slashed in half. That's when the locals come and pick them up as they are still perfectly good to eat.

Eating out is incredibly expensive, with even fast food (think McDonald's) averaging between $10 and $15 and sit-down meals at a decent restaurant nearly always $30 or more for just a main course. For a cheap, quick snack, Norwegian-style, look no further than the nearest streetside vendor or convenience store, where you can eat a hot dog or sausage for around $8. Fish-and-chip meals are around $20.

Bottom line, the only way to eat on a budget in Norway is to cook all your meals.

In Sweden, you'll find the food to be cheaper. Grocery shopping here will cost $70 per week for the same type of food that I mentioned above. You can get cheap meals from outdoor street vendors starting at $8, such as wraps, sandwiches, and burgers. For something really cheap, you can get hot dogs and sausages starting at $3. Whole pizzas start around $13, while most sit-down restaurant meals begin at $20 for a main dish.

In Denmark, if you are going to eat out in a restaurant, be prepared to pay around $17 for a cheap meal with a main course and a drink. If you are looking for something fancier, meals including a drink start at $25. You can find some lunchtime buffet specials for $12, which allow you to eat out without breaking the bank. You can find vendors lining the streets of the bigger cities selling cheap hot dogs for $5. Groceries will cost around $80 per week. When I come to Denmark, I tend to eat out for lunch and cook my own meals for dinner. That way I can average about $15 per day for food.

Since Finland is on the euro (and not their own currency like the other countries in the region), food is cheapest here. Grocery shopping will cost you $60 per week for a fairly robust shopping list of vegetables, meats, pasta, snacks, and the like. You'll be able to feed yourself well for a week with that budget.

Inexpensive food—mostly pizza, kebabs, and sandwiches—will cost $6–$10 for a tiny lunch special. Sit-down restaurant meals will cost $17 for a small meal and drink. During the lunch hour, many restaurants offer a lunchtime buffet costing about $13, and Stockmann supermarkets also have a wide variety of premade meals for around $7. Helsinki has a lot of nice restaurants, and meals at high-end establishments begin at $35.

Tap water is very safe to drink throughout this region. Since a bottle of water is generally $3, save money and reuse your water bottle. You aren't going to get sick from drinking the tap water.

Buying groceries and cooking your own meals in Scandinavia is a must if you want to save money. Locals in this region of the world cook far more than they eat out simply because of costs. All my friends in the region would never dream of eating out as often as we do in the United States—they simply couldn't afford to do so. During the summer months, farmers markets offer a plethora of berries and fresh fruit that can be good and cheap snacks.

If you do have to eat out, quick meals such as pizza, kebabs, fast food, burgers, or outdoor sausage vendors will be your cheapest food. (This region of the world isn't a culinary dream anyway, so you aren't really missing out by not dining out or by sticking to the cheap eats.)

TRANSPORTATION

Local transportation is relatively inexpensive in Scandinavia. Subways and buses in the cities are around $4 per trip. All the major cities in this region offer daily and weekly metro passes that are cheaper than purchasing single-ride tickets. If you are in a place for a while, consider buying them.

Trains

In Sweden, the majority of intercity trains cost $40–$75. They will cost $100–$160 if it is an overnight sleeper train, like the fourteen-hour trip from Stockholm to Luleå up north. If you want cheap train tickets, you need to purchase them at least one month before your departure date. Students and those under twenty-six are eligible for discounted train tickets.

Trains around Norway cost about $75 depending on the distance and when you buy your ticket. Booking your train at least a week in advance (a "minipris" ticket) will get you a 50 percent discount. For example, the train from Oslo to Bergen on the west coast costs $85 if you book the day of travel but closer to $50 if you book in advance. I always book in advance in Norway because the substantial savings are worth the lack of flexibility in my schedule.

Train travel across Denmark (Aarhus to Copenhagen) costs around $65 if you book the day of travel. Shorter distances of two hours or less are around $30 (or $40 if booked last-minute). Denmark is a really small country, so travel doesn't take that long. The closer you get to the travel date, the higher the cost.

The Danish rail system offers cheap tickets called "DBS Orange" tickets via their website (dsb.dk/find-produkter-og-services/dsb-orange). They are only available on the website, and you have to print out the ticket before you board the train, but these tickets are a third of the cost of what you can buy at the railway station.

In Finland, train tickets cost between $60 and $80 regardless of the distance you travel. Booking in advance will get you a 25 percent discount off the day-of price. Groups of three or more can also get discounts of 15 percent off the ticket price.

Intercountry travel in Scandinavia isn't that much more expensive than traveling around each country. A train from Stockholm to Oslo is about $80, while Stockholm to Copenhagen is around $80. Copenhagen to Oslo varies between $75 and $150.

Rail passes are offered for all the countries in the region. The Global Pass discussed in the Western Europe section also covers the region. Additionally, there is a regional pass (eurail.com/en /eurail-passes/one-country-pass/scandinavia) that begins at $203 for three days of travel in a second-class seat if you're twenty-seven years and below. For an adult second-class three-day pass, it costs around $235.

If you are going long distances or hopping between countries in the region, then the pass will likely save you money. After all, each train ride is "worth" about $80 and last-minute fares are often that high (or higher).

Buses

Buses are cheaper but slower than train travel. An extensive range of buses connects cities and even most national parks throughout the region. Buses booked a month or more in advance can be found for as cheap as $15 (however, these advance tickets are limited in number, so plan accordingly). Typically buses cost $35–$60 for a regular same-day ticket.

In Finland, student discounts are available if you show a valid ISIC card. There is also BusPass (matkahuolto.fi/passengers/bus

-pass), which offers unlimited travel for $159 for seven days and $267 for fourteen days.

Regional and national bus companies include:

- Abildskou: abildskou.dk
- Bus4You Sweden: bus4you.se
- Matkahuolto: matkahuolto.fi
- Nor-Way Bussekspress: nor-way.no
- Swebus: swebus.se
- Vy Express: www.vybuss.no

FlixBus is also widely available in Sweden and Denmark, though it is more limited in Finland and Norway.

Check out the website Busbud for timetables, routes, and prices.

Flying

Prices are generally more expensive here than elsewhere. You won't find very good flight deals, and unless you are really short on time (and long on money), buses and trains offer better value. The farther north you go toward the Arctic, the more expensive and infrequent flights tend to be. In Denmark, flights to some of the smaller islands cost as much as $200 for a forty-five-minute flight.

There are three large airlines based out of Scandinavia:

- SAS: flysas.com
- Finnair: finnair.com
- Norwegian Airlines: norwegian.no

The budget airlines discussed in previous sections of this chapter also have flights in and out of the region.

Refer to chapter six for info on how to get cheap flights.

ACTIVITIES AND ATTRACTIONS

Museums in Scandinavia typically cost around $13, and prices are pretty uniform from country to country. There are plenty of full-day activities to do in this region, and most involve exploring the beautiful countryside. Day trips will cost $50 or more.

The best way to save money on attractions in Scandinavia is to buy city tourism cards. Every big city or tourist destination offers one. Not only will they provide free public transportation, but they will save you a bundle on tourist sites. For example, in Oslo, I saved $30 with the pass plus got free public transportation. In Helsinki, I saved $20 on attractions, plus I got discounts on some buffets and free city transportation.

Additionally, these cards offer discounts on many of the day trips offered from the cities, such as boat tours or hikes. City tourism cards can be bought at the local tourist office and often in the airport. Using your ISIC, YHA, or IYC card will also get you a discount between 20 and 50 percent on public attractions, museums, and tours.

Free walking tours are also available in all the major cities in the region and you'll also find a lot of Airbnb Experiences.

Additionally, there are lots of free parks, museums, and attractions. It's very easy to keep your costs down in the region if you stick to free walking tours, free outdoor activities, and visit museums when they offer free entry or by using one of the city discount cards.

HOW MUCH MONEY DO YOU NEED?

Europe isn't the cheapest place to travel on $75 a day, and how much you spend will greatly depend on which countries or regions you visit. Spending all your time in Scandinavia? You're going to spend a lot. Same if you are going to mostly Western Europe, especially during the summer. Spending the majority of your time in Eastern Europe? You'll be in budget traveler heaven.

If you stick to hostel dorms, eat out at inexpensive restaurants for most of your meals, take free tours, get a rail pass, and do a few paid activities and museums, you'll need about $110 per day in Western Europe, $75 in Central Europe, $55 in Eastern Europe, and $130 in Scandinavia. This is your typical backpacker budget. You aren't going to have a fancy time, but you aren't going to want for anything either.

If you cook most meals and watch your spending, you could cut that down to $90 per day in Western Europe, $65 in Central Europe, $45–$50 in Eastern Europe, and $100 in Scandinavia.

If you wanted to stay in private rooms or hotels and not limit your spending on food or activities, you'd need about $200 per day in Western Europe, $140 per day in Central Europe, $75 per day in Eastern Europe, and about $250 per day in Scandinavia.

Most travelers spend about three months in Europe. By mixing destinations across the continent, you can keep your budget really low. Traveling around Scandinavia cost me a lot of money, but I headed to Eastern Europe next and I was able to lower my daily spending average to something more reasonable. While I may have spent $85 per day in Amsterdam, I spent only $50 per day in Greece (where everything is much cheaper), thus bringing my daily average down again. Mix, match, save.

Europe can be a very expensive destination, and because of that, it requires more work to stretch your money. But it can be done. By being conscious of when and where I'm spending my money, I've never had to turn down a wine tour in Italy or a night out on the town in Paris.

18

INDIA

There's an expression often said among travelers: there is the world and then there is India. Traveling around India is just *different*. It's almost mystical. India is big, chaotic, magical, beautiful, difficult, rich, poor, developing, developed, and everything in between. It tests travelers. Because of the vast distances, plethora of sites to visit, and slow travel time around the country, most visitors should spend at least a month or two here. Or, at the very least, break your trips up into smaller geographic sections. India is not a place for the rushed.

India has always been an inexpensive place to visit, but the recent steep decline in the Indian rupee has made this country very accessible for visitors. Throw in cheap flights (from anywhere), and you have the recipe for a very affordable destination. You can travel well here for very little money, and increasing your budget by just a few dollars can often lead to substantial increases in luxury.

ACCOMMODATIONS
Hostels

European-style hostels (think big dorms, common rooms, kitch-ens, organized activities) are not popular in India. Instead, small, family-run guesthouses are the preferred accommodation option. Accommodation is already so cheap that few people desire to stay in dorm rooms. New Delhi, a city with around twenty-two mil-lion people, had only twenty-six hostels in May 2024 according to the booking website Hostelworld. Paris, a city with a tenth of the population, had over forty!

As Derek Baron of Wandering Earl (wanderingearl.com) and a tour guide in India states: "When it comes to budget accom-modation in India, hostels are generally not the option of choice, even for the most budget-conscious traveler. They are harder to find, usually not of good quality, and they typically charge only slightly less than what it costs to have your own private room in a budget hotel."

While dorm beds can cost as little as $2 per night in rural destinations, they usually range between $4 and $8 per night in larger cities, making them just as expensive as a simple private room in a budget hotel. For example, Youth Hostels Association of India (yhaindia.org) has beds in non-air-conditioned dorm rooms ranging between $5 and $15 per night, which is about the price of a nice budget hotel. Why share a room when you can get your own room for the same price?

In short, while hostels do exist in India, they aren't worth staying in and there are better accommodation options you can choose from that are equally filled with travelers.

Budget Hotels

India is awash with affordable, family-run guesthouses and cheap budget hotels (and they are often interchangeable). These are a traveler's best accommodation option in the country. You can get a single or double room (the price is usually the same for both) between $5 on the low end in the countryside and $40 for something very nice in the city.

On average, you'll pay between $10 and $15 for something really basic, offering the best value for your money. At these prices, you get a large, semi-comfy bed, fan, and a bathroom with a Western toilet. The rooms are basic but they will be clean.

If you want something a little nicer and with a more comfortable mattress, you'll pay around $20 per night.

Hotels over $25–$30 a night will get you a more spacious room, twenty-four-hour hot water, a comfy mattress that won't kill your back, television, air-conditioning, and some additional furniture.

It is fairly easy to find rooms last minute in India so don't worry about booking too far in advance. This is especially true during monsoon season (late June through August) when many hotels have high vacancy rates and offer deep discounts.

Apartment Rentals

Apartment rentals were once a rarity in India. In the first edition of this book, written back in 2012, there were just nine thousand Airbnb listings in all of India. At the time of this writing, there are over seventy thousand, and that number keeps growing.

In big cities like New Delhi and Mumbai (formerly known as

Bombay), a private room will run about $10–$15 per night and an entire apartment costs about $24–$40 on average.

While you get all the amenities of home, these apartments cost more than budget hotels and, unless you are traveling as a family or in a big group, I would stay away from them as you get better value for your money at guesthouses and hotels.

Airbnb is the biggest apartment rental company in the country by far. Vrbo only has seven thousand listings at the time of publication. There's no India-centric company either, so I would stick to Airbnb if you're looking to rent an apartment.

Camping

Camping is also not very widespread in India. While there are a few places where you can camp, it's not something I would suggest doing (unless you are on an organized hiking/camping trip in the desert or mountain regions).

This is very important for female travelers. As Mariellen from the website Breathedreamgo cautions, "It's important to stick to the popular tourist-friendly areas of India for female travelers, especially solo female travelers." She suggests females avoid camping in rural areas alone.

Hospitality Exchanges

Couchsurfing is the most popular network in the country with are over 21,000 active Couchsurfing hosts (i.e., hosts who have logged in within the last month). That said, it's a country of a billion people, so that's not a lot on a percentage basis, but in most major cities like New Delhi or Bangalore (Bangaluru), you'll find lots of options. Indians are generally very hospitable to foreigners and really like sharing their culture, so it's quite easy to find hosts.

The other hospitality exchanges mentioned in other sections of this book don't have extensive networks in India. For example, BeWelcome only had a handful of active hosts in New Delhi and Travel Ladies only had a handful of people too. Couchsurfing is going to be your best option in the country.

House-Sitting

House-sitting, at the time of writing, is not very popular and there are only a handful of listings for the entire country. I wouldn't consider this when traveling in India.

WWOOF

There is no official WWOOFing in India. However, there is a privately owned "knockoff" called WWOOF India (wwoofindia.org). From just a few hosts at the start, it now has more than three hundred. It's a legitimate organization that you can use, even though it's not part of the official global organization.

However, Worldpackers, Workaway, and HelpX all have a large number of farm opportunities available and I would recommend using those three sites too.

Before you do any type of WWOOFing, do your research and pay special attention to the climate. It's not going to be a very comfortable experience during the heavy monsoon rains or when temperatures are over 40°C (104°F).

FOOD

Indian food is delicious, spicy, flavorful, and incredibly diverse. I love Indian food. From mouthwatering naan bread, to tongue-scorching chili-enhanced curries, to the soothing flavor of a lassi, Indian food blows my mind and there's nothing like getting it from the source.

One thing to consider is that Indian cuisine varies quite a lot by region. North Indian food uses a variety of lentils, gravies, chilies, vegetables, and bread. Dairy and wheat are very common in the north, and some prominent spices include fenugreek and garam masala as well as herbs and dried mango powder to add a touch of sourness to curries. Some typical dishes you'll stumble upon in the north include palak paneer, a creamy spinach dish with cubes of cheese (paneer), and aloo ghobi, a curry-spiked blend of potatoes and cauliflower. (Most Indian food in America is from northern India so this will be the most familiar to many travelers.)

By contrast, south Indian cuisine is much more rice-based and often consists of large dosas (big rice pancakes with filling) and nuts as well as traditional curries. Instead of dried mango powder to season curries, southern cooks opt for tamarind instead, and dried curry leaves are more typical in soups. The most common spice is huli pudi, a sambar powder.

All that said, it's really hard to generalize Indian cuisine. In the north, Punjabi cuisine is very different from the food of Awadhi. And then there's east and west India, which have their own unique dishes—Goan cuisine in the west is vastly different from Bengali cuisine in the east.

In India, there's food on every street corner. As Derek

describes his experience, "You can barely walk two meters without facing another street stall or restaurant serving up some kind of snack or dish that you suddenly want to devour. Whether it be samosas, pakoras, lassis, or momos, whether it be North Indian or South Indian cuisine . . . it is all so very tempting."

Restaurant meals cost between $3 and $6 for most main courses. At most restaurants in the north, you choose from a long list of dishes (like the ones I just listed) and then you order either rice or naan/chapati to go with it. For those who get easily overwhelmed, like me, there is always a thali, which means "plate" and usually comes with two or three curries, a lentil dish, rice, bread, a few other accompaniments, and often a dessert, making it a great overall value.

Oftentimes a particular restaurant might be known for a specific dish, whether it be their thali or biryani (rice mixed with vegetables and spices), a particular curry, or their massive masala dosas, so it often pays to ask what the specialty is before ordering.

If you're traveling with a friend or another traveler you just met, sharing dishes is the way to go. Order a couple of curries, some rice, and bread and just split it all so that you get to taste even more. Sharing Indian food is by far the best way to try a variety of dishes.

You'll generally find street stalls selling food on the cheaper end (and even less than that), while sit-down restaurants in bigger cities will be on the higher end. Here is an example of food costs in 2024:

- Samosas or pakoras from a street vendor: 50 cents to $1
- Thali (meal consisting of vegetable dishes, dhal, rice, roti, and more): $2–$4

- Dish of mattar paneer (peas and cheese curry): $2–$3
- Dhal and rice: 60 cents to $1
- Chicken tandoori (½ chicken): $2.50–$4
- Masala dosa: 50 cents to $2
- Chai from a vendor: ten to twenty cents
- Cup of tea: ten to twenty cents from a stall; more than $1.40 in a top hotel
- Beer (650-milliliter bottle): $1–$2 in a shop; $2–$4 in a bar

Pretty inexpensive, right? If you stick to Indian food, you are going to be able to eat for less than $10 a day.

From fast-food chains (McDonald's, Subway, and Domino's Pizza) to restaurants that cater to foreigners, eating Western food is an expensive affair in India by local standards. Prices for a plate of pasta will cost about $6, a six-inch sandwich at Subway is between $2 and $3, and Mexican is going to be between $3 and $6. While that doesn't sound like a lot, compared to the price of Indian food, it's a fortune! While Western food is abundant, the quality varies A LOT and you shouldn't expect anything extraordinary. Personally, I wouldn't come to India to eat bad pasta or questionable Mexican food.

Derek offers good advice for those looking for something besides curries: "If you need a break from Indian food, I recommend finding a Nepali-owned restaurant, which can be found in most destinations that are popular with backpackers. These places cater to foreigners and usually offer a wide range of inexpensive, typically delicious salads, sandwiches, Italian, Israeli, Mexican, Nepali, and other Western dishes, all prepared fresh, with all vegetables washed in purified water as well, so that you can enjoy a quality non-Indian meal."

It's important to keep in mind that the cow is sacred in India and thus burgers are very, very hard to come by. Don't expect to eat or find much red meat in the country.

Since food is so cheap, I don't recommend cooking for yourself. While there's nothing wrong with buying food from markets for snacks, if you try to cook meals you are going to end up spending more money than if you ate out. (But if you do plan to cook, you should do so with filtered water and nothing from the tap—ever!)

In fact, let's talk about food safety. The phrase "Delhi belly" exists for a reason. Food sanitation isn't top notch and a lot of people get very, *very* sick in India. I know experienced travelers who have been incapacitated for weeks. In order to minimize your chances of getting sick, follow these rules:

- Don't drink the tap water. *Ever.* This includes ice cubes. (Seriously, don't!)
- Make sure your bottled water is sealed before you open it.
- Avoid street food that nobody else is eating, and don't eat anything that hasn't been cooked.
- Minimize the amount of meat you eat.

I would also recommend taking probiotics two weeks before you travel to India. Take them every day before your trip and then every day throughout your trip as well. This significantly reduces any chance of getting "Delhi belly."

Common sense with street food goes a long way. Derek advises: "If a restaurant looks sketchy and has no Indian customers, it's a good idea to avoid it. But if a local hole-in-the-wall restaurant is full of local customers, you can try it out as well. Local people do not want to eat bad, non-fresh food either! So, if it's a popular place with locals, it's popular for a reason—good, fresh food is being served, and as a result, it would be safe for you to eat there too."

TRANSPORTATION

Transportation in India is slow. Painfully slow sometimes. Departure and arrival times are often mere suggestions. There are frequent stops and schedule changes. You aren't going anywhere fast unless you fly. Any overland travel will take time. And even when trains and buses stick to their schedule, the great distance involved combined with the slow speeds means it still takes a while to get to where you want to go.

Trains

Around 24 million passengers travel by train in India every day, and Indian Railways is one of the largest employers in the world with a staggering 1.6 million workers. There are, on average, about 13,000 train journeys per day in India. And India has yet to institute a high-speed rail across the country at the time of writing so don't expect to get anywhere fast.

But train journeys in India are more than the means to get from point A to point B—they are an adventure in and of themselves and an incredible way to meet and chat with locals.

"Train travel in India should not be viewed as a dreaded necessity. While it might not be the most comfortable or luxurious train system, you are bound to meet endless people on every journey, have some interesting conversations, see some beautiful countryside, and in the end, have some of the most memorable experiences of your entire trip," says Derek.

Service on the trains can range from rough, crowded, and smelly to relaxing and comfortable depending on your class of service.

For the cheapest travel, go third class. In third class, there are no assigned seats, it's unbelievably crowded, with people sleeping on the floor (and even on the luggage racks!), and there's poor ventilation. It's uncomfortable, rough, and tight, but tickets are dirt cheap—costing around $2 for most journeys, such as from Delhi to Varanasi or Goa to Kochi. For those on a tight budget, it's the best way to go.

The next class up is the second-class sleeper, which comes with assigned seats, beds, and a lot less people. It is more private and comfortable, and prices are around $6–$12 for a typical twelve-hour journey.

At the top end is first class, which actually has three different subclasses. The 3A has six beds in each compartment, the 2A has four beds, and the 1A has only two beds. They all have more comfortable beds than other classes, and come with sheets, pillow, a blanket, air-conditioning, and outlets. A 3A bed would cost about $17–$30 for an overnight journey, while 1A would cost around $35–$70.

As a budget traveler, the second-class sleeper is the best class to travel in—it's affordable, comfortable, and a great way to meet locals. For comprehensive timetables and routes, use the Indian Railways website (indianrail.gov.in) or the very user-friendly 1-2-Go (12go.asia).

In terms of travel safety for women, Mariellen never hesitates to travel by train in India by herself, even on long journeys. "I have never felt unsafe on a train," she says. "One time, I was booked into a second-class sleeper for an overnight journey, and I saw the compartment was filled with men. I asked to be moved and the conductor was very understanding. He put me in a first-class compartment with a family. Generally, I recommend second class for female solo travelers."

Buses

Government-run buses are cheap and their quality varies greatly as each individual state runs their own bus operation. The quality of private buses can vary as well. Ultimately, it's a gamble since there are no uniform standards (in terms of comfort and safety). In my view, trains are a much better option unless you *have* to take a bus.

A normal government bus from Delhi to Dharamsala (a journey of eleven hours) with super-crowded bench seats, no air-conditioning, and lots of stops will cost around $10, while a private bus with semi-reclining seats, (sometimes working) air-conditioning, limited stops, and no more passengers than the number of seats will be around $15 for the same journey. —

FlixBus (flixbus.in) also operates limited routes in northern India. Some example fares are New Delhi to Varanasi for $13–$16 (14 hours) and New Delhi to Kanpur for $9–$12 (8 hours). However, the bus company Vijayanand (vrlbus.in) has a more extensive route network. Going from Bangalore to Goa, for example, will set you back $15–$30 and take 13 hours, while Hyderabad to Mumbai will cost $10–$22 and take 15 hours.

On many long-distance buses, you can purchase a bed. The

double beds are a great value; there is enough space for two people and their backpacks.

One thing to keep in mind is that bus travel can be accident prone. In the mountains, the roads are perilous, buses are driven a bit recklessly, and accidents are always a risk. Try to avoid night buses unless there is no alternative as accidents are the most common then.

For bus routes and timetables, the website redBus (redbus.in) is really good.

Flying

The number of budget airlines in India seems to be growing all the time, and as a result, the fares are often remarkably low. Most intra-country flights range between $50 and $120, though deals often abound for much less than that and you can often find tickets for between $25 and $35.

The following are the major airlines in the country:

- AirAsia: airasia.com
- Air India: airindia.com
- Air Vistara: airvistara.com
- Alliance Air: allianceair.in
- IndiGo: goindigo.in
- SpiceJet: spicejet.com

Since travel around the country can be long and tiring, flights can be a quick and easy way to cut out a twenty-hour train journey. However, I'm not a huge fan of flying in India as I think a lot of the smaller airlines have spotty safety records. AirAsia and

Air India are my two favorites and, when you are pressed for time, flying is the best way to cover the vast distances in India.

For more information on how to find cheap fares, refer back to chapter six.

ATTRACTIONS AND ACTIVITIES

Like many "developing" countries, India has a two-tier fee system where foreigners pay significantly more than locals. However, prices are never that expensive and rarely more than $10 (and that's usually just for big attractions). The Taj Mahal costs around $15, Humayun's Tomb in Delhi is $7, the Red Fort in Delhi costs about $7, and Bundi Palace costs around $5.

Prices vary wildly depending on popularity, but overall, everything is incredibly affordable. One thing to note is that there may also be additional charges for photo and video cameras, and those fees can be pretty steep. For example, Ranganathittu Bird Sanctuary charges an additional $2–$7 if you have a DSLR camera.

Derek says, "Before buying an entrance ticket to any attraction, be sure to ask what it includes. Oftentimes your ticket will include the entrance fee to other nearby attractions as well, and sometimes you'll have the option of purchasing a package that, for a little more money, allows you to visit several sites on that one ticket as well."

Unlike other destinations in the world, India does not have any discount cards or offers that travelers can use.

Full-day excursions from most cities cost between $30 and

$40, while Airbnb Experiences (which are very popular in the country) cost between $15 and $30.

You can find a lot of free walking tours in all the major cities in India.

HOW MUCH MONEY DO YOU NEED?

For those on a really tight budget, you could survive in India for around $20–$25 a day. This would include staying at really cheap (and less than super) guesthouses, eating local food at cheap restaurants and street stalls, and traveling in third-class trains or on local buses. You can further reduce your costs by Couchsurfing or sticking to ultra-cheap street food and avoiding the major cities.

But on that kind of bare-bones budget, you wouldn't be able to do a lot of paid activities or day trips, and you would have to avoid drinking at bars or eating at more upscale restaurants. On a more comfortable and realistic budget of $30–$45 per day, you'll be able to travel significantly better and be a lot more comfortable—better food, better lodging, second-class sleeper, more activities. There will be room for the occasional beer and even first-class sleeper trains every now and then.

In the larger cities of Mumbai, New Delhi, and Bangalore as well as beach destinations like Goa, you can expect to spend around $45–$55 per day as costs are higher—more people, more tourists, and city life is just generally more expensive.

Overall, India is not expensive and anything above $35 per day would allow you substantial comfort and flexibility in traveling throughout the country.

19

JAPAN

Japan is one of the best countries on the planet. The food, the people, the service, the scenery, the temples—I've been seven times now and I could go seven hundred more. I've never met someone who absolutely didn't love their experience. It's a country of high expectations but it fulfills all of them!

For years, I put off visiting Japan because I was scared by rumors that the country was expensive. I've loved Japanese culture since the first time I ate sushi, and I knew any visit would involve gorging myself on seafood, visits to lots of temples, and extensive train travel through the countryside. And the thought of how much that would cost made me constantly think, "I'll wait until I have more money."

But when I decided to finally go, I found those rumors were dead wrong. Japan is not that expensive. Yes, the bullet trains are expensive, and yes, the international hotel chains are expensive, but everything else is very cheap. Bus, train, food, activities, and locally owned accommodation are all very affordable. Japan is simply not as expensive as the myths would make you believe, and, with a few ninja (see what I did there?) travel moves, you can turn this seemingly expensive destination into one any budget traveler could love.

ACCOMMODATIONS
Hostels

Hostels in Japan are normally found in big cities like Tokyo or Osaka. Rarely will you find them in the more rural areas or smaller towns. You'll find that most hostels include a kitchen (which can save you money by avoiding eating out every day), a common area to relax and socialize, Wi-Fi, bike hire, and laundry facilities. Plus, sometimes they even have a Japanese onsen (spa).

A dorm bed typically costs around $25 per night (sometimes as low as $15 or as high as $45 in Tokyo), while private rooms can be as cheap as $50 or as high as $95 in major cities like Tokyo.

The hostel staff are also likely to speak very good English (which isn't common in Japan) and can be a lifesaver helping you get around.

Additionally, many hostels in Japan often let you stay for free if you are willing to clean up for a few hours a day. This is a great way to stay for no cost and, for those with more time than money, it's the easiest way to visit some of Japan's expensive megacities on a shoestring budget.

Budget Hotels

There are a lot of cheap budget hotels and traditional guesthouses in Japan for those who want a little more comfort.

First, you have ryokan, which are Japanese inns that provide an opportunity to experience traditional Japanese accommodations. They feature tatami mats, onsens, traditional futon beds, and sometimes include meals. Ryokan prices vary greatly and can cost as little as $50 a night to upward of $200, depending on how "spa"-like they are and if there's an onsen on-site. While they are not very budget-friendly accommodations, they are very unique and traditional and should be experienced at least once during a visit to Japan.

For more modern-style hotels, expect to pay from $50 per night for a small, private room. You'll have all the basic amenities but expect a tiny room (space is at a premium in Japan). Breakfast is usually served. However, the price depends heavily on the location. You'll find prices from $50 in smaller towns but in big cities like Kyoto, Osaka, Sapporo, or Tokyo, expect your starting price to be around $65–$70 per night.

Unless you are using hotel points (as discussed in chapter five), I would avoid the larger, international chains as they are very expensive in Japan and usually at least double the price of a Japanese-owned hotel.

While in Japan, I encourage you to try capsule hotels, which are exactly like they sound. You sleep in a little tiny pod. It's like being in a space capsule in a sci-fi movie. Your capsule has a light, outlet, and maybe a small television, and the bathrooms and common areas are all shared. They are frequently used by businessmen who work late and miss the last train home. They are a little weird to stay in, and if you aren't comfortable in tight spaces, they probably won't be for you. One night was all I could take, but it's definitely a unique experience and an inexpensive option for solo travelers. Capsule hotels start around $30 per night.

Booking sites like Agoda and Booking.com have the best rates in Asia for large hotels. Rakuten Travel (travel.rakuten.com) is a Japan-only website that features smaller hotels not found on the large booking sites. Some lesser-known hotel and ryokan websites include Jalan (jalan.net/en/japan_hotels_ryokan), Japanese Guest Houses (japaneseguesthouses.com), and the Japan Ryokan and Hotel Association (ryokan.or.jp).

One thing to keep in mind is that many small mom-and-pop hotels in Japan, especially those outside the big touristy cities, don't have English websites or aren't listed on global booking websites, so be sure to check the Japanese websites listed above.

Apartment Rentals

Apartment rental services in Japan are strictly regulated. As such, you will find very few classic Airbnb-style opportunities where people rent out a room or house while they travel. Due to those regulations, you'll find mostly entire rental homes and hotels on these platforms.

That can be good for big groups, but if you are traveling by yourself or as a couple, I wouldn't recommend using one of these websites. Just use a hotel booking website as the prices are generally the same.

Camping

Camping is allowed in Japan only in national parks. There are more than three thousand campsites scattered all over the country, owned and managed by local municipalities. Metropolitan areas don't have campsites, so don't expect to camp anywhere other than in the woods. In the national parks, camping outside the designated areas is strictly prohibited.

It costs about $4 per night for a basic plot (you bring your own tent and equipment) or about $25 per night for a pre-pitched tent site.

Hospitality Exchanges

Hospitality exchanges are not as widespread in Japan as elsewhere in the world, but there is still a small but active Couchsurfing community in the country, most of whom are expats living in Japan. There are not many hosts outside of Tokyo, so make sure you request rooms well ahead of time to increase your odds of success, as the response rate is often very low.

Couchsurfing has the largest community in the country, while BeWelcome and Travel Ladies have a lot of hosts in Tokyo.

House-Sitting

At the time of writing, house-sitting was not a thing in Japan and there were no active hosts.

WWOOF

WWOOF Japan (wwoofjapan.com) has hundreds of hosts all over the country. WWOOFing is very, very new to Japan so there are not that many options, but you'll find a variety of farms, health centers, and traditional homesteads looking for workers. But, to WWOOF in Japan, you will need a work visa, which isn't always easy to get. The same is true for any opportunities you find via Worldpackers, HelpX, or Workaway.

FOOD

Japanese cuisine is world-renowned and has even earned a spot on UNESCO's Intangible Heritage List. While each region has its own specialties, rice, noodles, seafood, and seasonal produce all feature heavily no matter where you are. Plus, there's izakaya (small plates), yakitori (grilled food), curry bowls, BBQ, and so much more. One of the best things about visiting Japan is the food.

From melt-in-your-mouth sushi to silky miso soups, curry bowls, and hearty ramen, I find Japanese food to be delicious and a flavorful delight. There's nothing better than sitting down in a traditional little hole in the wall with Japanese businessmen washing their meal down with a beer while everyone looks at the gaijin (foreigner) trying to navigate the menu. I remember being in Kanazawa staring bewildered at a menu when the guy next to me helped me out. We struck up a conversation and, over sake, I learned his story as well as about life in Japan. It's one of my favorite memories.

Since Japan imports most of their food, I was afraid of paying through the nose for even the most basic meal, but surprisingly, I found food to be inexpensive. It is a common misconception that food in Japan is universally expensive, so if you stick to non-imported food (especially fruits), you can eat pretty cheaply.

If you want to eat cheap, stick to the trifecta of curry, ramen, and donburi. Curry bowls are as cheap as $3.50 per plate.

Donburi bowls with meat and rice are between $4 and $5. Ramen is usually never more than $8. These are the best ways to eat cheap and filling meals while in Japan. You'll find places all over Japan, especially in train stations, that offer these dishes at an affordable price.

And that's an important part I want to bring up—if you want to eat cheap and well, head to a Japanese train station. These are not just train stations but huge complexes featuring shops, restaurants, and takeaways. Here you will always find a ramen, 7-Eleven, sushi train, supermarket, or whatever else to meet your food budget needs. They are incredibly popular with locals who stop for a delicious and inexpensive meal on their way to and from work.

Most other traditional Japanese meals such as tempura, iza-kaya, and bento boxes cost between $10 and $15 for lunch, while dinners usually start from $20. Most sit-down restaurant meals are going to cost you $13–$20, while quicker lunch spots are going to be around $10.

Domestic beer is around $3–$5 and sake is about $6 per glass. A cocktail will set you back about $8, although expect to pay closer to $11 per drink at the famous cocktail bars in Tokyo.

For Western food, you can expect to pay $4 for a small plate of pasta; other Western meal set menus (sandwich, burger, or pizza with drink) begin around $12.

For those who love sushi (who doesn't?), there are delicious options at all price levels. While I had a few fancy sit-down meals, you can't beat the sushi trains for value. At $1–$4 per plate, I could stuff my face for less than $15. Traditional sushi sets will cost around $16 or more. If you want a nice restaurant with wait-staff and a formal setting, be prepared to pay $75 or more for a filling sushi dinner. The fish market in Tokyo also has cheap sushi served in the morning after the fish auction.

If you're just looking for a light meal, head to the convenience stores. They often have fresh fruit, prepared meals, and sandwiches for only a few dollars. Many locals stop by here for prepared meals on their way home from work. There are a lot of incredible options so don't sleep on convenience store food. It's a very big cultural thing here. Popular convenience stores include 7-Eleven, Food Mart, Family Mart, and Lawson.

Self-catering is the most effective way to eat on a budget in Japan. As noted above, convenience and other corner stores have a lot of prepared meals for $1–$3 that make for a cheap lunch option.

Hostels have kitchens where you can cook and cut your food expenses to less than $8 per day, especially by shopping at the 100 Yen Stores (the Japanese equivalent of dollar stores). Buying groceries costs around $45 per week for basic staples like rice, vegetables, and fish. At the end of the day, most grocery stores discount their fresh meals by between 30 and 50 percent. It's a good way to get cheap, delicious meals for dinner. However, given the availability of such cheap food, it's doubtful you'll go grocery shopping to prepare your own meals.

TRANSPORTATION

Most of the city metro tickets cost $1–$2 for a single journey. (The price varies by distance and may be higher.) Additionally, in most major cities, you can buy a day pass that gives you unlimited travel for twenty-four hours for $5–$8.

You can also use a prepaid and rechargeable PASMO passport card for use on the subway, rail, and bus. It costs $10. For more information, visit pasmo.co.jp/visitors/en/buy.

The Suica card is another prepaid option. It can be used on the metro, buses, some commuter trains, and even at 7-Elevens and vending machines. Think of it like a prepaid debit card. You can buy it at jreast.co.jp/multi/en/pass/suica.html.

Neither the PASMO nor the Suica card saves you money, but they do make things quicker since you don't have to buy a ticket every time you are at the station.

Trains

Train travel in Japan is punctual, comfortable, and extremely fast. But it's not cheap. Individual tickets can cost hundreds of dollars.

The best thing to do is get a Japan Rail (JR) pass (jrpass.com). But, like the Eurail pass, the decision to get one comes down to money. The pass used to be a no-brainer but, in 2023, they raised the prices substantially and now the choice comes down to how long you'll be in Japan, how many times you'll be taking a train, and whether those trains are high-speed shinkansen trains.

The JR pass gives you unlimited journeys on all JR trains, JR ferries, and JR buses throughout the country. These passes cost $336 for seven days, $537 for fourteen days, and $671 for twenty-one days. All passes are for consecutive travel days. The Green Pass is the first-class option but, given the cost and the comparable comfort of second class, I wouldn't get one.

One thing to keep in mind is that you have to buy your JR pass before you arrive in Japan. This is because the pass is available only to non-Japanese travelers who are visiting for a limited time.

Once you get to Japan, you will exchange your order for a pass at a JR office.

So, should you get the pass? Let's discuss.

The JR pass is good on several types of JR trains. After the shinkansen, the next fastest is the tokkyu (limited express). The kyuko express train comes next, followed by the kaisoku and fut-su-densha (local trains that make every stop).

Here are prices for popular routes without the pass:

- Tokyo–Kyoto: $105
- Tokyo–Osaka: $115
- Tokyo–Hiroshima: $120
- Kyoto–Hiroshima: $80
- Osaka–Hiroshima: $64

If you're going to Japan for two weeks and averaging three or four days in a city, that means you'll take about five train rides at an average of $113 using your JR pass. That's about breakeven with the prices above. However, since you can also use the pass on smaller trains for day trips and some metro lines, the pass is worth it for that and the increased flexibility of traveling whenever you want.

Even buying a seven-day pass and taking any three of these routes will save you money.

But, if you're just going for a few days and maybe just going from Tokyo to Kyoto and back, the pass isn't going to save you money.

So only get the countrywide pass if you are doing multiple destinations.

If you're not traveling the entire country, there are region passes that will save you even more money since they are cheaper than the regular JR passes. Currently there are two JR East passes, seven JR West passes, one JR Central pass, and one Kyushu pass. Regional passes generally range from one to seven days in length and cost between $17 and $226 for unlimited rides during the specific duration (e.g., seven days). You can learn more about what each region covers here: jrailpass.com/regional-passes.

If you're just going to be focusing on one region of the country, consider buying a JR regional pass. If you want to explore everywhere, get the regular JR pass.

Japan also has regular limited express and regional trains. Naturally, they are much slower than the shinkansen, but they are also cheaper and only used on certain non-major lines. (And, even then, the prices aren't *that* much cheaper.) One thing to keep in mind is that once you get off the main bullet train lines, it can be complicated getting into very rural towns due to all the transfers and connections you have to make.

Regardless of what you do, use the website NAVITIME (japantravel.navitime.com/en/) to find train times and schedules in English. It's an invaluable resource.

Buses

Buses are a much cheaper alternative to the bullet train system in Japan. But, while the cost is less, the trip will take considerably more time. For example, the two-hour bullet train ride from Tokyo to Osaka becomes a ten-hour bus ride.

Long-distance highway buses service many of the intercity routes covered by trains at significantly lower prices. Bus journeys around the country begin around $25. For example, Tokyo to Nagano is $33, while Osaka to Hiroshima is $24. There are a multitude of operators, including Star Express and Willer Express (willerexpress.com/en), Kansai Bus, and the bus company operated by the Japan Rail group (the company that runs the trains).

A few overnight buses are women only, such as the Dream Sleeper Osaka bus service between Tokyo and Osaka.

Willer Express offers a Japan Bus Pass (willerexpress.com /st/3/en/pc/buspass) at $77 for three days or $97 for five days. Travel days are nonconsecutive, but passes must be used within two months. (Note that at the time of writing it did not include routes in Sapporo on the northern island of Hokkaido.)

Keep in mind that the bus pass restricts you to seats that are four in a row. It also can't be used during major holidays, and it often has blackout dates (you need to check with the company for the exact dates).

With all that in mind, if you have time in Japan and aren't in a rush, buses are the cheapest way to travel the country. I tend to use buses for shorter trips (three hours or less) or for routes that require a lot of train connections to make the journey simpler and quicker (like between small countryside towns).

Flying

Flying between most cities is not necessary as the bullet trains are pretty fast and prices are comparable to flights. You get all the speed without the hassle of going through airport security! If you are hopping between the islands of Japan, you'll need to fly (unless you want to take really long train rides).

The main airlines of Japan are:

- JAL Group: jal.co.jp
- ANA Group: ana.co.jp
- Skymark Airlines: skymark.jp/en
- Peach Aviation: flypeach.com/en
- Jetstar Japan: jetstar.com
- Air Do: airdo.jp
- StarFlyer: starflyer.jp/en
- Fuji Dream Airlines: fujidream.co.jp

Most flights within the country are between $40 and $80. There are frequent departures between all the major (and not so major) cities in Japan, which, combined with all the competition, helps keep prices down. You can refer back to chapter six for information on how to find cheap flights.

ATTRACTIONS AND ACTIVITIES

Most of the attractions in Japan are very cheap. Admission to famous temples costs between $1 and $7. Most museums and castles charge $2–$10 per person. Shinto shrines are free throughout Japan. Most full-day excursions (like visits to mountains, day tours, hiking excursions, etc.) cost between $60 and $100. For example, a trip to Mount Fuji from Tokyo is about $70. Food tours, cooking classes, sumo matches, or kabuki theater shows will be between $40 and $100, with food and drink tours on the higher end.

There aren't a lot of city tourism or discount cards in Japan. In fact, I only know of two at the time of writing. The Hakone Free Pass gives you multiple discounts on excursions in Hakone (an hour outside Tokyo in the mountains near Mt. Fuji) and is valid for two days. Additionally, with this pass, you'll be able to enter and use the transportation service in the area, which includes the train, the ropeway, the sightseeing boat, and the different buses.

The Grutto Museum Pass (rekibun.or.jp/en/grutto) provides free or discounted admission to over seventy-five attractions in the Tokyo area. The pass costs $16.50 and is sold from April through January. It's valid for two months after purchase. For those doing a lot of sightseeing in Tokyo, it's a must-buy.

Some tourist attractions distribute coupons and discount cards at local tourist information centers and hotels. Be sure to stop in to check what is currently offered as it can change frequently.

Free walking tours are just starting to take off, and at the time of this writing, there were three major options to choose from in Tokyo as well as some in Kyoto, Hiroshima, and Osaka. See Appendix A for my favorites.

Airbnb Experiences are widespread in all the major cities in Japan and are a fun and unique way to meet locals. These are excellent for getting to know Japanese culture, which can be hard to break into. Experiences usually start at around $60 for a half-day trip, $100–$200 for a full-day trip, and $55–$100 for something related to food and drink. Similarly, the company GetYourGuide (getyourguide.com) has a lot of activities to choose from that are run by more traditional operators.

HOW MUCH MONEY DO YOU NEED?

Japan has an image of being one of the most expensive countries in the world—and it can be. If you are staying in Western hotels, eating luxury omakases, doing lots of excursions, and moving around a lot, you can easily spend $350 or more per day.

But it doesn't have to be that way.

If you're staying in a hostel dorm room, buying a rail pass, eating relatively inexpensive local food like ramen or donburi with the occasional nice meal, and visiting a few attractions and doing a couple of day tours, you could spend between $90 and $100 per day. You wouldn't live large or be able to eat any high-end meals or drink a lot, but it's a totally doable backpacker budget. If you want to fit in more food or drinks, you could take the bus instead of the train depending on how much time you have in the country.

Trains (i.e., the rail pass) are going to be over a third of your daily budget given they are just expensive, so if you plan on taking high-speed trains, it's going to be hard to go lower.

If you were to stay in private hostel rooms or budget hotels, eat more sushi and nicer meals, drink more, take a few taxis, and just generally sightsee more, you'd need to budget around $170 per day. At this range, you'll be staying in simple accommodations (no Park Hyatt for you!) but you won't want for anything when it comes to activities or local cuisine.

In the end, Japan will never be a "dirt cheap" place to visit but it doesn't need to break the bank thanks to affordable accommodation and lots of inexpensive ways to eat and drink.

20

NEW ZEALAND

New Zealand is another country that can destroy your budget. Day-to-day life here isn't expensive—the problem is that New Zealand has so many outstanding outdoor activities that it sucks your money out of your wallet. This country is known for its natural landscape, and adventure activities here—like caving, skydiving, bungee jumping, fishing, and glacier trekking—can really add up.

While those costs can accumulate and travelers need to pick and choose their battles, New Zealand's jaw-dropping beauty makes any visit there worth it. Anyone who has ever seen *Lord of the Rings* knows just how beautiful this country is with its towering mountain ranges, green forests, pristine meadows, remarkable caves, and inviting lakes that shimmer under clear blue skies. New Zealand is a country that may not always be friendly to your wallet but will always be friendly to your eyes.

ACCOMMODATIONS
Hostels

Hostels in New Zealand feature a lot of amenities such as common rooms, comfortable beds, bars, tour booking desks, and work placement help. (One thing that is not common in hostels here is free breakfast. It's very rare so don't expect it.)

In recent years, more and more hostels have started to have "pod"-style dorm beds with enclosed beds, privacy curtains, and outlets. While it's not widespread and you'll still find *plenty* of hostels with old-school metal bunks (and no privacy), pods are becoming more common, especially in New Zealand's bigger cities.

Hostels in New Zealand cost on average $25–$35 per night for a bed in a dorm room (though, depending on the season, you can sometimes find hostels higher or lower than that range). Private rooms in hostels range from about $60–$90 per night, though again, it might be slightly higher or lower than that depending on the season.

Since the country is so small, prices are pretty uniform regardless of whether you're in the city or countryside. The popular hostels will be on the higher end of the listed range.

There are three big hostel chains in the country: Haka House (hakahouse.com), YHA (yha.co.nz), and Nomads (nomadsworld.com). They have locations in all the major tourist destinations throughout the country. If you become a member of YHA, you'll get a 10 percent discount on all YHA accommodations. At Nomads, you can buy a bulk of nights in advance and save money via the Bed Hopper pass discussed in the chapter about Australia.

There's also The Backpacker Group (thebackpackergroup .co.nz/hostels-savings-nz/), which has its own discount card and network of thirty-five hostels. A one-year membership is $15 and saves up to 30 percent on hostel-organized activities, up to 25 percent on buses and tours, and up to 20 percent on accommodation.

Budget Hotels

Traditional B&Bs are very common in New Zealand, especially in the small towns and countryside (which, admittedly, is a lot of the country). Here you'll get those picturesque homes with antique-looking rooms, big comfy beds, and a home-cooked breakfast by lovely owners. Prices for a double room cost about $130 or more. While quaint and unique, this accommodation is not very affordable. Generally, I would choose a private room in a hostel because they are cheaper. However, in small towns, you don't always have that option and, if you wanted a more unique stay, this would be it.

The country is also awash in generic two- and three-star hotels. These properties tend to be small and come with all the basic amenities of a hotel but aren't going to "wow" you with luxury. You can expect to pay between $80 and $100 per night for a double room.

I personally prefer private hostel rooms over hotels because hostels are a great way to meet other travelers and the prices are similar.

Apartment Rentals

Apartment rental prices average about $50 per night for a private room in a home, while entire apartments tend to cost $70–$100 per night. These rental services have become really popular in the last few years, but if you are spending a lot of time in small towns and in the countryside, traditional B&Bs are a better choice because you'll just get a warmer and more welcoming experience.

However, New Zealand has a lot of really cool and unique homes (like tree houses, huts, tiny homes) listed on apartment rental websites.

Airbnb is the largest operator in the country, while Vrbo mostly has options in resort and beach towns. A local alternative is Holiday Houses (holidayhouses.co.nz), but like Vrbo, they primarily focus on vacation rentals in resort and beach towns.

Camping

Camping is a great budget accommodation option in New Zealand. Because the country is so outdoor-friendly, you will find a lot of campgrounds as well as car and camper van parks. Kiwis (the slang name for New Zealanders) love to be outdoors and they have lots of opportunities for camping.

Campsites cost around $13 per night. You can rent cabins with a bed for two people starting at $37, though you're more likely to pay around $50–$60. The price includes use of all communal facilities, such as kitchen, showers/toilets, and laundry. Everyone staying in the parks has access to the public facilities. Many of these sites have deluxe apartments that can accommodate two to eight people with their own shower, cooking, and laundry facilities. Prices begin at $70 for this option.

The NZ Department of Conservation (doc.govt.nz) runs public camping facilities throughout the country. Holiday Parks (holidayparks.co.nz) is a collection of 260 family-run holiday parks throughout New Zealand.

Hospitality Exchanges

Hospitality exchanges used to be widespread in this country. There were so many people signed up for the service that you'd never have a problem finding a host, even in off-the-beaten-path destinations.

However, that has all changed in recent years and these services are not really used anymore. Couchsurfing still has the most hosts, but they are all concentrated in Auckland. At the time of writing in May 2024, they had fifty-eight hosts who were accepting guests that had logged in within the last month. For the rest of the country? Fewer than five. Super popular Queenstown had only three hosts.

BeWelcome only had twenty hosts in Auckland and none in most other places.

Servas has a large number of hosts in the country, but those hosts tend to be older. For solo female travelers, the app Travel Ladies has a lot of hosts here.

If you're looking for hosts, check out Facebook Groups as there are usually a number of "backpacking New Zealand" groups filled with locals who host. But, overall, you won't find many opportunities here.

House-Sitting

House-sitting is somewhat popular in New Zealand and you will find a lot of hosts looking for sitters, especially in vacation areas such as the Bay of Islands, Queenstown, and the Coromandel. As Kiwis tend to book long-term overseas trips, house-sitting opportunities here tend to be for longer periods of time. Because this is another popular destination for sits, I recommend inquiring about opportunities far in advance. Having references will increase your chances of finding a sit.

WWOOF

Like its neighbor, Australia, there's no official WWOOFing in New Zealand but there are abundant farm work opportunities here. Much of the local economy is agricultural with sheep farms, fruit farms, and wineries dotting the countryside (in fact, there are ten times more sheep in New Zealand than people), so you will find a high demand for willing farmworkers. With so many travelers using this option in New Zealand, and with the transient nature of the workers, there is always at least one farm looking for help.

Workaway, HelpX, and Worldpackers will have a lot of options for you to look through. Moreover, hostels in the country can help point you in the right direction.

FOOD

There's a lot of mouthwatering food and world-class wine in New Zealand. While you can splurge here and there, eating out in New Zealand is always expensive. Even humble cafés offer delicious gourmet options, and New Zealanders take a lot of pride in their food. I remember a beautiful summer salad with nuts, apples, and blue cheese I ate in Auckland. Or that wonderful lamb steak I had in Queenstown while sitting outside sipping a nice glass of white wine. That said, food is very expensive in New Zealand, and if you eat out, you're going to spend a lot of money quick. Most travelers simply stick to cheap pub food or buying all their groceries.

Cheap and inexpensive meals such as sandwiches, pizza, and grab-and-go eateries abound in this country. A few examples of food costs in New Zealand: A pizza is going to run you about $10, fish and chips are about $10–$12, a burger will set you back about $10, and a meal at a Thai restaurant is about $20. Kebabs and noodle shops are usually $10–$12. Sushi is also very popular and there are a lot of fast-food sushi joints that serve premade rolls in the $6–$9 range. When I got tired of cooking, all of these shops kept me fed on a budget.

Cafés are very artisanal but sadly also very expensive. An average meal will cost around $30 for a starter and main course and up to $50 if you add in wine.

While those prices don't seem like a lot (except for the cafés), they will add up quickly if you eat out for every meal. You can look to be spending $30–$50 per day on food if you decide you want something somewhat healthy.

The best way to save money on food is to grocery shop, which will cost between $70 and $100 per week. You'll be able to get the basics: pasta, meats, vegetables, and breads. I often found myself cooking a lot while there. I don't find the restaurants in New Zealand to be as good of a value as in the United States, so you aren't missing out on a host of cultural dishes if you cook most of your own food.

Besides grocery shopping, if you are looking to eat out in New Zealand and want to save money, do so during lunchtime. Cafés and restaurants have lunch menus until about 3 PM that cost as little as $15, which is still expensive compared to grocery shopping but about half the price of dinner. I like to mix eating out during lunch with cooking my own food for dinner. That way I enjoy some of New Zealand's delicious cafés while still saving money.

TRANSPORTATION

The best way to get around cities in New Zealand is via their extensive bus network (cities in New Zealand don't have subway systems). Local buses and trams cost about $1–$2 per trip for a ride around the city center.

Trains

New Zealand has a train line that goes from Auckland down to Wellington in the North Island and from Picton to Christchurch across the South Island. Though scenic, both routes are ridiculously expensive. A train from Christchurch to Picton takes six hours and costs about $115. However, the bus, which takes the same amount of time, only costs $50.

The trains here are meant more for scenic tourism than a practical mode of transportation. They are beautiful and I loved cruising around the country in a train for the experience, but they are not a good budget travel option. Skip the train and take the bus if you are on a budget.

Buses

New Zealand only has one main bus company: InterCity (intercity .co.nz). Fares are typically between $15 and $25.

InterCity offers a bus pass called the FlexiPass (intercity.co .nz/bus-pass/flexipass-overview). The FlexiPass is an hour-based pass for from ten to sixty hours. Prices begin at $85. Your pass is good for a set number of hours that are calculated based on the hours per trip (i.e., time it takes to get from point A to point B). This pass sounds like a good idea but is in fact quite the opposite. For example, a regular fare from Auckland to Wellington is $40 and takes eleven hours. If you were to get the fifteen-hour pass at $103, this trip would cost you $75 on the pass. With regular bus prices so cheap, it doesn't make sense to get this pass, so I would skip it.

InterCity also offers a TravelPass that allows you to stop anywhere along the route. For example, if your pass includes travel between Picton and Christchurch, you could do Picton to Blenheim, Blenheim to Kaikoura, and Kaikoura to Christchurch all on one trip. TravelPasses start at $75. While these passes often include day tours, I don't find this pass good value either and would also skip this.

A popular method of transportation among younger travelers are backpacker bus tours such as Stray Travel (straytravel.com) and the Kiwi Experience (kiwiexperience.com). These buses are a substitute for the local bus and are strictly used by tourists. Often included in your pass are meals, activities, day trips, and discounts on attractions. Prices vary greatly depending on the pass, and prices are a lot higher during peak tourism season in December through February. The most basic passes start at $150 for a four-day trip.

I am a huge fan of these bus tours. If you have the time and want to meet a lot of other travelers, I think they are better than the public bus. There are a lot of communal activities and events that get people socializing, and you can always get off if you don't like the crowd or want to travel at your own pace. Years later, I'm still good friends with the people I met on a Kiwi Experience bus. While the general age range for travelers on these buses is from eighteen to thirty, I found many older travelers on them too.

The Kiwi Experience is the biggest and most popular backpacker bus in New Zealand. It attracts mainly young gap-year travelers. I like how they go out of their way to make sure everyone socializes and gets to know each other: the drivers play a lot of games and icebreakers, and there are group dinners most nights.

The downside is that: (a) the buses seat around fifty-five people, and when they're full, they get a little bit cliquey (and during the busy season, the bus is pretty much always full); and (b) the passengers are really focused on getting drunk (the Kiwi Experience's affectionate nickname is "The Green Fuck Bus")—hence why so many young people take it. I'd say if you're twenty-five or younger (or just looking for a party), this bus is for you.

Tours range from two to twenty-eight days and fares range from $416 to $1,150 per person for hop-on/hop-off tours, while small group tours range from two to eighteen days and cost between $2,750 to $3,600 per person.

Stray has smaller buses, providing a more intimate setting and making it easier to meet people. While there are many gap-year travelers on the bus, Stray also attracts older, independent travelers. The bus drivers don't play as many games or have as many icebreakers, making it a bit awkward when you first step on the bus alone and aren't an extrovert.

If you aren't really looking to party a lot or want to spend time with more mature travelers, Stray is for you. Tours range from nine to twenty-four days and cost between $1,825 and $3,900 per person.

Camper Vans

A lot of travelers rent cars and vans in New Zealand because it's easy to get around and there are a ton of campsites along the way. This is a very economical (and popular) way to travel because the country is small and the weak New Zealand dollar makes it even cheaper to rent the cars and sleep in campsites. The biggest rental companies are:

- Britz: britz.com/nz
- Hippie Campers: hippiecamper.com
- Jucy: jucy.com/nz
- Spaceships: spaceshipsrentals.co.nz
- Wicked Campers: wickedcampers.com.au

Using the companies above, you can rent cars and vans for as little as $35 per day. You can also find tons of travelers selling their old cars on sites like AutoTrader (autotrader.co.nz), Turners (turners.co.nz), and Trade Me (trademe.co.nz).

By getting other travelers to come with you and using these vans for accommodation, you can drastically reduce your accommodation and transportation costs!

If you are interested in buying a van, websites like Gumtree NZ (gumtree.com/all/new+zealand) and hostel message boards are full of posts from travelers who are finished with their trip and looking to sell their vehicle. Within hours of arriving at my hostel in Auckland, I was offered about three cars by people looking to sell.

Flying

Flying around New Zealand is expensive despite the short distances. New Zealand only has two countrywide carriers: Air New Zealand (airnewzealand.co.nz) and Jetstar Airways (jetstar.com). Since there is no competition, fares stay relatively high, especially on less trafficked routes. However, on heavy traffic routes like from Auckland to Christchurch or from Christchurch to Queenstown, you can find very cheap fares. The two airlines really fight it out for customers, and between big cities you can find fares as low as $55, especially if you book far enough in advance.

While I think New Zealand is best seen from the ground, if you are short on time, flying would be just as cost-effective as taking a bus from one end of an island to the other (or the bus and ferry between islands).

You can refer to chapter six for tips on how to find cheap flights.

Hitchhiking

Hitchhiking is very popular in New Zealand and a relatively safe method of travel. You see a ton of travelers hitchhiking around the country. And they get picked up a lot! As with hitchhiking anywhere in the world, however, you need to use common sense when getting into a stranger's car, especially if you are a solo female traveler. Not everyone will feel comfortable doing this, but if you are thumbing it by the side of the road, you'll find plenty of people will pull over and give you a lift.

The best website for learning more about hitchhiking in New Zealand is Hitchwiki (hitchwiki.org/en/New_Zealand). As hitchhiking is extremely popular and very safe here, this is also a good country to get comfortable hitchhiking if you've never done it before.

Ridesharing

Ridesharing is huge here. You can easily find rides (or riders) since so many travelers rent cars and vans. I've never had a problem finding a ride. Beyond the websites listed in chapter twelve, hostels have message boards where people post rides, or you can just ask around.

ACTIVITIES AND ATTRACTIONS

Activities in New Zealand will really drive your costs up. This country revolves around outdoor activities, and its tourism industry markets it as one of the top adventure travel destinations in the world. Most activities tend to cost between $100 and $300. For example, the Waitomo Glowworm Caves and a Maori cultural show are both around $100–$120, and bungee jumping is typically $150. Skydiving costs about $300.

The main museum in the whole country is Te Papa in Wellington. It's free, but most other history or art museums have an entrance fee around $5.

Occasionally, you'll find special offers from the companies that offer activity tours (see Appendix A for a list of companies), and you can sometimes get discounts through travel agencies or hostels. You may also find activity discounts if you buy a lot of tours at once.

BBH, ISIC, and HI cards all offer some discounts for selected providers of up to 10 percent. If you are using any of the back-packer buses, they also have partnerships with tour operators for similar discounts.

Because of the high cost of tours here, you really need to pick and choose your battles. And if you start doing multiple bungee jumps or skydives, all hope is lost. I suggest choosing the five major outdoor activities you want to do before you travel—and then sticking to them.

New Zealand has a much more centralized tourist industry than Australia, but unlike many destinations in the world, they have not caught on to the tourist card trend. At the time of this writing, there's no national or city pass.

HOW MUCH MONEY DO YOU NEED?

If you're backpacking New Zealand, you'll likely spend around $75 per day. On that budget you would be staying in hostel dorms, eating cheap food and cooking some of your meals, traveling by bus, and doing two or three big activities.

Most travelers spend at least a month here, which averages about $30 per day in accommodation, $20 per day for food (assuming a mix of grocery shopping and eating out cheap), $15 per day on activities (a mix of adventure activities, museums, and tours), and $10 per day on transportation, for a total of $75 per day. If you are planning to party (and most people who visit do), I would bump your budget to around $100 per day.

It's a tight budget, but it can be done. A lot of backpackers survive here on this much (if not less).

Your biggest expenses will be accommodations and activities. There are a lot of free sights, parks, and hiking in New Zealand that can fill your day and not empty your wallet. If you get a camper van, you can lower your accommodation costs. If you cooked all your own meals on top of that, you'd lower spending to between $60 and $70 per day, especially if you are sharing the van with a friend or other travelers you meet along the way.

For someone who wants to be frugal but not go completely backpacker, I would plan on an average of $160 per day. This would get you a private hostel or hotel room, more restaurant meals, some adventure activities, and just a bit more wiggle room.

New Zealand is a country designed to suck your money away. You don't want to be indoors here—you want to be out exploring, eating at boutique restaurants, and drinking wine. And that destroys your budget. Budgeting here takes a lot of work because there are so many opportunities to spend money, but it's not impossible to do New Zealand on a budget if you pick and choose your battles properly.

21

SOUTH AMERICA

Argentina, Bolivia, Brazil, Chile, Colombia, Ecuador, Paraguay, Peru, Uruguay

From the landscapes of Patagonia to the jungles of the Amazon to the deserts of Bolivia, from the tango scene of Argentina to the gregarious culture of Brazil to the culinary treats of Peru, there is a lot of variety in South America. I have loved every trip here and am always fascinated by the diverse landscape, food, and culture.

While there's still some political volatility in the region and you have to be very mindful of petty crimes (I'm not fearmongering here; that's just a reality), you will find some of the most welcoming people in this region.

Moreover, this is an area of the world where your money goes very far. Though costs vary dramatically by country and prices have risen substantially over the last few years, you can still find a lot of value here. More expensive cities and regions like Rio de Janeiro, Buenos Aires, Santiago, and Patagonia will eat into your budget, as will big trips like the Galápagos Islands, Easter Island, and Machu Picchu. However, countries such as Ecuador, Peru, and Bolivia are very affordable and will offset the costs of the other destinations.

Given its vast size, be sure to budget a lot of time on this continent.

ACCOMMODATIONS
Hostels

Hostels in this region provide a host of amenities—free breakfast, internet access, bars, game rooms, tour organization, and large kitchens. However, outside major cities or popular tourist destinations, most hostels in the region are pretty bare bones. They are getting better and more luxurious, but for the most part, they are quite simple compared to hostels in other parts of the world.

In Argentina, the peso moves like a yo-yo as economic instability changes the value of the currency almost daily. You can expect to pay about $10–$15 for a bed in a dorm room and about $30–$50 for a private room, but given the rampant inflation in the country as I write this, prices could change dramatically by the time you travel.

In Brazil, hostel prices vary significantly depending on the city or region. In general, expect to pay between $12 and $20 for a bed in a dorm and $25–$45 for a private room with a private bathroom. Large cities like Rio de Janeiro or beach destinations like Florianopolis will be on the upper end of that range

Hostels in Chile are around $15 per night for a dorm and between $35 and $40 per night for a private room. In Peru, expect to pay about $10 per night for a dorm room and around $30 per night for a private room. Bolivia and Ecuador are roughly the same price and have dorms as little as $5 and private rooms for $15 and up. Because Paraguay is relatively off the beaten path, hostels are similarly priced, if not just a few dollars more. In Uruguay, dorms go for around $15 per night, while private rooms in hostels go for about $45 per night.

Colombia is a budget traveler's oasis in terms of hostel accommodation, offering the most options and some of the most luxurious digs. It's become a mecca for digital nomads and has some of the nicest options around. Dorms usually range between $10 and $20, while private rooms start around $50 (though the more upscale hostels in Medellín can cost close to $100 per night).

Budget Hotels

Small, family-owned budget hotels are widely abundant and a cheap accommodation option if hostels don't interest you. For a double room, you'll likely get a private bathroom, breakfast, TV, and air-conditioning. The decor in these establishments is usually out of date and bare bones, but they are comfortable, plentiful, and safe. Plus, you'll get to interact a lot with the families that own the places. They are very personable places to stay.

Generally, decent quality hotels (clean, comfy bed, safe) in Argentina, Chile, Colombia, and Brazil start at around $45 per night. In Bolivia, Ecuador, Paraguay, and Uruguay, you'll find guesthouses that start closer to $30 a night. You can definitely find places that are cheaper (some budget hotels in the region are under $20 per night) but just keep in mind that you get what you pay for in South America, and places get sketchier the cheaper you get. If you wanted a little more three-star luxury, I'd add $15 per night to these numbers.

In popular touristy destinations, beach locations, and Patagonia, expect to pay around 30 percent more per night.

While rates for large international hotels are really pricey compared to small, family-run establishments, the point redemptions in the region are some of the lowest in the world. If you have hotel points, this would be a great region to use them. Refer to chapter five for more on collecting hotel points.

Apartment Rentals

When I first wrote this book in 2012, there weren't that many apartment rental options around the continent. In recent years, these services have exploded, especially as COVID untethered people from their desks and freed them to become digital nomads. Most of the listings are still in the capitals or large cities with slim pickings in smaller towns, but that changes daily as more and more places become available.

Generally, you'll find very few private room rentals and a lot of private apartment rentals. Prices in the region for this are pretty uniform, with most places around $20 per night. In Argentina, Brazil, Chile, and Colombia, expect prices to be around $30 or more. In Rio or beach destinations in Brazil, expect $50 per night. In parts of Colombia, which is now a digital nomad hot spot, prices begin at $60 per night.

At the time of writing, there were no local alternatives to Airbnb or Vrbo. Moreover, while this region doesn't suffer from the overtourism and housing stock issues other parts of the world experience, the influx of Westerners in many cities has dramatically raised the cost of living for locals and created a lot of backlash against these services. I would research how locals feel about these services before using them.

Hospitality Exchanges

Couchsurfing is still very popular throughout this region and you'll find an abundance of hosts on the platform, especially in the larger cities. For example, Buenos Aires had over four hundred active hosts at the time of writing, which is more than most cities in Europe! Even little Lima, Peru, had over three hundred hosts! Most major cities have at least one hundred active hosts, so I'd definitely consider using Couchsurfing for this region of the world.

Servas also has good networks in this area of the world. Be-Welcome doesn't have many active members in this region and you're unlikely to find a host. Buenos Aires only had sixteen active hosts at the time of writing, which is far below what Couchsurfing had. Travel Ladies has a small but active user base here and is worth looking into.

House-Sitting

House-sitting isn't as popular in the region. While you may find some options in large capital cities, it isn't something that you should rely on as there are very infrequent opportunities here. However, homestays are very popular in South America, as they are in Central America. Homestays are usually done for a minimum of one week; they cost $75–$150 per week and include three meals a day. You can find homestays on the websites Workaway, Homestay Web (homestayweb.com), or People Like Us (peoplelikeus.world). Any Spanish language school can also help you find one.

WWOOF

WWOOFing exists in the region, but it's not very popular. Chile has the largest network on the continent, and it only has 143 hosts! Most other countries have fewer than 50. You can find hosts if you're diligent, but don't expect an abundance of opportunities. And most opportunities are in really rural places.

That said, there is an abundance of opportunities on World-packers and Workaway throughout the continent. You'll likely have better luck there. HelpX has listings, too, but they aren't in as large of numbers as the other two services.

FOOD

It's hard to spend a lot of money on food in South America if you stick to local markets and street stalls. I remember when I was in Ecuador and found sandwiches for a dollar and delicious ceviche for fifty cents. Even in a local diner, a large meal with chicken, rice, and a drink cost me $3. Eating at local food stalls will cost you about $2 per meal for a hearty plate of meat and rice. You'll find these vendors in the local markets or on the side of the street selling dishes like empanadas or BBQ skewers. In more expensive countries like Chile, costs will be closer to $3. In inflation-plagued Argentina, you won't find cheap street food as sometimes food prices increase in that country as much as 100 percent per month.

Small, locally owned restaurants throughout the region cost around $5 for a local meal that includes a couple of courses and a drink. Even in Puna, Peru, home to touristy and popular Lake Titicaca, you can get a complete three-course meal for $5. Nicer meals at a casual restaurant with attractive decor will cost around $12. In Argentina, again due to inflation, meal prices for even a cheap restaurant will begin at around $15 and move up from there.

Throughout the region, local eateries are easy on the wallet. Look for signs that say "Menus Ejecutivos," which are the best budget option for eating out and usually only available for lunch. They will include a starter, main course, dessert, and usually a drink. They are simple meals, but they are simply wonderful on the wallet.

Western food is going to cost the most, especially if you want something that actually tastes like it does back home. Most restaurants can't do a good burger to save their lives. However, if you're really desperate, most Western dishes will cost about $7 for a burger, sandwich, or pizza, with higher-quality meals costing $10–$17. If you are looking for a nice sit-down meal with good steak and wine, expect to pay $25 and up. Prices in Argentina, Uruguay, and Brazil will cost about 25 percent more.

Grocery shopping is very cheap, costing $15–$25 per week. In expensive Argentina, groceries cost about $40 per week. Colombia and Chile are also more expensive, and you will most likely spend $50 per week in both countries. I personally don't do a lot of grocery shopping while in South America since I can eat well for about $15 per day by sticking to lunch specials, street food, and the occasional nice meal. If you do choose to cook, the local markets will provide a large array of beans, rice, vegetables, meats, and fruits. Fresh food will be very cheap, but anything that needs to be imported will only cost slightly less than it would at home.

Simply put—eat at the vendors, enjoy the local cuisine and culinary style, and save some money.

TRANSPORTATION

Local buses are the most effective way to get around in South America. Most cities, even large ones, lack extensive commuter rail systems. The buses are typically old tour or school buses from the United States. Buses cost around fifty cents inside a city. Taxis are available everywhere and cost $3–$7 per trip within a city's limits. Larger metropolitan and capital cities have subway systems that cost around $1 per ride.

Trains

Trains in this region are virtually nonexistent. There are no inter-country trains anywhere on the continent, and there only a few intra-country in Ecuador, Argentina, Brazil, Peru, and Chile (but generally these are scenic tourist trains, not long-haul passenger trains).

Trains in Argentina are experiencing something of a revival though. There is now rail service between the country's three largest cities: Buenos Aires, Córdoba, and Rosario. The trip to Mar del Plata is fast (six hours), very popular with Argentinians, and half the price of taking the bus if you ride the low-cost Tren Diario that runs daily.

The most popular train service right now is the Train to the

Clouds, called El Tren a las Nubes (trenalasnubes.com.ar). This is a scenic tourist train that runs from Salta in northern Argentina and takes about a day to go round-trip. It costs between $130 and $185, depending on the month. Operation is seasonal so be sure to check if the train is running ahead of time.

In Chile, passenger trains (efe.cl) only operate in a few places. The state railway runs a train from Santiago to Temuco once a day, and there is also train service between Santiago and Chillán. It's fast and mostly reliable. Trains connect Arica in Chile with Tacna in Peru and La Paz in Bolivia. However, trains are about 20 percent more expensive than buses, and with very limited departure, I generally would avoid train travel in Chile in favor of the bus.

There are two train companies in Bolivia, Eastern (fo.com.bo/Paginas/Inicio.aspx) and Ferroviaria Andina, which shuttles passengers through the Andes (ferroviaria-andina.com.bo/). The latter network is more tourist-oriented. There is also a working branch line to Calama in Chile, but this only runs rarely, perhaps once a week. The main line in the west runs from Oruro to Tupiza almost daily.

In Brazil, train service is also very poor. Service is mostly limited to the tourist-oriented steam train that offers transportation between the Brazilian tourist towns São João del Rei and Tiradentes. There is also train service between Vitória and Belo Horizonte. Fares for both lines begin at $27.

Trains in Peru (perurail.com) go from Cusco to the tourist towns of Machu Picchu and Puno. They are tourist trains. Tickets begin at $50 and go all the way up to $125, depending on the time and what level of luxury you want.

Countries not listed here do not have train service.

At the time of this writing, long-distance train travel should be avoided in the region. There are few tracks, limited departures, and poor rail conditions, making train travel much slower and far more expensive than buses. While countries are trying to improve train travel, currently it will be cheaper and easier for you to get around by bus.

Buses

Bus transportation is the cheapest—and best—option for getting around South America. Domestic bus travel costs start around $10, while international or fancier buses (with air-conditioning, fully reclining beds, and even meals) start around $80. For example, a twelve-hour bus ride in Argentina might cost $50–$60, while in Bolivia the same journey might be $20. Generally, Ecuador, Peru, Bolivia, and Paraguay are cheaper and you can get fares for as little as $1 per hour of travel. In the larger countries of Chile, Argentina, Colombia, and Brazil, which use full-service, double-decker sleeper buses, expect to pay $5 or more per hour of travel.

A few countries have bus networks specifically worth talking about.

Argentina boasts an outstanding short- and long-distance bus network. The more expensive buses generally offer high-quality service, and for distances longer than 125 miles, it is common to have food served on board as well as Wi-Fi and alcohol. There is generally a good amount of legroom, and many buses have seats that recline horizontally into beds (camas), making the experience a lot like traveling business class on a plane. The best category, with completely reclining seats, is normally called a cama suite, but other names such as tutto leto, executive, or salón real are also in use. Somewhat cheaper seats only recline partially (semi-camas) or not at all (servicio común). Information about buses and timetables can be found on the Omnilíneas website (omnilineas.com).

In Brazil, long-distance buses are a convenient, economical, and sometimes rather comfortable (if you buy the most expensive ticket) way to travel between regions. For example, the six-and-a-half-hour ride from Rio to São Paolo is just $15 when booked in advance. You should check distance and time while traveling within Brazil; going from Rio de Janeiro to the southern region could take more than twenty-four hours, so it may be worth going by plane if you can afford it.

There is no one bus company that serves all of Brazil, so you need to identify the company that services your departure and arrival cities by calling the bus station in one of those cities. ANTT, the national authority for land transportation, has a search engine for buses (antt.gov.br), but it is only in Portuguese. Big cities like São Paulo and Rio have more than one bus station, each covering certain areas of the city. Be sure to check in advance which bus station you are going to.

Bus prices are quite expensive in Colombia by regional standards but long-distance trips rarely cost more than $35 one way. The eight-to-nine-hour trip from Medellín to Bogota, for example, costs around $30. Long-distance bus travel tends to be very slow because main highways are two-lane roads with lots of truck traffic. Budget airlines are often comparable in price to long-distance buses in Colombia, so make sure to check the airline websites listed later in this section for fare information.

In Peru, colectivo buses (e.g., they pick up people as they go) are the cheapest option, following the general rule of $1 per hour of travel. For some routes in Peru, such as from Lima to Mancora or Cusco, there are more expensive buses run by private companies that have first- and second-class service. Light meals and snacks are provided, and there may be private security guards on board due to bandits. These buses cost upward of $50, though you can usually find tickets for as little as $25 if you book early.

One thing to remember is that in many of these countries, you will be traveling long distances and through winding mountains, so bus journeys can be eighteen hours or more. The roads in South America are not well kept, the distances are long, and the terrain is difficult, so it is often better to get a plane ride if you are short on time. If you have to take the buses, plan accordingly with water, snacks, comfortable clothing, and entertainment.

Hitchhiking

Hitchhiking is not recommended anywhere in South America. I don't do it and I know few people who do. It's simply not safe due to kidnappings, robberies, and theft. It's especially unsafe if you are a single female. Additionally, drunk driving is a big problem in many parts of South America. It's just too dangerous to hitchhike here and you do so at your own risk.

Flying

Flying around this region is expensive compared to the cost of living, but given the vast distances between destinations, it can be a good option for travelers with limited time. As I said, bus rides can be eighteen-plus hours here and often on dangerous and winding roads. Sometimes it is worth it to spend the extra money on a flight to avoid traveling for two days.

For example, the bus from Buenos Aires to Santiago takes 21 hours and costs $100, whereas flying only takes 2.5 hours and costs $120. Likewise, the bus from Rio de Janeiro to Salvador takes over 24 hours and costs $60, while the flight is only $100 and takes 2 hours. There's no need to be a travel hero if you're short on time or just want a little more comfort.

The major airlines in South America are:

- Aerolíneas Argentinas: aerolineas.com.ar
- Avianca: avianca.com
- Copa Airlines: copaair.com
- GOL: voegol.com
- LATAM: latamairlines.com/us/en

For ways to find a cheap ticket, refer back to chapter six.

ACTIVITIES AND ATTRACTIONS

Museums and city attractions cost around $5–$10. There are a number of good art and historical museums throughout the region, and I love the museums that give insight into the fabulous Inca civilization and the Spanish occupation of the region.

The tourism cards in other parts of the world are not in use here. While there are some private tour companies that offer limited passes, at the time of writing, there's no city tourism cards offered by any of the tourism boards. What is offered by the private companies is very limited in scope and often not a good deal, so I would skip them.

Simple day tours cost around $40–$50. These will include wine tours in Argentina, a day trip to Rainbow Mountain in Peru, coffee tours in Colombia, a visit to the salt flats in Bolivia, and short hikes into the Amazon.

Whereas in other parts of the world you can find tours for backpackers and budget travelers, there are no specific budget options in South America. That's simply because, for most places, everyone wants to go and there are restrictions on visitor numbers. For example, a weeklong Galápagos tour costs about $2,400, a three-day Amazon tour is $225, and a weeklong Machu Picchu trek starts at $500.

You'll save the most money by taking your own transportation to tourist hot spots. Many attractions like wine tours, salt flats, or national parks can be easily driven to from nearby cities.

For epic adventures like Antarctica, Galápagos, Amazon River tours, and, of course, the Inca Trail, you will get the best prices if you book far in advance or arrive last-minute, which can cut prices down by 50 percent. However, with this latter option, you run the risk of having to wait while a spot opens up on an unfilled tour (but honestly, that's where you get the best deals).

Being flexible, waiting until the last minute, and visiting a local travel agent will allow those amazing dream tours you see advertised in the States to become far more affordable and realistic.

HOW MUCH MONEY DO YOU NEED?

South America is still relatively inexpensive, but countries like Brazil, Chile, and Colombia are becoming increasingly expensive by the day.

There's also a big price divide in the continent. You'll be hard pressed to eat for less than $40 per day in Argentina, while, on the other hand, you'll be hard pressed to spend more than $40 per week on local food in Peru.

Most travelers spend three to six months traveling around the continent (it's pretty big, after all). Assuming you were going to travel around and hit expensive and inexpensive countries, you'd need a budget of about $55 per day. You'd be staying in dorms ($20 per day), eating mostly local food ($16 per day), taking the bus ($10 per day), and doing a few museums, day tours, and one or two big activities like Galápagos Islands and Machu Picchu. To give yourself some buffer room, I think $60 per day on a backpacker budget would be more realistic.

If you plan to have more sit-down restaurants or stay in the occasional private rooms in hostels or in hotels, you'd want to budget closer to $90 per day.

However, there are a lot of variables to budgeting here. Do you spend more time in cheaper countries like Peru or Bolivia, or more time in Brazil or Argentina or Colombia? Do you live off street food or do you splash out? Do you decide to book a last-minute hike through Patagonia or head to Antarctica? These questions can greatly change your daily budget.

Travel in South America, like travel in Europe, is about balancing expensive countries with inexpensive countries. If your whole trip is in Chile, Brazil, and Argentina, taking tours and drinking a lot, you'll spend more than $75 per day. But if you balance out these countries with the more inexpensive ones, your average will drop way below that.

22

SOUTHEAST ASIA

Cambodia, Indonesia, Laos, Malaysia, Singapore, Thailand, Vietnam

Southeast Asia is one of the most affordable regions in the world, with the typical traveler spending way less than $75 per day. I'm always shocked when people tell me they've spent more than that in this region. Yes, if you stay at international brand hotels, fly between destinations, and eat the same food as you do back home, you can spend a lot of money. But this is a region where the average yearly salary in some countries can be as low as $2,000. In Thailand, one of the most developed countries in the region, the average annual salary is just $7,600! So, if you follow my rule about traveling as locals live, you won't spend a lot of money here.

Costs in Southeast Asia can vary wildly. Singapore, a highly developed shipping and financial center, is *vastly* more expensive than rural countries like Cambodia or Laos. Rural Thailand is a fraction of the cost of popular tourist and resort islands like Koh

Samui. Vietnam is pennies compared to Bali. You're going to get big swings in prices as you travel around, but the relatively inexpensive nature of the majority of the region (outside of the major cities and developed tourist centers) makes it an affordable place to visit. It's why the region is so popular with young travelers.

ACCOMMODATIONS
Hostels

Hostels in the region have really exploded in the last five years. And they can be really luxurious too! Throughout the region, you'll find hostels with pod-style dorm rooms, kitchens, tour desks, bars, and communal spaces. Free breakfast is common and many hostels even have pools.

Whereas ten years ago European-style dorms were a rarity because guesthouses and hotels were so cheap, they are now common as the cost of other accommodation has risen. Generally, you can find hostel dorm rooms for between $6 and $9 in Cambodia and $7–$10 in Laos. In Thailand, four-to-six-bed dorm rooms are $8–$12, while in Vietnam you can expect to pay $5–$10. In Indonesia (outside of Bali), prices range between $8 and $12. In Singapore, where accommodation costs are the highest in the region, you can expect to pay between $25 and $40 per night for a dorm room.

Pretty much every hostel in the region has private rooms as hostels are usually old converted guesthouses. Private rooms in hostels generally start at $100 per night in Singapore, $30 in Thailand, $15 in Cambodia, $25 in Vietnam, and $25 in Indonesia, Laos, and Malaysia. As with dorm rooms, prices in cities will be about 20 percent higher—and double the price on some of the more popular islands and bigger destinations.

In the major metropolises and touristy hot spots, expect dorms to be on the higher end of that range (or slightly above it). On Thailand's famous islands like Koh Phangan, Koh Samui, or Koh Phi Phi, expect to spend at least $15 per night. In pricey Bali, prices will be between $10 and $25 for a dorm room.

During peak season (November–April), expect to spend about 20 percent more no matter where in the region you stay. Most hostels have air-conditioning but, in more rural areas, they might charge you extra for it—or not have it at all.

Given the similar price point to budget hotels (see the following section), I try to stay in private rooms in hostels as much as possible because of the social component. You'll meet more people for a similar price and service.

Budget Hotels

In Southeast Asia, you'll hear people talk a lot about guesthouses. Think of them like European pensions: small, family-run establishments with basic amenities and a few rooms. And like in Europe, there's not too much difference between them and a cheap hotel—except that a hotel is going to be larger, have more standardized amenities, and be a little less homey.

Simple guesthouses throughout Southeast Asia generally cost $12–$20 per night for a basic room, fan (sometimes air-conditioning), and hot water. If you want a nicer guesthouse that includes a more comfortable bed, air-conditioning, and a TV, expect to pay $25–$35 per night. You won't get five-star luxury here—the beds are probably uncomfortable, the water pressure low, and the rooms small. But if you are on a budget, they'll provide a good night's sleep in a clean environment.

Expect prices in bigger cities or on the popular tropical islands like Koh Phi Phi, Bali, or the Perhentian Islands to cost around 25 percent more. In Singapore, you're going to spend at least $100 per night for a cheap hotel.

Air-conditioning is standard in the large cities but might not be included in rural areas as well as on some tropical islands unless you pay extra, so it's always a good idea to check when you book.

When booking hotels in Southeast Asia, I like to use the website Agoda (agoda.com). Agoda focuses on accommodations in Asia and has the most robust listings for guesthouses and hotels in this region. They regularly have sales and cheaper prices than those found on worldwide sites like Hotels.com or Booking.com.

Apartment Rentals

Apartment rentals are huge in the region. Apartments usually come fully furnished in buildings with doormen, and often include maid service for long-term stays. Rooms to rent in people's homes are not as common outside very touristy destinations (Bangkok, Bali, Hanoi, etc.), but you'll find plenty of full apartment rental options throughout the region, including in the countryside.

While Vrbo has a presence here, you'll find the largest selection of places on Airbnb (and generally Airbnb is cheaper). Apartment prices vary wildly in the region. In Thailand, full apartments cost about $40 per night, though in Bangkok prices start around $60 per night. On the Thai islands, I'd expect to pay about $80 per night. In Laos, private rooms start from $35, while an entire apartment goes for as little as $50. In Vietnam, a private room costs at least $15 per night, while an entire home or apartment is around $25. In Singapore, private rooms start at $18 per night (though they average closer to $44), while entire apartments average $120 per night.

In Indonesia, private rooms start from around $15 per night. For entire apartments, expect to pay at least $25 per night. Specific to Bali, you will find a lot of options available as the destination is a digital nomad hub and a lot of expats buy property there to rent. Prices here start around $28 for a private room, while entire homes/ apartments start around $100 (though they are usually double that or more). But I wouldn't recommend any apartment rental services in Bali because of the overtourism issues discussed in chapter ten.

Hospitality Exchanges

Using hospitality networks is a wonderful way to have someone help you navigate the initially overwhelming nature of Southeast Asia. As with other regions in the world, hospitality networks aren't as popular as they used to be and most hosts tend to be Westerners. You'll find hosts in all the major and capital cities, but outside that, hosts will be few and far between.

BeWelcome, Travel Ladies, and Couchsurfing will be your best options for finding a host. It's easiest to find hosts in larger cities as well as Bali, Thailand, and Singapore.

House-Sitting

House-sitting is also not very common in the region and you won't find a lot of opportunities here. I would avoid using this method of finding lodging in Southeast Asia.

WWOOF

WWOOFing is not that common in the region. While there are both official and some unofficial WWOOFing organizations, there aren't a lot of hosts and listings aren't often updated. That said, there are more active and updated listings on Workaway and Worldpackers. HelpX has the least number of opportunities for any country in the region.

FOOD

Food is very inexpensive in Southeast Asia. If you are spending a lot of money on food, you are simply eating too many Western meals. If you're sticking to local cuisine, you're unlikely to average more than $15 per day.

In Southeast Asia, street food is the most popular form of eating. Outdoor food stalls line the streets of Asia where residents eat snacks, have dinner, and buy prepared meals. I love nothing more than heading to the local market, sitting down, and grabbing a delicious plate of fried rice, pad Thai, noodle soup, or stir-fried noodles. Walking through the markets and grabbing skewers of BBQ meats, fresh fruit shakes, and spring rolls makes Southeast Asia one of the most delicious regions of the world.

Many travelers are worried that street food isn't safe, but I assure you it is. If it made people sick, people wouldn't eat at these stalls in such large numbers. Your risk of food sickness is no greater than in a restaurant (actually, it's probably even less common). After all, food at the stalls is cooked fresh in front of you and used every night. It doesn't sit around. Plus, there are no cabinets for rats or bugs to get into. I eat street food wherever I can and prefer street stalls to sit-down restaurants.

On average, street food costs around $2 per dish. You will find these stalls throughout Southeast Asia, lining major streets and markets. In Thailand, street food markets abound. There's the famous Thong Lor food market in Bangkok and the big night market at Chiang Mai Gate in the northern city of Chiang Mai. It seems that on the corner of every street in Vietnam is a pho (noodle soup) seller. In Singapore, you'll find street food (or "hawker stands" as they are called there) to be around $3 for a meal. (Singapore also has cheap Chinese and Indian food in Chinatown and Little India, respectively, where you can get meals from $5.)

Even if you eat at restaurants serving local cuisines, prices don't increase that much. What is $1.50 at a street stall is only $3–$5 at a restaurant. If you went into a restaurant in Thailand, you'd pay around $4 for a pad Thai that would have cost $1.50 on the street. In Cambodia, street food (which isn't as abundant as I would like it to be) is around $1, while restaurants charge around $3 for a local dish like amok (coconut milk dish) or luc lac (pepper gravy beef).

Western dishes like burgers, pizza, and sandwiches cost around $5 per dish (though they aren't really that tasty). If you want something that actually tastes like it does back home, you're looking at spending at least $10 for your meal. In the mood for a really nice bowl of pasta? About $8. Want a deliciously made steak? At least $20. Sushi? Expect to spend around $30. Even though the food is cheaper than back home, it is expensive by local standards, and eating a lot of Western food will vastly increase your food budget.

There are a lot of Michelin-starred and other high-end

restaurants in Southeast Asia, especially in touristy and ex-pat-filled places like Singapore, Bangkok, Kuala Lumpur, and Bali. I've had some of the best sushi of my life in Thailand and amazing Italian in Bali. Some of the best BBQ ribs I've had in my life (and I say this as someone who used to live in Texas) were in a small beach town in Cambodia. But while the food is delicious, the price is only a little cheaper than what you would pay back home—and in some cases, even more.

If you're visiting a lot of island destinations (regardless of country), expect to spend about 20–30 percent more on food regardless of what you get.

TRANSPORTATION

It is very cheap and easy to travel around Southeast Asia. Hub cities like Bangkok specialize in getting tourists to their next destination, even if it's two countries away. There is a whole industry in Asia meant to keep you, the tourist, happy and on the move.

Local public transportation ranges from a few pennies to a few dollars. In Bangkok, the public bus costs $0.22, while the metro train system costs $0.50–$1.50 per ride. In Singapore, the local train system starts at $2.75. In Cambodia, a bus ticket in Phnom Penh costs just $0.40 per ride. In Vietnam and Laos, a bus ride will cost you the same. No matter where you are in the region, you'll find yourself spending very little on local city transportation.

Taxis (metered taxis) and tuk-tuks (small shared taxis with no meter) are normally double to triple the local transportation costs and you often have to haggle over the fare. One of the best ways to call a cab in the region and ensure you aren't getting ripped off is to use the Grab app. It's prolific in the region and the price is set via the app. I highly recommend using it.

Trains

There aren't a lot of train networks in Southeast Asia, especially if you want to go between countries. In terms of true intercountry travel, there is a train that runs from Singapore to Bangkok, though you have to switch trains twice in Malaysia (once in the capital, Kuala Lumpur, and once more at the border town of Butterworth). That train costs about $75 and takes a day and a half of travel. It's a beautiful scenic journey through the countryside, but if you are pressed for time, the three-hour flight from Singapore to Bangkok costs the same.

You can buy train tickets at the station or on the Malaysian Railways (KTMB) website (www.ktmb.com.my) if you are going north to Bangkok. If you are going south to Singapore, you can visit the website Thailand Train Ticket (thailandtrains.com) or simply book at the train station.

Thailand has the most robust train system in the region. There are trains all around the Bangkok region, up to Chiang Mai, over the border into Laos, or across into Cambodia. There's also the line that goes to Malaysia with stops along the east coast.

Train travel in the country, while slow, is actually one of my favorite ways to get around. It's a lot more comfortable than buses, there are always vendors selling tasty local specialties, and you get to see the countryside more than you do from the highways.

Day trains cost as little as $1 if you're not going far, but expect to realistically pay $10 for a train that is just a few hours long.

Night trains start at $20 for second class with air-conditioning (the air-conditioned night trains can be freezing, so be prepared). A train from Bangkok to Chiang Mai takes eleven to thirteen hours and costs $20–$27, while Bangkok to Pattaya takes four hours and costs $5. The Bangkok to Vientiane (Laos) train takes eleven to thirteen hours and costs around $30.

In Vietnam, there's a train that goes up and down the coast, which a lot of people love because it's safe, affordable, and comfortable. Although it might be slow, I would have to agree as you'll get some amazing views of the Vietnamese countryside. A train journey between Ho Chi Minh and Hanoi (which nearly spans the entire length of the country) starts at $40 for a soft seat (not a berth). The journey takes three days but hardly anyone does it straight though because you stop along the way. Hanoi to Hue costs around $24 and takes around thirteen hours, while Ho Chi Minh City to Nha Trang costs around $10–$20 and takes eight hours. I personally like to take the overnight berths because the roads in Vietnam are a little wild and the bus drivers tend to drive like they are F1 racers. For a soft sleeper bed with air-conditioning, expect to pay around $44 for the journey from Hanoi to Hue. For the same bed on the train from Ho Chi Minh City to Nha Trang, expect to pay around $30.

In Laos, a China-funded high-speed rail opened in 2021 and takes people from Vientiane to Vang Vieng and then into Boten on the Laos-China border. It's very nice and very fast. Tickets from Vientiane to Vang Vieng start at $15, while trips all the way to the border at Boten start at $25 for second-class tickets.

In Cambodia, there is a new train from Phnom Penh to Battambang, but it's not that comfortable. There is also a train from Phnom Penh to Sihanoukville. Tickets cost $5–$7, though departures are not very common so you'll need to plan ahead. The journey takes about six hours. While improvements are being made, there is still a general lack of upkeep of the rail infrastructure and much of it is in bad shape, so you'll get places faster if you take the bus.

In Indonesia, the cities of Java are well linked by train. Economy class from Jakarta to Surabaya takes eleven hours and costs about $42, while an eight-hour executive-class trip costs $96. Surabaya to Banyuwangi (for Bali) takes six to seven hours and costs as little as $16 for economy and $25 for executive class. You can reserve your tickets at tiket.com. Outside of Java, you won't find much train service.

Generally speaking, you don't need to prebook unless you are doing overnight sleeper trains. I find it easier to go to the train station and book the ticket there, as the online websites are very confusing and the price is the same online as it is in person.

Any country not listed here doesn't have trains.

Buses

Buses are the best way to get around in Southeast Asia and will likely be your most common means of transportation. Bus costs vary between $5 and $8 for a five-to-six-hour journey. Overnight buses cost $10–$15 depending on distance. Buses go everywhere you want to go, and since there isn't a comprehensive train system in the region, they are the main form of transportation for locals and tourists alike.

Buses are operated by a plethora of small operators. There is no version of Greyhound. You simply go with the operator who services the route you want or with the company the tourist agency / guesthouse sets you up with. All you do is show up at the bus station and book your ticket. You don't need to book them in advance or online (and, at the time of writing, few companies even offer online booking).

Moreover, the backpacker trail in Southeast Asia is so well established that there is a very well-oiled "tourist bus" system here. These buses (often called "VIP" buses) will pick you up at your accommodation or have a set meetup point in the tourist area and take you directly to your next destination. For example, if you need to go from Bangkok to Chiang Mai, you'd buy a ticket, meet the bus (probably on Khao San Road), and enjoy the night ride up to Chiang Mai with other travelers. No stops at other bus stations—just a straight shot to Chiang Mai.

While they are very convenient, they are usually about 25 percent more expensive than the local buses. As Stuart, owner of the Asia travel website Travelfish.org, says, "Saving money by taking local transportation can often be a false economy as it can take a lot longer than something more tourist-focused. It may be worth spending the extra $2 if it means you are on the beach four hours earlier."

While local buses are much cheaper, they aren't often direct. They always stay full, so they will pick up people along the way, drop people off, and then pick up new people. This often means slower travel. As someone who has done this before, I can tell you it can be annoying after a while and you'll likely wish you splurged on a direct tourist bus.

Ferries

Ferry prices vary greatly throughout the region and depend on the popularity of the island you are going to. As with buses, there are no recommended lines. There is just the company that services the route you want, or the guesthouse that runs a boat from the mainland to your island paradise.

It's worth noting that ferries in Southeast Asia don't often adhere to Western safety standards, and lack of life jackets is an issue. Some people recommend staying on the top deck so it's easier to quickly leave the boat if necessary.

While it's not necessary to book in advance, it's a good idea during peak season or on more popular routes to book your tickets the day before you plan to travel. You can buy tickets on the ferry company's website or via a ticket agent like 12go.asia. However, every agent or hostel or hotel can get you a ferry ticket too.

You might also consider doing a multi-day cruise on popular waterways like the Mekong River or Halong Bay. On the Mekong River in Laos, slow boats from Huay Xai will drop you off in Luang Prabang. Slow boats take two or three days, stopping at guesthouses for nightly accommodation. Prices vary depending on the quality of the company, but you can expect to pay around $50–$80 for the entire journey. Halong Bay tours from Hanoi start around $140 for two-day, one-night trips and increase exponentially from there.

Flying

You'll find a lot of inexpensive budget airlines that service the region, making it really affordable to fly around if you're in a rush. Some of the biggest carriers are:

- AirAsia: airasia.com
- Nok Air: nokair.com

- Jetstar: jetstar.com
- Lion Air: lionair.co.id
- Nok Air: nokair.com
- Scoot: flyscoot.com/en
- Vietjet: vietjetair.com

These airlines often run deals as little as $10 if booked in advance. Generally speaking, fares are closer to $30 per one-way trip. Last-minute fares can cost more than $100. On all of these airlines, you'll need to pay a bag fee to check a bag, book a seat, as well as pay a "convenience fee" (really a not-so-convenient fee!) for using a credit card. These airlines, like most, nickel-and-dime you on all sorts of fees.

AirAsia is the biggest and most popular airline in the region. I like flying with them a lot. You don't get much with them, but their planes are comfortable, and with such cheap fares, there's really nothing to complain about. All the airlines will get you from point A to point B. I will note that safety standards in Indonesia and the Philippines are a little lax and I would look up the safety record of the airline you're flying before you book.

ACTIVITIES AND ATTRACTIONS

Activities and attractions in this region have a wide range of prices depending on how touristy the destination is. Most Buddhist temples are free to enter, though some of the more famous and larger ones (like Wat Phnom in Phnom Penh, Wat Pho in Bangkok, the Temple of Literature in Hanoi, and Wat Xieng Toung in Luang Prabang, Laos) cost $3–$5 to enter. One thing to note is that most attractions as well as national parks have a higher price for foreigners than they do for locals so double-check the entrance fee before you visit.

Large temple complexes such as the ultra-famous world heritage sites of Angkor Wat in Cambodia ($37–$72), Borobudur in Indonesia ($25), or Sukhothai Historical Park in Thailand ($3–$15) do cost a lot more money than smaller temples. Scuba diving in the region costs $300–400 to get your three-day open water PADI certificate, which will allow you to dive anywhere in the world. The island of Koh Tao in Thailand is the cheapest place in the world to get your certification because there are more than fifty dive shops on the island and competition is very fierce. If you want to learn to dive, learn here.

The region is also filled with other day activities that cost an average of $20 for a one-day tour. If you are going jungle trekking, seeing elephants, climbing mountains, or doing overnight trips, prices can go as high as $70.

Travel agents are the mainstay of travel in this region. You step inside, tell them where you want to go, and they book your bus or train or ferry for you. Want to do a tour somewhere? You can book that there too. Unlike in many parts of the world, there isn't a lot of online booking and do-it-yourself travel here, so you rely on these companies a lot. Most are simply nameless mom-and-pop establishments that are just as good as one another.

Guesthouses can also help you book tours or transportation. Typically, there is one company and all the tour agents around town sell that tour. You'll find a bus full of people on the same tour who all booked at different places. If you are in a large group of people booking together, you can usually haggle down a price from the tourist agency. Appendix A lists some tour operators I like.

Free walking tours exist only in capital and large touristy cities.

One thing to note is that there is a lot of animal tourism in this region and a lot of it is very abusive. Skip any elephant rides, tiger temples, monkey parks, or dolphin tours. If you want to see the animals, make sure there is very little human interaction. There are a lot of wonderful elephant rescue parks in the region that are worth checking out, but don't do anything that involves riding them. Anything that involves animals in a cage or that you touch usually means they are drugged. Be a responsible tourist and avoid this stuff.

HOW MUCH MONEY DO YOU NEED?

Southeast Asia is one of the most affordable regions of the world to explore. It's why it's probably the number one region in the world for backpackers. It's easy to visit, there are lots of travelers, and it's cheap.

Most travelers spend a few months roaming the region. If you stick to dorm rooms ($15 per night), inexpensive local food from markets and restaurants ($15 per day), buses, temples, and a few day tours, you'll spend about $50 per day. That's your typical backpacker budget and give or take what most people spend. If you splurge on some nicer meals or drink more, you'll probably get closer to $60 per day.

If you get nicer accommodations such as private rooms with air-conditioning, indulge in the widespread partying in this region, or start eating more Western food, expect to spend $85 per day.

If you start heading to only overly touristy places or some of the more expensive destinations like Bali or the Thai islands, your daily average will go up a lot and you'll likely need around $100 per day.

Like most of the places discussed in the book, a lot of your daily budget will depend on how much comfort you want to have on your trip. That said, you get outstanding value from this region of the world, so if you're spending a lot of money it's likely you're partying too much or eating too many Western or upscale meals!

23

PUTTING IT
ALL TOGETHER

This book has laid out a lot of numbers, like pieces of a puzzle. Now it's time to put those pieces together. The promise of this book is that you can travel around the world for $75 per day, or $27,375 per year. Now, that number didn't just come out of thin air. I picked it because my own years of travel experience have taught me that it's exactly how much money you need for a world trip. But, remember, it's a daily average. Some days you may spend more; some days you may spend a lot less. If your whole trip is just to Southeast Asia, you'll spend less than that in one year. But if you are going away for a shorter time period or spending two weeks in expensive Norway, it will be harder to stay around $75 per day.

After years of traveling the world, I've realized that there are so many easy ways to save money that don't require a lot of work. So long as you get out of the "expensive hotel/dinners/flights" mentality, you'll find incredible value for your money throughout the world and ways to spend less money than you would living back home.

In this last chapter, I'd like to turn all the costs and expenses peppered throughout this book into a yearly budget.

First, let's discuss pre-trip expenses. As we saw in Part One, there aren't many of them. There are a few big things, but mostly your days will be spent organizing your life in preparation for your big journey. Your biggest pre-trip expenses will be:

- Travel insurance: $700
- Flights (a mix of points, international flights, and budget airlines): $1,500
- Backpack: $200
- Miscellaneous (chargers, locks, visas, vaccinations, gear, etc.): $250

Note: Flight costs can vary due to where you are going, time you are booking, and how many reward miles you use for free flights. If you don't use my tips on getting free flights, you'll end up spending a lot more.

So, even before we go away, we are looking at spending around $2,650. That's a lot of money, but it takes care of all our sunken costs, and the also previously discussed discount cards will end up saving us more on the road than they cost.

Next, let's talk about expenses on the road, because this is where you are going to spend most of your money. In this book, I included the most popular destinations people visit on a round-the-world trip.

For the purposes of adding it all together, I'm going to use the most common route people take around the world along with the time and money they typically spend in each region. Your route may be different, but this is generally what people do. (Note: The budgets used here are all the backpacker budgets from each section.)

South America: $60 per day x 90 days = $5,400

Europe (assuming a mix of regions): $70 per day x 90 days = $6,300

Southeast Asia: $60 per day x 90 days = $5,400

Australia: $100 per day x 45 days = $4,500

New Zealand: $75 per day x 30 days = $2,250

China: $60 x 14 days = $840

TOTAL = $24,690

Adding this number to our pre-trip expenses gives us exactly $27,340, or about $75 per day.

Now, of course, we all have different travel styles and budgets. As I mentioned at the start of Part Three, I didn't include many parts of the world outside the normal "backpacker route." If you were to travel around those regions, that would change the daily amount you need.

Moreover, where you go and what you do greatly factor into the final amount you need. As you can see above, you can spend three months in Southeast Asia for a lot less than you can spend three months in Europe. If you were to spend more time in China or India ($40–$50 per day), that would also lower your expenses considerably. Conversely, spending a lot of time in Japan or Australia would increase your daily average. You could decide to do it even cheaper, using the "tight" budget numbers I listed and cut out thousands of dollars from this figure.

My numbers are a guideline and my tips will help you reach those numbers. What you do with the information I give you is up to you, so the actual amount of money you spend will depend on how many of my tips you use and where you go.

I would also consider saving about 10% extra, over whatever total you determine you need, as a buffer for unexpected expenses and splurges. While this tactic isn't a necessity, I always found that something—a fun activity, a flight, a fancy dinner—does come up on the road that you didn't plan for.

I once went to London for ten days and spent $700 (including my flight) simply by using miles for free flights and rooms, cooking my meals, sticking to lunch specials, and staying with a friend. So, you can really go frugal if you want.

What these numbers illustrate is that traveling the world can be as cost-effective as living at home, and that you shouldn't think travel is unaffordable. As I've shown throughout this book, there are a number of ways to save money when you arrive at your destination.

It is possible to travel. The world is affordable. We don't have to be afraid that we don't have enough money to see it. Even if you can't find the money for a year of travel, all of these destinations can be seen on their own. If you only have a few weeks, you can find a cheap flight and use my tips to save money. You can skip expensive Europe and Australia and spend more time visiting cheaper countries. This book's tips are universal.

I firmly believe that travel is not expensive. My own personal motto is: "Travel cheaper, longer, and smarter." As I've traveled, I've come to realize that you can have a first-class travel experience on an economy-class budget as long as you are flexible and think outside the box. This book is my attempt to break down that perception and show that with a little knowledge and flexibility, your dream trip around the world or honeymoon in Italy doesn't need to be a dream at all—it can be an affordable reality.

Whether or not you decide to go around the world, or spend $50, $75, or $100 per day, remember to look for value when you travel. Don't just go with the first pick. Traveling the world on the cheap is as much about finding value as it is about saving money.

And after reading this book, I hope you've realized that travel is within your grasp.

See you on the road!

—Matt

Appendix A: Resources

The following are lists of all the travel companies, tour operators, hostels, and booking sites that I use and recommend, whether they have been included in the book or not. Restaurants and bars are not included here, though please refer to NomadicMatt.com for an updated list of all my favorite dining establishments.

GLOBAL RESOURCES
ACCOMMODATIONS

Agoda: agoda.com
Airbnb: airbnb.com
BeWelcome: bewelcome.org
Booking.com: booking.com
Campspace: campspace.com
Couchsurfing: couchsurfing.org
Hostelworld: hostelworld.com
Hotels.com: hotels.com

Hotwire: hotwire.com

HouseCarers: housecarers.com

LastMinute: lastminute.com

LateRooms: laterooms.com

MindMyHouse: mindmyhouse.com

Nomador: nomador.com

Priceline: priceline.com

Servas International: servas.org

Traveling Ladies: travelladies.app

TripAdvisor: tripadvisor.com

TrustedHousesitters: trustedhousesitters.com

Vrbo: vrbo.com

Warm Showers: warmshowers.org

WWOOF: wwoof.net

DISCOUNT CARDS

Hostelling International Card: hihostels.com

HostelPass: hostelpass.co

ISIC Student/Teacher/Youth Card: isic.org

FLIGHT RESOURCES

Airfarewatchdog: airfarewatchdog.com

Expedia: expedia.com

Going: going.com

Google Flights: google.com/flights

Holiday Pirates: holidaypirates.com

Momondo: momondo.com

Oneworld: oneworld.com

Skyscanner: skyscanner.com

SkyTeam: skyteam.com

Star Alliance: staralliance.com

The Flight Deal: theflightdeal.com

Thrifty Traveler: thriftytraveler.com

CAR RENTAL AND RIDESHARING

BlaBlaCar (Europe): blablacar.com

Bushride (Australia): bushride.com

Coseats (Australia): coseats.com

Discover Cars: discovercars.com

Grab: grab.com

Gumtree (UK/Australia/NZ): gumtree.com

Hello Ride (China): helloride-global.com

Kangaride (Canada): kangaride.com

Liftshare (UK): liftshare.com/uk

Lyft (US): lyft.com

RV Share: rvshare.com

Uber: uber.com

GEAR

Backcountry: backcountry.com

Campmor: campmor.com

Eastern Mountain Sports (EMS): ems.com

Mountain Equipment Company (MEC): mec.ca

Recreational Equipment Inc. (REI): rei.com

Sierra Trading Post: sierratradingpost.com

MEAL SHARING SITES

Eatwith: eatwith.com

Traveling Spoon: travelingspoon.com

With Locals: withlocals.com

TOUR COMPANIES

Airbnb Experiences: airbnb.com/experiences

Devour Food Tours: devourtours.com

GetYourGuide: getyourguide.com

Intrepid Travel: intrepidtravel.com

Walks: takewalks.com

TRAVEL INSURANCE

Clements Insurance: clements.com

IMG Insurance: imglobal.com

InsureMyTrip: insuremytrip.com

Insured Nomads: insurednomads.com

MedEx: medexassist.com

Medjet Assist: medjetassist.com

Safety Wing: safetywing.com

World Nomads: worldnomads.com

TRAVEL CREDIT CARD
AND POINT-RELATED RESOURCES

Awayz: awayz.com

FlyerTalk: flyertalk.com

One Mile at a Time: onemileatatime.com
Point.me: point.me
Prince of Travel: princeoftravel.com
The Points Guy: thepointsguy.com
View from the Wing: viewfromthewing.com

MISCELLANEOUS

Busbud: busbud.com
Cruise Sheet: cruisesheet.com
Ferryhopper: ferryhopper.com
GetByBus: getbybus.com
Lonely Planet Guidebooks: lonelyplanet.com
Rome to Rio: rome2rio.com
The Man in Seat 61 (trains): seat61.com
Trainline: trainline.com

DESTINATION-SPECIFIC RESOURCES
AUSTRALIA
Accommodations

Aussie House Sitters: aussiehousesitters.com.au
Beaches of Broome (Broome): beachesofbroome.com.au
BUNK Surfers Paradise (Gold Coast):
    bunksurfersparadise.com.au
Camps Australia Wide: campsaustraliawide.com
City Backpackers HQ (Brisbane): citybackpackershq.com
Nomads Magnetic Island Hostel (Magnetic Island): nomadsworld
    .com/australia/nomads-magnetic-island

Nomads Noosa Hostel (Noosa): nomadsworld.com/australia/nomads
 -noosa
Nomads St Kilda Hostel (Melbourne): nomadsworld.com/australia
 /nomads-st-kilda-melbourne
Wake Up! Sydney Hostel (Sydney): wakeup.com.au

Tour Operators

Adventure Tours Australia: adventuretours.com.au
Darwin Walking Tours: darwinwalkingtours.com
Fraser Island Tours: fraserexplorertours.com.au
Melbourne Street Art Tours: melbournestreettours.com
OzSail Whitsunday Tours: ozsail.com.au
Tusa Diving Great Barrier Reef: tusadive.com

Transportation

Greyhound Australia: greyhound.com.au
Journey Beyond Rail: journeybeyondrail.com.au
Spaceships: spaceshipsrentals.com.au
Travellers Autobarn: travellers-autobarn.com.au
Wicked Campers: wickedcampers.com.au

Walking Tours

Bonza Bike Tours: bonzabiketours.com
Dark Stories: darkstories.com.au
I'm Free Walking Tours: imfree.tours
Locl Tour Sydney: locltour.com

Melbourne Street Tours: melbournestreettours.com

MelTours: meltours.com.au

CENTRAL AMERICA
Accommodations

Alajuela Backpackers (Costa Rica): alajuelabackpackers.com

Costa Rica Backpackers (Costa Rica): costaricabackpackers.com

PachaMama (Nicaragua): pachamama.com

Roatan Backpackers' Hostel (Honduras): roatanbackpackers.com

Tour Operators

Alton's Dive Center (Honduras): diveinutila.com

Raggamuffin Tours (Belize): raggasailadventures.com

CHINA
Accommodations

Dayin International Youth Hostel (Shanghai): No website. Book via Hostelworld.

Great Wall Box House (Beijing): No website. Book via Hostelworld.

Han Tang Inn Hostel (Xi'an): No website. Book via Hostelworld.

Hop Inn (Hong Kong): hopinn.hk

Kelly's Courtyard (Beijing): No website. Book via Hostelworld.

Lazy Gaga Hostel (Guangzhou): No website. Book via Hostelworld.

Poshpacker Flipflop Hostel (Chengdu): chengduhostel.com

YHA Mei Ho House (Hong Kong): yha.org.hk/en/hostel/yha
   -mei-ho-house-youth-hostel

Tour Operators

Free Tours China: freetourschina.com
Hong Kong Free Tours: hongkongfreetours.com
Walking Tours Beijing: beijingwalkingtours.com

Transportation

Air China: airchina.com.cn
Cathay Pacific: cathaypacific.com
China Highlights: chinahighlights.com/china-trains
China Southern Airlines: csair.com/en
China Ticket Online: chinaticketonline.com
ETrip China: etripchina.com/bus
Hainan Airlines: hainanairlines.com
Hello Ride: helloride-global.com
HK Express: hkexpress.com/en-hk
Sichuan Airlines: global.sichuanair.com
Spring Airlines: en.ch.com
Trip.com: trip.com/trains/china

EUROPE
Accommodations

Balmers Herberge (Interlaken): balmers.com
Camping Key Card: campingkeyeurope.com
Carpe Noctem (Budapest): budapestpartyhostels.com/hostels/carpe
    -noctem-original
Castle Rock Hostel (Edinburgh): castlerockedinburgh.com
City Backpackers (Stockholm): citybackpackers.org

Clown and Bard Hostel (Prague): clownandbard.com

Francesco's Hostel (Ios): francescos.net

Gallery Hostel (Porto): gallery-hostel.com

Generator Hostels: generatorhostels.com

Goodnight Hostel (Lisbon): goodnighthostel.com

Hostel Archi Rossi (Florence): hostelarchirossi.com

Hostel Mostel (Bulgaria): hostelmostel.com

Kabul Hostel (Barcelona): kabul.es

Miss Sophie's (Prague): miss-sophies.com

Nest Hostels (Spain): nesthostelsvalencia.com

Pink Palace (Corfu): thepinkpalace.com

Snuffel Hostel (Tallinn): snuffel.be

St. Christopher's: st-christophers.co.uk

The Flying Pig (Amsterdam): flyingpig.nl

The Madhouse (Prague): themadhouseprague.com

The Monk's Bunk (Tallinn): toth.ee/hostel/the-monks-bunk

Viru Backpackers (Tallinn): toth.ee/hostel/viru-home

Wombat's: wombats-hostels.com

Yellow Square (Rome): yellowsquare.it

Walking Tours

Athens: athensfreewalkingtour.com

Belgrade: belgradewalkingtours.com

Bratislava: befreetours.com

Budapest: triptobudapest.hu

Devour: devourtours.com

Edinburgh: cityofthedeadtours.com

Krakow: freewalkingtour.com

Ljubljana: ljubljanafreetour.com

New Europe Walking Tours: neweuropetours.eu
Prague: newpraguetours.com; extravaganzafreetour.com
Sarajevo: sarajevowalkingtours.com
Take Walks: takewalks.com
Tallinn: traveller.ee/tour/tallinn-free-tour

Tour Operators

1 Big Night Out: 1bignightout.com
Cracow City Tours (Poland): cracowcitytours.pl
Divina Cucina Tuscany Food Tours: divinacucina.com
Fat Tire Bike Tours: fattirebiketours.com
Haggis Adventures (Scotland): haggisadventures.com
Ultimate Party Pub Crawl: joinultimateparty.com

Transportation

Ecolines: ecolines.net
Eurail: eurail.com
FlixBus: global.flixbus.com
Interrail: interrail.eu
Megabus UK: uk.megabus.com
Rail Europe: raileurope.com
Trainline: trainline.com

INDIA
Accommodations

Bombay Backpackers (Kolkata): bombaybackpackers.com
Joey's Hostel New Delhi (New Delhi): joeyshostel.com

Namastey Mumbai Backpackers (Mumbai): No website. Book via Hostelworld.

The Funky Monkey Hostel (Goa): thefunkymonkeyhostel.com

The Little Blue Window Hostel (Bangalore): No website. Book via Hostelworld.

Zostel Mysore (Mysore): zostel.com/zostel/mysore/mysore-mysh811

Transportation

AirAsia: airasia.com

Air India: airindia.com

Air Vistara: airvistara.com

Alliance Air: allianceair.in

BlaBlaCar: blablacar.in

FlixBus: flixbus.in

Indian Railways: indianrailways.gov.in

IndiGo: goindigo.in

SpiceJet: spicejet.com

Tour Operators

India for Beginners: indiaforbeginners.com

Intrepid Travel: intrepidtravel.com/en/india

Wandering Earl Tours: wanderingearltours.com

JAPAN
Accommodations

Backpackers Hostel K's House: kshouse.jp

J-Hoppers Hostels: j-hoppers.com

Khaosan Tokyo Guesthouse (Tokyo): khaosan-tokyo.com

Tour Operators

Arigato Travel: arigatojapan.co.jp
Klook: klook.com
Rakuten Travel Experiences: experiences.travel.rakuten.com

Transportation

Japan Bus Lines: japanbuslines.com/en
Japan Rail Pass: japanrailpass.net
Japan Travel by NAVITIME: japantravel.navitime.com
Willer Bus: willerexpress.com/en

Walking Tours

Kyoto Free Walking Tour: kyotofreewalkingtour.com/kyoto-tours
-schedule
Osaka Free Walking Tour: osakafreewalkingtour.com
Tokyo Free Guide: tokyofreeguide.org
Tokyo Free Walking Tour: tokyolocalized.com

NEW ZEALAND
Accommodations

Finlay Jack's Backpackers (Taupo): finlayjacks.co.nz
Haka House: hakahouse.com
Mountain View Backpackers (Wanaka): mtnview.co.nz

New Zealand Department of Conservation Campsites: doc.govt.nz

Nomads Queenstown (Queenstown): nomadsworld.com/new-zealand
/nomads-queenstown/

Urbanz (Christchurch): urbanz.net.nz

Tour Operators

AwesomeNZ: awesomenz.com

Tamaki Maori Village: maoriculture.co.nz

Taupo Tandem Skydiving: tts.net.nz

The Legendary Blackwater Rafting Company: waitomo.com/black
-water-rafting

Ziptrek Queenstown: ziptrek.com

Transportation

Hippie Camper Hire: hippiecamper.com

InterCity: intercity.co.nz

Kiwi Experience Bus: kiwiexperience.com

Kiwirail: kiwirail.co.nz

Spaceships: spaceshipsrentals.co.nz

Stray Travel Bus: straytravel.com

Wicked Campervans: wickedcampers.com.au

Walking Tours

Auckland Free Walking Tours: aucklandfreewalkingtours.com

I'm Free Walking Tours: imfree.tours

Kiwi Crawl: kiwicrawl.co.nz

SOUTH AMERICA
Accommodations

America del Sur Hostel (Buenos Aires): americahostel.com.ar
CabanaCopa (Brazil): cabanacopa.com.br
Home Stay Web: homestayweb.com
La Casa Filipe (Santa Marta): lacasadefelipe.com
Loki Hostel (Peru): lokihostel.com
Media Luna Hostel (Colombia): medialunahostel.com
Milhouse (Buenos Aires): milhousehostel.com
Pariwana Hostel (Cusco): pariwana-hostel.com/en/hostels/cusco

Transportation

Berlinas: berlinasdelfonce.com
Bolivariano: bolivariano.com.co
Chile: efe.cl
Coomotor: coomotor.com.co
Copetran: copetran.com.co
Expreso Brasilia: expresobrasilia.com
Omnilineas: omnilineas.com
Perurail: perurail.com
Rápido Ochoa: rapidoochoa.com
Train to the Clouds (El Tren a las Nubes): trenalasnubes.com.ar

Walking Tours

Beyond Colombia: beyondcolombia.com
Buenos Aires Free Walks: buenosairesfreewalks.com
Free Walker Tours: freewalkertours.com

GuruWalk: guruwalk.com
Inkan Milky Way: inkanmilkyway.com
Real City Tours: realcitytours.com
Red Cap Tours: redcapwalkingtours.com
SP Free Walking Tour: saopaulofreewalkingtour.com

SOUTHEAST ASIA
Accommodations

Funky Monkey Hostel (Vientiane): No website. Book via
Hostelworld.
Honey Inn (Nang Rong): honeyinn.com
Indigo House (Luang Prabang): indigohouse.la
Kodchasri Thani (Chiang Mai): kodchasri.com
Mut Mee (Nong Khai): mutmee.com
Pooh's (Koh Lipe): poohlipe.com
Real Vang Vieng Backpacker Hostel (Vang Vieng): No website.
Book via Hostelworld.
Sairee Hut Dive Resort (Koh Tao): kohtaosaireehutresort.com
The Green Kiwi (Singapore): greenkiwi.com.sg
The Magic Sponge Guesthouse (Kampot):
magicspongekampot.com

General Information

Travelfish: travelfish.org

Tour Operators

Bali Discovery Tours (Bali): balidiscovery.com
Elephant Nature Park (Chiang Mai): elephantnaturepark.org
NS Travel & Tours (Bangkok): nstravel.com
The Gibbon Experience (Laos): gibbonexperience.org

Appendix B: Suggested Packing Lists

A lot of people ask me what they should pack when they travel. That's a hard question to answer because we all have our own clothing and style preferences. I subscribe to the general rule of packing light. You quickly learn when you travel that you don't need a lot of stuff. You can wear that shirt and those pants for a few days in a row. As the saying goes, "Take twice as much money and half as much stuff."

To help you with your packing, below is a list of what I carry with me (one of the reasons I like small backpacks is because it forces you to pack light):

CLOTHES

5 T-shirts
1 long-sleeved T-shirt
1 pair of jeans (Heavy and not easily dried, but I wear them a lot—a good alternative is a pair of khakis.)
1 pair of shorts
7 pairs of underwear

1 bathing suit

1 pair of flip-flops

1 pair of sneakers

8 pairs of socks (I always lose my socks so I take extra! I have no idea where they go.)

1 pair of dress shoes (Heavy to carry around, but when I visit friends, we usually go somewhere not sneaker-friendly. This is destination dependent. I do this more in Australia and Europe and less so everywhere else.)

1 dress shirt (For going to a respectable place in the evening.)

1 pair of black dress socks

TOILETRIES

1 toothbrush

1 tube of toothpaste

1 razor

1 package of dental floss

1 small bottle of shampoo

1 small bar of soap

Deodorant

SMALL MEDICAL KIT

Band-Aids

Hydrocortisone cream

Antibacterial cream

Eyedrops

Earplugs

Doctor-prescribed antibiotics / medication

Tylenol
Hand sanitizer

MISCELLANEOUS

A key or combination lock (Everyone should have this!)
Zip-top bags
Plastic bags
Sleep mask
Any necessary chargers

I've met a lot of travelers who take even less than the above, but I've found that this list leaves me wanting for nothing when I am on the road. If something does come up (like if I stay somewhere where it is cold), I simply buy what I need on the road—light jackets and sweaters can be found anywhere.

ADDENDUM FOR FEMALE TRAVELERS

Kristin Addis from *Be My Travel Muse* has suggested additions for women travelers:
5–7 thin and simple tank tops and T-shirts
2 pairs of shorts of varying lengths
2 long skirts or dresses
2–3 pairs of light cotton pants and/or leggings
1 set of sleepwear
Sufficient underwear to last you at least a week (I suggest 7 pairs of panties, 2 bras, and 2 sports bras.)
2 sets of interchangeable swimwear

1 sarong or big scarf when modest dress is called for and cooler
   evenings

2–3 long-sleeved shirts for layering

2–3 pairs of leggings for layering

TOILETRIES

Solid shampoo

Facial moisturizer

Razor refills

Birth control for the length of your trip (If you take it, or consider
   monitoring your cycle with a free app and using condoms,
   which are available almost worldwide.)

Tweezer

Nail clippers

Makeup

A reusable menstrual cup, disc, or other necessary products

Appendix C: Vaccinations and Medicine

VACCINATIONS

I've been sick many times on the road. Once in Costa Rica, I had bad sushi and ended up in a hospital for three days. I've gotten mild food poisoning in Thailand that woke me up in the middle of the night—I clutched my stomach, ran to the bathroom, and drank Pepto-Bismol like it was going out of fashion. I had a flu in Romania that required me to find a pharmacy in the middle of the night in a town where no one spoke English. I got COVID while traveling. Germs are everywhere, and as travelers we are often more susceptible to them. We expose our bodies and specifically our immune systems to germs we aren't used to. Staying healthy on the road is important because you don't want to end up like me and spend your time in bed for the week in a beautiful historic village in Europe.

I get asked a lot about which vaccinations you should or should not get or if you need malaria tablets everywhere. I am not a doctor, so before you go, you should consult a medical expert as well as do research on the areas you are going to find the latest information. The US Centers for Disease Control has a detailed section on medicine and travel at wwwnc.cdc.gov/travel/page /vaccinations.htm and a complete list of vaccinations at cdc.gov /vaccines/schedules/hcp/adult.html.

You can also consult the World Health Organization's website for additional information (who.int/ith/en), which features a free digital book for travelers.

If you don't have a doctor, many hospitals have travel clinics where you can visit a doctor and get any shots or vaccines that you need. You'll have to pay for this out of pocket if you don't have insurance, and it's usually not covered by US health insurance plans. There are also a number of private travel clinics around the country where you can get the medical advice you need. Some of these clinics are even free. You can get a list of these clinics from the CDC website (wwwnc.cdc.gov/travel/page/travel-clinics.htm).

While you need to consult with a doctor, I would make sure you get a typhoid, tetanus, hepatitis, and, if you are traveling in Asia, a Japanese encephalitis shot. Those four shots are basic and will cover you for the most common of illnesses and problems that might occur on the road. You'll need to get any of these vaccinations months in advance, and some require a second follow-up shot. You should see your doctor or visit a travel clinic at least six months prior to your trip.

One of the biggest concerns among potential travelers is the threat of malaria, especially in developing countries. When I first went away, I had the malaria drug Malarone with me for when I went to Southeast Asia. I was told there was malaria in some parts of the area and I'd need the medication. I took it for a while, until I realized that none of the Westerners who lived in Asia took it. I stopped taking it, and I didn't get malaria. In my nonmedical opinion, while you can never fully get rid of the threat of malaria, if you are going to very touristy, popular, and developed destinations, your risk of catching it is minimal. What you decide to do should be based on your conversations with a medical professional and your feelings about taking medicine every day, but in all my years of travel, outside of Africa or the jungle in the Amazon, I've never known people to take malaria medication.

If you do decide to get vaccines, you will get a small yellow book listing all your vaccinations. This is for your records as well as for health officials in other countries in case they need to know (for example, at a border crossing or a doctor's office). Make sure you carry this book around with you.

WHAT ABOUT MEDICINE?

People always ask me—what do you do when you get sick while traveling? Well, I do the same thing I do when at home. I rest, take medicine, drink lots of fluids, see a doctor if I have to, and watch movies until I get better. We live in the twenty-first century. Globalization and technology have made medicine and treatment widely available throughout the world. In fact, one of the fastest-growing areas of the tourism industry is medical tourism, in which people travel to destinations around the world in search of affordable health care. Mexico is popular for dental work (many of their doctors are trained in the United States), Israel for in vitro fertilization, Argentina for plastic surgery, and Thailand for just about everything.

There is a common misconception that the United States is the only place you can get good health care. That is not true.

Most countries in the world actually have a first-class health care system, even in what we would consider "developing" countries. Think of all the Westerners who live in non-Western countries around the world—they aren't going to live in a country where they will get poor-quality medical care. After all, it would be too expensive to fly back home every time they got sick.

I spend a lot of time in Bangkok. It's like my second home, and while I'm there, I often get medical treatment. I spent $40 for a dermatologist appointment, and getting my eardrum looked at after my scuba diving accident (plus the follow-ups and medicine) cost me less than $200. I've had dental work done for $20. And these aren't at back-alley places. They are at internationally accredited hospitals and clinics, like Bumrungrad Hospital and Samitivej Hospital.

Just because you are overseas, don't assume you can't get any quality treatment. You can, and if you need something done, you can look up international accredited hospitals (jointcommission international.org/JCI-Accredited-Organizations).

Outside of some very rural areas of the world, you will be able to find all the basic supplies you need at a local pharmacy. I have never encountered a problem where I couldn't find cold medicine, ointments, or allergy medicine.

It's important to remember that the whole world doesn't call every product by the same name. Oftentimes, travelers will ask for Tylenol or Benadryl, find the pharmacy doesn't have it, and leave discouraged. Well, they do have it, but they just call it by a different name. We are used to calling medicines by their brand names and not their medical name. To ensure I get the medicine I need, I simply google to find the active medical ingredient in the product I'm looking for, give that name to the pharmacist, and get what I need. Same thing, different name. Here are some examples of popular drugs and their medical names:

Tylenol is often called acetaminophen or nurofen. Pepto-Bismol is bismuth subsalicylate. Neosporin is a simple antibacterial ointment. Sudafed is pseudoephedrine. Benadryl is diphenhydramine.

The point is that you'll find what you are looking for overseas, so don't feel the need to overload on medicine before you leave.

Acknowledgments

Writing a book takes a lot of work, and there are a lot of people I want to thank for helping me put this together, especially since this book has gone through four editions.

First and foremost, I'd like to thank my original editor, Maria Gagliano, for approaching me (all the way back in 2012!) about turning my old online e-book into the book you just read. She saw the potential for this book to be even more than it already was, and I thank her immensely for her support. I'm still unsure how she stumbled across my website, but I'm glad she did. Without her, this book wouldn't be here. Plus, she spent time editing my verboseness into something concise and coherent!

I'd like to thank my current editor, Keith Gordon, for helping me finesse this new edition, which was heavily rewritten for the post-COVID world.

Next, I'd like to thank my literary agent, David Fugate, for handling all the contract issues and my annoying questions. He's a great agent in case anyone wants one!

I'd really like to thank my friend and mentor Jason Cochran (found at JasonCochran.com). As a fellow travel writer who has done this before, his edits, guidance, and criticisms were instrumental in getting me to where I am today. Writing a blog is not like writing a guidebook, and he helped me through this process more than anyone else. He picked me apart, lifted me up, and provided invaluable notes. And, along the way, he made me a much better writer.

Additionally, I would like to thank fellow travel writer David Farley for helping with my research for this new edition. There's a lot of work that goes into updating a book after a global pandemic and his expertise was incredibly invaluable. I'd also like to thank my team members Andrea Hunt, Chris Oldfield, and Samantha Anthony for their help in fact-checking and researching information.

I'd also like to thank those who helped build the book into what it is today with their feedback, comments, and quotes: David Whitely, Audrey Scott and Dan Noll, Chris Guillebeau, David Lee, Brooke Schoeman, Matthew Khynn, Amanda Williams, Steve Kamb, Tim Leffel, Brook Silva-Braga, Marina Villatoro, Dani Heinrich, Jessica Ainlay, Jeff Jung, Molly McHugh, Marcello Arrambide, Stuart McDonald, Dani and Craig James, Sean and Dawn Lynch, Benny Lewis, Brian Kelly, Bethany Salvon, Nora Dunn, Raymond Walsh, Lawrence Norah, Lee Abbamonte, Michael Hodson, Sarah Muir, Kristin Addis, Mariellen Ward, Joel Ward, Derek Baron, and Chris Walker-Bush.

I'd also like to acknowledge everyone who reads my website as there would be no editions of this book without their support over the years. You've continued to read my information and trust me with your trip planning, and I don't take that responsibility lightly. My team and I are committed to always being as accurate as possible because we know that a bad trip is one of the worst things in the world. Thank you for placing your continued trust in us.

Finally, I'd like to thank all the travelers I've met since I left that day in 2006. You are an inspiration to me. Thank you for teaching me so much. Thank you for all the good times, the hangovers, the lifelong friendships, and the wonderful and exciting adventures. Every part of this book is based on experiences shared with you. Thank you.

About the Author

Matthew Kepnes didn't take his first trip overseas until he was twenty-three, but this trip to Costa Rica got him hooked on traveling. Like most Americans, he only had two weeks of vacation per year and didn't know any of the genius ways to save money and travel longer. Everything changed in 2005 on a trip to Thailand. After that, he came home, quit his job, finished graduate school, and in July 2006 embarked on a trip around the world that lasted eighteen months. In 2008, he started his website, Nomadic Matt, to help others travel better, cheaper, and longer. In 2019, he published his memoir, *Ten Years a Nomad*, about his decade backpacking the world. He is deathly afraid of heights and, ironically, a really nervous flier. When he isn't traveling, he resides in New York City, where he likes to eat lots of sushi, catch up with friends, and enjoy the fact that movie theaters are open at 11 PM.

He can be found at his website, NomadicMatt.com, as well as on Instagram at @nomadicmatt.